The Evangelical Origins of the Living Constitution

The Evangelical Origins *of the* Living Constitution

JOHN W. COMPTON

Harvard University Press

Cambridge, Massachusetts
London, England
2014

Library of Congress Cataloging-in-Publication Data
Compton, John W., 1977- author.
The evangelical origins of the living constitution / John W. Compton.
pages cm
Includes bibliographical references and index.
ISBN 978-0-674-72679-6 (alk. paper)
1. Religion and law—United States—History. 2. Evangelicalism—
United States—History—19th century. 3. Constitutional law—United
States—History. 4. United States—Religion. 5. Church and
state—United States—History. I. Title.
KF4869.E93C66 2014
342.7302'9—dc23   2013029764

For Heidi

Contents

The Evangelical Origins *of the* Living Constitution

Introduction

In twenty-first-century America, religion seems to go hand in hand with veneration of the Constitution and its framers. Devout believers overwhelmingly endorse the view that the Constitution should be interpreted "as originally written." Socially conservative politicians promise to oppose the nomination of judges who are not "dedicated to the original document and its original meaning." And every year, dozens of books portraying the founders as orthodox Christian believers and the Constitution as divinely inspired appear in bookstores.[1]

As natural as it may seem today, however, the connection between religious faith and constitutional faith is a relatively recent development. In fact, for much of American history prominent religious activists were almost as likely to condemn the Constitution as to praise it. In 1843, for example, the abolitionist William Lloyd Garrison read the Constitution's fugitive slave clause as evidence that the Founding generation had entered into "a covenant with death and an agreement with hell." Carrying this belief to its logical conclusion, Garrison and other abolitionists burned copies of the Constitution in public meetings.[2] And while the Garrisonians' sensationalist methods were widely condemned, their willingness to subject the Constitution to moral criticism was far from atypical. Indeed, religiously motivated opponents of drinking, lottery gambling, and Sabbath-breaking were equally convinced that the nation's constitutional system suffered from flaws that threatened to undermine the moral health of the republic. In the words of New Hampshire Senator Henry Blair, a leading Gilded Age prohibitionist, the Constitution was "the great legal fortress of intemperance" and "the great almighty obstacle in the way of . . . reform."[3] Significantly, Blair and other nineteenth-century evangelicals did not believe, as many modern-day social conservatives do, that judges or elected officials had adopted a flawed *interpretation* of the nation's fundamental law. Rather, like Garrison, they laid responsibility for the nation's woes directly at the feet of the Founding generation.

Why did the nation's earliest religious activists often express disdain for a constitutional inheritance that their twenty-first-century successors regard with awed reverence? In order to answer this question, we must rediscover a largely forgotten characteristic of the early American polity—a tension between rapidly evolving mores, on the one hand, and the generally rigid principles and institutional structures of the constitutional order, on the other. To put the point more concretely, Americans living in the aftermath of the great religious revivals of the early nineteenth century came to regard as sinful many activities and forms of property that the Founding generation had tolerated, or even actively promoted. And yet these same Americans inhabited a polity whose basic institutions were ill equipped to accommodate a radical shift in mores. For while the designers of the American constitutional order did not set out with the aim of inhibiting the moral development of future generations, they did envision a republic whose fundamental law would hinder efforts to interfere with settled property rights or restrict the flow of goods in interstate markets. And for this reason, efforts to rid the nation of newly immoral forms of property—from liquor, to lottery tickets, to slavery—were from the outset hampered by serious constitutional obstacles. Thus, where modern-day social conservatives tend to believe that the route to moral improvement runs *through* the constitutional principles of the framers, many of their nineteenth-century forebears believed precisely the opposite: that any hope of national regeneration depended on a turn *away* from the inflexible property protections and jurisdictional boundaries of Founding-era constitutionalism.

The present study argues that the tension between nineteenth-century mores and Founding-era constitutional commitments holds the key to a fuller understanding of American constitutional development. In fact, I shall argue that this tension was perhaps the most important force shaping American constitutional development in the period between the Founding and the 1930s. And it is only by recovering this tension, I argue, that we can arrive at a satisfactory answer to the question of why a traditional constitutional order oriented to the protection of economic rights and the rigid separation of state and federal authority suddenly collapsed in the New Deal period.

The Second Great Awakening as a Critical Juncture in American Constitutional Development

It would be difficult to overstate the extent to which American social mores were transformed in the early decades of the nineteenth century.[4] Lottery gambling, for example, was not only tolerated by Founding-era Americans but regarded as an indispensable form of revenue generation. Alcohol was similarly ubiquitous: the laboring classes fortified themselves with liquor at set intervals throughout the day, political elites operated taverns and distilleries, and clergymen were, by all accounts, among the nation's most enthusiastic drinkers. During the first third of the nineteenth century, however, the nation was swept by a wave of religious revivals that simultaneously increased rates of church membership and transformed the theological foundations of American Protestantism. By the 1840s the percentage of Americans attached to religious congregations had doubled relative to 1776, and millions of believers had exchanged the Founding generation's relatively lax Calvinism for a more demanding evangelical worldview that emphasized the possibility of moral perfection at both the individual and societal levels.[5] A central tenet of the new evangelical theology was that the nation's political institutions should brook no compromise with immorality. Thus, where the Founding generation had for the most part turned a blind eye to drinking, lottery gambling, and even Sabbath breaking, the new generation of evangelicals reconceived these activities as "national sins."[6] Moreover, where Founding-era morals laws, when enforced, had aimed at social control—by, for example, punishing *public* drunkenness—post-Revival Americans increasingly believed that the proper function of law was not to control vice, but rather to eradicate it altogether. Laws that licensed liquor sellers or lottery operators, on this view, were not sensible social controls; they were affronts to the Almighty.

At first glance, it may not be immediately apparent why this shift in mores should have impacted the constitutional realm. After all, the Constitution of 1787 is silent on subjects such as liquor and lottery regulation; and to the limited extent that the framers discussed these subjects, they clearly expected that states and localities would continue to regulate public morality as they had since the early colonial period. But as scholars of American political development are increasingly discovering, the effects of significant ideological change are rarely confined to any single sphere of the polity. As Karen Orren and Stephen Skowronek have explained, polities are generally "intercurrent," or characterized by "multiple orders of authority whose coordination with one another cannot be assumed and whose outward reach and impingements . . . are inherently problematic."[7] Because the institutions that compose a polity are historically constructed and interconnected, a revolution in one institutional order—be it the economy, the party system, or the religious sphere—will likely reverberate throughout the entire system. "[B]uilding something new," they write, usually "entails bumping against authority already in existence."[8]

This observation is clearly borne out in the post-Revival transformation of American mores. For as nineteenth-century Americans soon discovered, the basic structures of their constitutional system worked in myriad ways to reinforce the moral status quo. Lottery opponents watched in disbelief as legislative victories were nullified by the federal Contract Clause, which barred lawmakers from impairing the rights of currently licensed lottery operators. Anti-liquor crusaders similarly found their efforts blocked by the due process clauses of the state and federal constitutions, which were initially held to bar the summary destruction of legally acquired liquor. Efforts to combat the interstate market in "immoral" commodities, in turn, forced reformers to contend with a federal system whose rigid jurisdictional boundaries prohibited state regulation of commerce and federal regulation of morality. Viewed collectively, these features of the constitutional system convinced some evangelicals that the founders had indeed struck a deal with the Devil—that they had, in effect, mortgaged the nation's soul in a bid for national prosperity. Others merely lamented that the framers were products of a benighted age that had yet to perceive the inherently sinful nature of activities such as drinking and lottery gambling. But to the modern student of political development, these incidents suggest nothing so much as a classic case of "intercurrence"—that is, of governing institutions outliving their creators, shackling a new generation with the ideals and purposes of their forebears.

In any event, the emergence of a novel conception of the social order placed the constitutional order under enormous strain. Indeed, the legitimacy of the nation's nascent constitutional system depended in significant part on the idea that the jurisdictional boundaries articulated in the Constitution's text were susceptible to fixed and precise definition.[9] So long as this was the case, as Madison explained in *Federalist* 39, the task of delineating the "boundary between . . . jurisdictions" could be safely entrusted to the judiciary, where any constitutional disputes would be "impartially" resolved.[10] The anti-lottery and prohibition movements were particularly problematic because they forced jurists to consider whether the concepts and categories that undergirded the constitutional system were in fact fixed and unchanging. It was undeniable, for example, that the Founding generation had considered liquor a perfectly valid form of property. And yet millions of nineteenth-century Americans plainly thought otherwise, viewing "demon rum" as a common nuisance on the order of diseased goods or counterfeiters' tools. (The hatchet-wielding prohibitionist Carry Nation summed up the basic conundrum following one of her famous saloon-smashing episodes. Jailed for "malicious destruction of property," Nation quipped that the judge must have misstated the charge. Her only crime, if the label even applied, had been the "destruction of malicious property.")[11] The question of whether constitutional provisions that protected vested property rights should be applied to liquor therefore placed nineteenth-century judges on the horns of a dilemma: to invalidate laws that destroyed property rights in liquor would be to risk the wrath of millions of politically active evangelicals. But to sanction the outright destruction of a traditionally valid commodity would be to call into question the idea of fixed and unchanging categories on which the stability of the constitutional edifice depended.

Over time, I argue, the disjunction between Founding-era constitutional commitments and post-Revival mores gradually undermined the stability of the traditional order. For although antebellum jurists generally refused to bend the rules of constitutional adjudication on behalf of moral reform, the post-Civil War judiciary ultimately acquiesced in the destruction of "immoral" forms of property, thereby casting doubt on the permanence and objectivity of the traditional order's doctrinal underpinnings. To be sure, few postwar jurists saw reason to believe that a series of seemingly narrow doctrinal exceptions involving liquor and lottery regulation would threaten the stability of the larger constitutional order. And yet the decision to accommodate post-Revival mores ultimately forced the judiciary into the awkward position of explaining why property protections and federalism constraints could be dispensed with in cases involving liquor and lotteries, but not in cases involving labor relations, railroad rates, or antitrust regulation. By the turn of the twentieth century, I argue, the contrast between the judiciary's deferential attitude towards morals regulation and its rigid opposition to industrial regulation had begun to undermine the legitimacy of the traditional order's organizing concepts, thus paving the way for the reconceptualization of the Constitution as a "living" document whose key provisions should be understood to evolve in tandem with changing social and economic conditions.

Public Morals and Private Rights in the Nineteenth Century

Admittedly, this account of American constitutional development cuts against the grain of an entrenched scholarly consensus. Most studies of constitutional development in the period between the Founding and the New Deal offer little, if any, discussion of subjects such as liquor and lottery regulation. And indeed, conventional wisdom holds that the period's myriad moral reform movements were constitutionally insignificant, at least in comparison to rate regulation, labor organization, antitrust reform, and other constitutional controversies engendered by the rapid industrialization of the late nineteenth century.[12] Only recently have a few historians of religion begun to grapple with the legal and constitutional implications of nineteenth-century evangelicalism. Studies by Steven Green and David Sehat, in particular, have drawn attention to the contrast between Founding-era and nineteenth-century conceptions of religious liberty.[13] But these studies, while certainly improving our understanding of nineteenth-century political development, have focused almost exclusively on evangelical efforts to restrict free exercise rights through the enforcement of blasphemy laws, Sabbath laws, test oaths, and similar measures. Left largely unexplored is the question of how the Revival-era shift in mores impacted constitutional structures and doctrine beyond the narrow confines of church-state jurisprudence.[14]

Why have scholars generally failed to perceive any connection between the moral and religious upheavals of the nineteenth century and the constitutional transformations of the New Deal period?[15] There are, I believe, two reasons for this failure. The first stems from a deeply ingrained misconception regarding nineteenth-century constitutional law. More specifically, scholars have long described religion and morality as "local" matters that were all but excluded from the purview of constitutional law during the pre–New Deal period. As one scholar has observed, states and localities functioned within the nineteenth-century constitutional order as "keepers of morality and community" who were empowered "to deal with their citizens as they saw fit."[16] On this view, the evangelical-led moral reform movements of the nineteenth century were of little constitutional significance, since states and localities already enjoyed plenary authority over the regulation of morality.

Perhaps the clearest statement of this view is found in the work of William Novak. In his influential and carefully researched study *The People's Welfare,* Novak argues that the apparent tension between liberal constitutionalism, on the one hand, and draconian morals laws, on the other, was far from obvious to nineteenth-century Americans. In particular, Novak contends that jurists in this period did not regard the individual rights enshrined in the state and federal constitutions as "trumps" or absolute checks on the power of legislatures or local officials. Nineteenth-century governance, he writes, was "predicated on the elemental assumption that public interest was superior to private interest. Government and society were not created to protect preexisting private rights, but to further the welfare of the whole people and community." In practice, this meant that public officials enjoyed near-total freedom to restrict personal liberty and property rights, so long as there existed a plausible connection to public morality. Indeed, Novak concludes that "of all the contests over public power" in the nineteenth century, morals regulation was "the easy case"—the one regulatory sphere in which American jurists unwaveringly subordinated private rights to the public good.[17]

Novak is hardly alone in this assessment. Even scholars who are not inclined to describe the nineteenth-century legal order in communitarian terms nonetheless agree that, at least in the realm of morals regulation, public officials enjoyed considerable freedom of action. Thus Herbert Hovenkamp concludes that nineteenth-century legal culture reflected a dualistic ideology of "economic individualism" and "moral collectivism." Although judges were generally skeptical of government intervention in the market, they viewed morals regulation as a different matter altogether. So long as liquor, lottery, and other "police" measures were directed at upholding the moral standards of the wider community, they were likely to survive judicial scrutiny, regardless of the consequences for private rights.[18] James W. Ely echoes the point, noting that the same judges who vigorously protected property rights in other contexts "consistently repulsed [constitutional] attacks against morals . . . laws" and "allowed the states wide discretion to control individual behavior."[19] Lawrence Friedman, in his influential *History of American Law,* reaches a similar, if more concise, conclusion. The idea of "vested rights in liquor, lottery tickets, gambling, and sex," he writes, "never appealed much to nineteenth-century judges."[20]

One burden of this study, therefore, will be to demonstrate that the conventional scholarly wisdom greatly overstates the nineteenth-century judiciary's affinity for morals regulation. Although there is a grain of truth in the claim that nineteenth-century officials enjoyed considerable leeway in the policing of moral deviants, the body of case law examined below will show that this freedom of action was not unlimited. Part of the confusion may stem from a failure to clearly distinguish between two forms of morals regulation. As we shall see, Novak and like-minded scholars are correct to assert that nineteenth-century judges rarely questioned the legitimacy of *traditional* forms of morals regulation—from liquor license laws to prohibitions against operating a "disorderly" house—which had deep roots in both English common law and colonial-era custom. And yet nineteenth-century judges adopted a very different attitude when confronted with truly *novel* forms of morals regulation—that is, with laws criminalizing activities and forms of property that had traditionally enjoyed some degree of legal protection. In keeping with the evangelical theology of the Revival, the new measures typically aimed at the eradication of vice rather than the maintenance of public order. And because these laws unceremoniously abolished long-established property rights, many judges perceived a direct challenge to the constitutional order. Keenly aware of the need to resist any incursion upon the principles of the framers—lest the objectivity of those principles be called into question—*antebellum* jurists, at least, did not hesitate to set aside innovative morals laws. Indeed, far from affording state legislatures carte blanche in the regulation of personal morality, the judiciary soon came to be viewed as among the most serious obstacles blocking the path to moral regeneration.

The Moral Origins of the New Deal Revolution

But there is a second—and arguably more important—reason why scholars have generally failed to appreciate the Second Great Awakening's impact on constitutional development, namely, the enduring tendency to view the first 150 years of American constitutional development through the ideological prism of the New Deal. For while there is certainly no shortage of studies on constitutional development in the pre–New Deal period, most such studies are self-consciously framed in terms of the Roosevelt administration's battle with the Hughes Court. Modern critics of the New Deal revolution thus endeavor to prove that the collapse of economic rights and federalism constraints was, in effect, a constitutional coup. On this view, the New Dealers were motivated by blind devotion to a set of economic policies—centralized planning, labor regulation, economic redistribution—which they knew to be patently incompatible with the first principles of the republic. But instead of conceding defeat in the face of judicial resistance—or pursuing the intellectually honest remedy of an Article V amendment—the progressives used a combination of political pressure and judicial appointments to "rewrite" the Constitution.[21] At the opposite end of the ideological spectrum, modern-day defenders of the New Deal Court seek to establish the popular bona fides of the constitutional revolution.[22] Although these scholars often concede that the New Deal Court departed radically from the constitutional vision of the framers, they nonetheless argue that the revolution was a broadly participatory event in which "we the people" self-consciously opted for a new constitutional order.[23]

Occupying a middle position between these extremes is a growing body of revisionist scholarship which rejects the characterization of the constitutional revolution as a response to specifically *political* pressures (whether from the electorate or elite supporters of the New Deal). Although the revisionist scholars are far from a monolithic group, most agree that the doctrinal shifts of the 1930s were the culmination of a gradual process of constitutional change, a process triggered, in significant part, by changes in the structure of the American economy. In the wake of the rapid industrialization of the late nineteenth century, the argument goes, constitutional concepts and categories that had functioned perfectly well in the agrarian society of the early republic became increasingly problematic. Indeed, traditional principles often produced absurd decisions when applied under modern conditions, with the result that legal actors gradually lost faith in such traditional doctrinal tenets as the distinction between "commerce" and "production," or that between public and private economic concerns.[24]

One major achievement of the revisionist literature has been to lay to rest to the long accepted view of the early twentieth-century Court as a pro-business body that reflexively opposed all efforts to mitigate the human costs of industrialization and economic integration. Scholars including Howard Gillman, Barry Cushman, Owen Fiss, and Julie Novkov have convincingly demonstrated that decisions such as the Court's much-maligned 1905 ruling in *Lochner v. New York*—which blocked the state of New York's attempt to regulate the working hours of bakery employees—were not, in fact, motivated by class bias or a simple preference for laissez-faire economic policies. Rather, the "conservative" justices of the *Lochner* era seem to have been driven by a desire to prevent a total collapse of a constitutional order that had indeed been stretched to the breaking point by economic change. That the Court ultimately abandoned this effort in the late 1930s was not due to fear of political repercussions so much as the gradual realization, on the part of certain justices, that the doctrinal underpinnings of the Court's federalism and economic due process jurisprudence had become unworkable.

The present study joins earlier revisionist efforts in conceiving of the New Deal "revolution" as the culmination of a decades-long process of doctrinal evolution and not as the product of a sudden, politically motivated "switch in time." At the same time, I attempt to redress what I see as a significant limitation in the existing revisionist literature: namely, the tendency to focus almost exclusively on economic developments as the drivers of constitutional change. Perhaps because the critical decisions of the late 1930s and early 1940s involved efforts to address problems such as labor unrest and agricultural overproduction, scholars have tended to assume that these "underlying" economic problems must have functioned as the primary *causes* of the constitutional revolution. And in light of this assumption, it is only natural that revisionist scholars should focus their efforts on a narrow range of Court rulings dealing with questions of commodity regulation and industrial organization. But while it is clear that the constitutional revolution was in some sense a response to developments in the economic sphere, there is reason to believe that an *exclusive* focus on economic controversies has produced a misleading picture of constitutional development. In particular, it is important to remember that constitutional orders are complex, and seemingly disparate doctrinal areas are often interconnected. Indeed, one need only consider slavery's pervasive influence on antebellum jurisprudence to appreciate that the underlying causes of constitutional change are often quite remote from the immediate contexts of particular landmark decisions.[25]

One scholar who has focused much-needed attention on "doctrinal synergies" in the constitutional jurisprudence of the early-twentieth-century Court is Barry Cushman. In particular, Cushman has argued that the Court's rulings on the scope of the commerce power cannot be understood in isolation from contemporaneous rulings on economic due process. As Cushman has shown, the two lines of doctrine were intertwined to such an extent that, when the Court began to abandon the due process distinction between "public" and "private" economic concerns, the effect was simultaneously to undermine much of the Court's Commerce Clause jurisprudence (which had implicitly relied on the public/private distinction to determine when intrastate economic activities could be reached by the federal commerce power).[26] Although my analysis in no way contradicts this insight, I hope to push the scholarly discussion in a new direction by highlighting doctrinal synergies involving Court decisions that are typically viewed as far removed from the New Deal revolution. In particular, I shall argue that a complete explanation of the constitutional crisis of the 1930s must take into account the tension between the early-twentieth-century Court's deferential response to innovative morals laws, on the one hand, and its rigid opposition progressive economic regulations, on the other. Stated differently, we shall see that it was the *disjunction* between the Court's moral and economic rulings—and not the economic rulings in isolation—that bears much of the responsibility for the old order's collapse. For example, I demonstrate in chapter 5 that the unraveling of the pre-New Deal Court's Commerce Clause jurisprudence was driven, in significant part, by the perception that the Court's infamous 1918 decision invalidating federal child labor legislation (*Hammer v. Dagenhart*) was incompatible with earlier decisions upholding the federal regulation of lotteries, liquor, and prostitution. In the traditional conception of the federal system, after all, both manufacturing and morality were classed under the "police" power—a power that was understood to belong exclusively to the states. In the aftermath of the *Hammer* decision (holding that child labor laws were "police" regulations and therefore beyond the reach of the federal commerce power), many commentators concluded that the Court was selectively applying federalism limitations. How else, they asked, could one explain the Court's decision to invalidate the federal child labor law while simultaneously permitting Congress to use its commerce power to reach other traditional "police" subjects?

In short, the Court's accommodation of moral reform produced a series of doctrinal disjunctions that the justices could neither explain nor resolve, thus lending credibility to the Legal Realists and others who argued that legal rules were often indeterminate and the task of judging inherently subjective. By the 1930s, it was apparent even to casual observers that key constitutional concepts like "property" and "commerce" did not correspond to fixed and unchanging categories found in nature; and from here it was a relatively short step to the idea that key constitutional provisions should be understood to evolve in tandem with the moral and economic development of the nation.

Why Liquor and Lotteries?

Whether focused on slavery, liquor, lotteries, prostitution, or Sabbath obser-vance, the myriad religiously inspired social movements of the nineteenth century shared a great deal in common. All drew inspiration from the evan-gelical theology that rose to prominence during the early-nineteenth-century revivals. Most received the bulk of their manpower and resources from the nation's Protestant congregations and denominational organizations. Perhaps most important, all encountered serious obstacles in the courts—usually in the form of constitutional provisions that, at least according to opponents of moral reform, were intended to protect the rights of unpopular minorities (in-cluding slaveholders).[27] But although the myriad moral reform movements of the nineteenth century are rightly characterized as different dimensions of the same broader phenomenon, this study places the prohibition and anti-lottery movements at the heart of the story.

The reasons motivating this choice may not be immediately apparent. Most studies of American constitutional development, to the extent that they take notice of nineteenth-century moral reform movements, focus exclusively on the antislavery movement.[28] The tendency to associate antislavery, rather than the prohibition or anti-lottery movements, with significant constitutional change is not surprising. It was, after all, in the context of the slavery contro-versy that antebellum Americans were most likely to enter into debates over the meaning of the nation's fundamental law. Moreover, it is clear that antislavery thinkers made important and lasting contributions to constitutional thought, with some going so far as to articulate a dynamic or aspirational understand-ing of the nation's constitutional experiment.[29] And yet, in the end, it is clear that the antislavery movement ultimately failed in its attempt to transform the constitutional system. Whether because of the Supreme Court's narrow interpretation of the Reconstruction amendments or Congress's eventual in-difference to the problem of racial subordination, the nation emerged from the slavery crisis with most of its original constitutional architecture intact.[30] The rigid distinction between the state and federal spheres, which had appeared vulnerable during Reconstruction, reemerged with a vengeance in late-nine-teenth-century jurisprudence.[31] And although the Thirteenth Amendment eradicated an entire class of property rights, the Reconstruction amendments had little broader impact on property owners—except, perhaps, to grant them added protection through the Fourteenth Amendment's due process clause.

In light of these facts, scholars have begun to reevaluate the conventional periodization of American constitutional history, with its emphasis on the Civil War and Reconstruction as the critical turning points in constitutional development.[32] To be sure, the successful dismantling of the legal underpinnings of slavery marked a significant and durable change in the nation's governing arrangements, but the promise of the Reconstruction amendments would remain largely unfulfilled until the mid-twentieth century, when the political and constitutional transformations of the New Deal period at last made federal enforcement of civil rights a realistic possibility.[33]

There is, however, a critical difference between the antislavery movement and the movements examined below: where the constitutional pressures arising from the slavery crisis were eventually addressed (albeit incompletely) through *formal amendments* to the constitutional text, those arising from the prohibition and anti-lottery movements were accommodated, in the first instance, by shifts in constitutional doctrine and interpretive methodology. In the liquor and lottery cases, formal amendment was simply not a viable option for most of the nineteenth century, in part because of the widespread conviction that the amendment process was a device for correcting relatively minor structural flaws in the constitutional system and was therefore not to be used for addressing substantive policy concerns.[34] And while post-Civil War Americans warmed to the idea of using the amendment process for substantive ends, the unique circumstances that had facilitated the adoption of the Reconstruction amendments—namely, the exclusion of the Southern states from the Union—were no longer present. As a result, state and federal judges faced increasing pressure to find doctrinal solutions to problems that, in the case of slavery, had been addressed by formally amending the constitutional text. In the end, *judges*—rather than Article V actors—bent the constitutional framework to accommodate a series of ever more restrictive state and federal morals laws. And although it is true that national liquor prohibition was eventually enacted through an Article V amendment, the Eighteenth Amendment's purposes were largely symbolic. By the time of the amendment's ratification in 1919, most of the nation was already "dry" as a result of state and local regulations, and the Supreme Court had recently endorsed the constitutionality of federal laws that banned the shipment of liquor into dry areas. (Ironically, the true purpose of the prohibition amendment, in the eyes of many anti-liquor crusaders, was to insulate the liquor question from electoral politics, thus ensuring that the nation would remain permanently dry.)[35]

One potential drawback of using doctrinal shifts to accommodate social change, however, is that even the narrowest of exceptions to the prevailing rules of constitutional interpretation may spread beyond its original context to affect other, seemingly remote, doctrinal areas. As we shall see in chapters 4 and 5, shifts in the judiciary's treatment of prohibitory liquor and lottery laws worked in unexpected ways to erode the foundations of the Supreme Court's Contract Clause, due process, and Commerce Clause jurisprudence—the three pillars of the nineteenth-century constitutional order. Thus, without denying the constitutional significance of antislavery and the other major moral reform movements of the nineteenth century, it is my contention that the prohibition and anti-lottery movements played a more integral role in laying the groundwork for the interpretive revolutions of the New Deal period.

Contemporary Relevance: Reexamining the Origins of the Living Constitution

The study's implications for contemporary constitutional theory will be considered in some detail in the conclusion. Yet it is worth noting at the outset that American political discourse has been dominated in recent years by questions concerning the legitimacy of the modern—that is, post-New Deal—constitutional order. For present purposes, the important point to note is that normative debates concerning the legitimacy of the modern order often hinge on the empirical question of how that order came into being. Many critics of the modern order have therefore labored to link the progressive vision of a "living" Constitution to a series of apparently insidious foreign intellectual traditions, from Darwinian evolution to Hegel's theory of the state. This is true not only of socially conservative politicians—who regularly describe the idea of the living Constitution as "un-American"—but also of a number of recent academic works on American constitutional development.[36] Richard Epstein, for example, has argued that that Progressive-era reformers rejected the property-centered constitutionalism of "Locke and Madison" in favor of a dynamic constitutionalism inspired by "Bismarckian social initiatives."[37] James Stoner, in turn, explains that Progressive-era intellectuals modeled their constitutional theory on "the concept of a living species" as understood in "Darwinian evolution."[38] Bradley C. S. Watson likewise traces the birth of the living Constitution to "the arrival on the [American] intellectual scene" of "Social Darwinism" and "Hegelian idealism."[39] According to Christopher Wolfe, the decline of the traditional constitutional order began when leading Progressives, including Woodrow Wilson, rejected the framers' "Newtonian theory of government in favor of a more Darwinian theory."[40] Finally, Paul Carrese levels a similar charge against Justice Oliver Wendell Holmes, who replaced the traditional order's "careful equilibrium of powers" with a constitutional theory modeled on "Darwinian evolution" and "Hegelian liberal progress."[41]

The point is not that these scholars are completely mistaken; it is beyond dispute that Progressive-era constitutional thought owed a significant debt to pragmatist philosophers who, in turn, owed a great deal to Darwin and Hegel. But when scholars attribute the demise of the traditional constitutional order to the force of these Anglo-European intellectual traditions, we are again left with the impression that the Progressives and New Dealers engineered a sort of constitutional coup. Such narratives, in other words, are not content merely to highlight the normatively problematic aspects of the modern constitutional order. Rather, with their frequent invocations of "foreign" antecedents, they go much further, casting a pall of illegitimacy over the entirety of twentieth-century constitutional development.

In reality, however, the organic conception of the constitutional enterprise that rose to prominence in the 1930s was not a straightforward outgrowth of Hegelian idealism or Social Darwinism; nor was it the sole creation of Progressive-era academics. In fact, the idea emerged gradually over the course of the nineteenth century, and largely as a result of the evangelical effort to eradicate immoral forms of property. Although few nineteenth-century evangelicals consciously envisioned an outright abandonment of economic rights or federalism constraints, evangelical reformers and their allies nonetheless developed a range of arguments that pushed in the direction of a dynamic conception of constitutional meaning. They argued that the will of democratic majorities should be afforded greater weight in constitutional adjudication; that the ideals of the Founding generation should not be permitted to bar the moral progress of future generations; and that the meaning of constitutional concepts should be updated to reflect advances in scientific knowledge. In the aftermath of the Civil War, this loosely related family of arguments gained a foothold in the judiciary, as the nation's judges began to acquiesce in the destruction of newly immoral forms of property. And although American jurists struggled mightily to prevent the spread of these novel doctrines beyond their original contexts, efforts at damage control were largely unsuccessful. Having opened the door to a dynamic understanding of the constitutional enterprise in the case of morals regulation, the judiciary was ill-positioned to resist the demands of those twentieth-century progressives who argued for a wholesale constitutional revolution.

One of this study's primary contributions to contemporary constitutional theory, then, is to suggest that the familiar characterization of the "living" Constitution as a foreign—and therefore presumptively illegitimate—import has little basis in fact. In reality, the disintegration of the traditional, static understanding of the constitutional enterprise began in the early nineteenth century, and millions of evangelical Protestants led the call for change. In light of this fact, we must acknowledge that the forces most responsible for severing the nation's fundamental law from its traditional moorings were no less "American" than the vision of limited government and inviolable property rights espoused by the Founding generation.

Organization of the Study

This study is organized chronologically and consists of five chapters. Chapter 1 examines the period from the Founding to the 1830s, paying particular attention to the ways in which the American constitutional order was shaped by the late-eighteenth-century society from which it emerged. As previous scholars have noted, the basic structures of the American constitutional system were designed to foster a "commercial republic"—a polity in which tendentious moral and religious concerns would be subordinated to the worldly goals of material prosperity and security. The creation of such a constitutional order was made possible, I argue, by a prior process of secularization which took place during the first three-quarters of the eighteenth-century. And yet the initial congruence of popular mores and constitutional principles proved tenuous. With the onset of the Second Great Awakening, rates of religious adherence soared, ecumenical projects flourished, and a morally demanding evangelical theology displaced the relatively lax Calvinism of the Founding generation. By the 1830s, Americans were beginning to press for policy changes—namely, the eradication of liquor, lotteries, slavery, and other "national sins"—that threatened to destroy the foundations of the commercial republic.

In Chapters 2 through 4, I turn to case law to document the effects of the emerging disjunction between post-Revival mores and Founding-era constitutional principles. Chapter 2 covers the period from 1830 to the mid-1850s, during which state judiciaries were inundated with constitutional challenges to innovative liquor and lottery laws. This chapter's most important finding is that state appellate courts generally resisted efforts to abolish property rights involving liquor and lotteries. Although it is true that the judiciary granted state legislatures wide leeway to *regulate* liquor sales and lottery drawings, judges typically drew the line at prohibition, striking down laws that revoked existing lottery grants (which were held to violate the Contract Clause) or ordered the summary destruction of property in liquor (which were held to violate the due process clauses of state constitutions).

As I demonstrate in Chapter 3, however, judicial attitudes towards moral reform began to shift in the mid-1850s, when the collapse of the Jacksonian party system produced the first significant cracks in the traditional constitutional order. Where Whigs and Democrats had for decades worked to exclude moral questions from the political sphere, the newly formed Republican party initially welcomed the support of evangelical reformers; indeed, Republican politicians regularly appointed prohibition-friendly judges to state appellate courts as a means of winning evangelical support. Not surprisingly, many state appellate courts—almost all of them in states dominated by the Republican party—now reversed course and endorsed the constitutionality of statewide prohibition. Ignoring or downplaying a half-century of contradictory precedent, many state-level judges now endorsed the view that any form of property that threatened the moral health of the republic could be abolished without regard for the constitutional rights of property owners.

Chapter 4 documents a similar shift in the Supreme Court's treatment of morals legislation. In decisions handed down during the 1870s and early 1880s, federal courts—including the Supreme Court—frequently resisted attempts to abolish property rights in liquor and lotteries. And yet, like their colleagues at the state level, the justices were ultimately forced to yield to the superior force of public opinion. As opposition to liquor and lotteries solidified, the Court handed down a series of decisions that unequivocally endorsed the constitutionality of state liquor and lottery bans, as well as federal restrictions on the interstate traffic in immoral commodities. Although scholars have generally described these rulings as run-of-the-mill restatements of existing doctrine, I demonstrate that the decisions were both innovative and controversial. In fact, contemporary commentators accurately predicted that the Court's deferential liquor and lottery rulings would make it difficult, if not impossible, for the justices to simultaneously uphold economic rights and federalism constraints in the industrial sphere.

Chapter 5 concludes the study by documenting the continued erosion—and ultimate collapse—of the traditional order's organizing concepts and categories. Beginning with Justice Holmes's influential *Lochner*-era dissents, we shall see that the Court's deferential treatment of morals laws lent credibility to those commentators who argued that traditional constitutional doctrine was little more than camouflage for the policy preferences of a conservative judiciary. By the mid-1930s, large swaths of the legal community were genuinely persuaded that the Court had so mangled the jurisprudence of federalism, economic due process, and the Contract Clause as to make a constitutional revolution all but inevitable. Moreover, we shall see that the revolution, when it came, was justified largely in terms of the Court's prior accommodation of moral reform. The Roosevelt administration lawyers who defended the New Deal before the Supreme Court frequently invoked the Court's liquor and lottery rulings to make the case for an expansive reading of the federal commerce power and a narrow conception of economic due process. And when the Court at last acquiesced in the birth of a new constitutional order, the justices grounded their transformative rulings squarely on the dynamic understanding of the constitutional enterprise originally articulated in the Court's turn-of-the-century liquor and lottery rulings.

{1}

The Evangelical Challenge to American Constitutionalism

A religious sect may degenerate into a political faction in a part of the Confederacy; but the variety of sects dispersed over the entire face of it must secure the national councils against any danger from that source.

—James Madison, *Federalist* 10

The constitutional system that emerged from the Philadelphia Convention has been aptly described as a "commercial republic."[1] The label highlights what is perhaps the most striking feature of the framers' handiwork: their subordination of traditional moral and religious purposes to the worldly goals of protecting property and promoting economic development. At a time when official references to the Almighty were commonplace, the framers took the surprising step of creating an essentially secular document: the text did not invoke God's blessing, nor did it even mention Him, save in a single reference in the signatory section to the "Year of Our Lord." More important, when leading Federalists were asked to explain the republic's ultimate purposes, they consistently spurned appeals to the divine in favor of appeals to their readers' material self-interest. As the authors of *The Federalist* explained, the principal purposes of the new governing arrangements would be to protect "private rights," promote "commercial prosperity," and bolster "the national security."[2]

This is not to suggest that the framers were hostile to religion or that they opposed efforts to promote a virtuous citizenry. Indeed, many clearly supported official regulation of religion and morality, at least so long as these functions were carried out at the state and local levels.[3] But they also recognized that traditional republican theories of politics, which viewed the cultivation of a virtuous and homogenous citizenry as the key to a republic's survival, were ill suited to American conditions. Simply put, the American nation was geographically larger, more populous, and more socially and economically diverse than previous republics. These factors made the cultivation of broadly shared norms and religious creeds—the traditional republican remedy for the evils of faction—practically impossible. Some other foundation for the American republic would have to be found, and so the framers turned to material prosperity and procedural consensus to serve as "surrogates" for the shared norms which classical thinkers had deemed so essential.[4] Turning the conventional republican wisdom on its head, they "reduc[ed] the scope of politics" to its lowest common denominators: "self-preservation and economic self-interest."[5]

But while the idea of the "commercial republic" may have seemed the perfect theoretical solution to the problem of reconciling republicanism with size and diversity, a successful transition from theory to practice was by no means assured. For, as Sheldon Wolin has written, the ratification process "did not adopt a constitution in anything but the most formal sense of a paper document." Rather, it endorsed "a sophisticated theory of a constitution, as represented most brilliantly by *The Federalist Papers*, but a theory with only a minimally developed practice or a supporting culture of its own."[6] Much would depend on the fit between the Constitution's institutional innovations, on the one hand, and existing political cultures and practices, on the other. And it is here that the Federalist vision was—perhaps unavoidably—shortsighted, in the sense that it assumed a background of social conditions that were in hindsight merely transient features of American life. In particular, it assumed an underlying society that would endorse, or at least acquiesce in, the severing of law and virtue and the identification of economic development as the primary end of national union.

These assumptions appeared reasonable enough in the early years of the republic. Indeed, at a time when a traditional, Puritan-inspired system of morals regulation was disintegrating and the influence of organized religion in decline, a Federalist-dominated judiciary experienced relatively little difficulty in translating the commercial republic ideal into the binding language of constitutional doctrine.[7] In particular, the landmark decisions of the Marshall Court firmly established congressional authority over interstate commerce, while also significantly restraining the power of state and local governments to interfere with vested property rights.[8] But the apparent fit between constitution and society proved fleeting. By the 1830s, organized Protestantism had reemerged as a significant political force, and large numbers of Americans were dedicating themselves to the task of abolishing liquor, lotteries, slavery, and other immoral forms of property. Where the framers had sought to protect established property rights and insulate interstate markets from excessive state and local regulation, the aims of the Protestant reformers were precisely the opposite: to constrain property rights and interstate markets in the name of the public good. The problem, of course, was that the first of these two policy visions was by this point thoroughly ensconced in state and federal constitutional doctrine. And for this reason, the reformers could not achieve their aims through moral suasion or statutory prohibitions alone. Rather, they would have to attempt to dismantle significant features of the Founding generation's handiwork.

In order to appreciate the full extent of the Revival's impact on American constitutionalism, however, we must also come to grips with a second critical feature of the Constitution of 1787: its assumptions regarding language. For it was not only the substantive policy choices of the framers that proved problematic in the wake of the Revival, but also their conviction that the meanings of key constitutional concepts like "property," "contract," and "commerce" were essentially static, or at least amenable to relatively precise definition.[9] Stated otherwise, the framers seem not to have contemplated the possibility that mores might evolve in ways that would reconfigure language itself, so as to render key constitutional concepts virtually unworkable. And yet American society underwent precisely such a revolution in the 1820s and 1830s. With the onset of the post-Revival reform movements, even constitutional categories with ancient lineages in Anglo-American common law were destabilized by the growing conviction that newly immoral forms of property should be excluded from the ambit of legal protection altogether. This was a deeply troubling development. Indeed, the idea that it was possible for a given entity to move between constitutional categories—to move, for example, from the category of "property" to the category of "nuisance"— threatened to discredit the very idea of what Hamilton termed the "limited constitution."[10] For how could textual provisions serve as meaningful constraints on official power if the Constitution's most basic concepts and categories were constantly in flux? Although the full extent of this problem will become clear only when we turn to case law in Chapters 2 through 4, the present chapter concludes by identifying three specific "sites" of constitutional conflict, or points where the new post-Revival morality tested the limits of Founding-era constitutional principles.

The Demise of the Puritan Worldview and the Enervation of the Religious Sphere

The institutionalization of the Federalist constitutional vision would not have been possible if not for the prior marginalization of an older and once-powerful strand of American political thought, one that rejected as illegitimate all attempts to separate the moral and legal spheres. In the Puritan worldview, which pervaded American intellectual life through the middle of the eighteenth century, political authorities were expected not only to secure the property and bodily safety of the citizenry but also to make "a regular effort to establish and uphold high standards of [citizen] conduct."[11] Thus the Cambridge Platform of Church Discipline, drafted by John Cotton in 1648, explained that it was "the duty of the Magistrate" to enforce "the duties commanded in the first, as well as . . . the duties commanded in the second table [of the Decalogue]."[12] During the seventeenth and early eighteenth centuries, the influence of the Puritan worldview was evident in the famously rigid criminal codes of the American colonies, which typically punished a range of "crimes" that would today be regarded as minor vices. Regional variations existed, of course, but virtually all of the colonial statute books contained prohibitions against blasphemy, profanity, Sabbath-breaking, gambling, and marital infidelity.[13] Such laws were designed to transform colonial villages into tiny, self-policing communities of virtue, and there is good evidence that they succeeded in this regard, at least for a time. Legal historians have demonstrated that, through the mid-eighteenth century, laws governing personal morality were strictly enforced; indeed, morals offenses appear to have made up the bulk of the judicial workload at the lower levels of government in most of the colonies.[14] Moreover, because colonial-era morals laws depended upon citizen informers to report abuses, there is reason to believe that efforts to police personal morality enjoyed broad public support.[15]

By the revolutionary period, however, a subtle transformation had taken place in Americans' understanding of the law-morality relationship. While leading ministers and other public figures continued to condemn the usual list of vices, calls to subject personal moral failings to *civil* punishment became increasingly rare.[16] Moreover, the underlying rationale for holding one's self (and others) to a high standard of moral conduct began to evolve as well. In particular, the classic Calvinist virtues of hard work, temperance, and frugality ceased to be viewed as ends in themselves, that is, as ends that were to be pursued solely for the glory of God.[17] In the new understanding, the primary motive for adhering to the traditional virtues was not because they "functioned in the divine plan of salvation," but rather because debt, idleness, and intemperance were viewed as the most common causes of earthly "dependence and misery." Pursuit of the traditional virtues thus became "a device for procuring [one's own] security and advantage."[18] This is not to suggest that Founding-era Americans were indifferent to the moral character of their society; on the contrary, improving the morals of the citizenry remained an *instrumentally* important goal, since the pursuit of virtue allowed "individuals and the nation as a whole [to] grow more prosperous, safer, and stronger in world trade." But furthering this goal would henceforth be the responsibility of private individuals and religious societies rather than the state.[19] Even John Adams, the founder who was perhaps most influenced by the Puritan worldview, conceded in 1778 that in America "the foundations of national Morality would be laid in private Families" and not in the statute books.[20]

That the demise of the Puritan worldview affected all levels of American society is confirmed by evidence demonstrating a near-total collapse of morals enforcement in the decades preceding the Revolution. Studies of local court records in Massachusetts, for example, have found that the judicial caseload in the early eighteenth century was dominated by morals offenses, with more than half of all prosecutions involving sexual crimes (adultery, fornication, prostitution) or religious offenses (blasphemy, Sabbath-breaking, profanity). Remarkably, prosecutions for strictly moral and religious offenses declined to a miniscule portion of total prosecutions in the decades following the Revolution, as prosecutors shifted their attention to economic crimes such as theft.[21] In addition, the same period witnessed what might be termed a routinization of morals enforcement: adultery and fornication were increasingly addressed with fines (designed to prevent illegitimate offspring from becoming public charges) instead of corporal punishment or public humiliation.[22] Similarly, the formerly cumbersome process of applying for a liquor license—a process designed to establish the moral character of the applicant—was in many areas reduced to a simple administrative proceeding.[23] As Lawrence Friedman has written, American law had by the Revolutionary period ceased to function as "guardian of a code of sexual and social behavior" and become instead the "defender of an economic and political order."[24]

The first precondition for the institutionalization of the commercial republic, then, was the erosion of the Puritan ideal of the virtuous, self-policing community. Absent this sea change in American thinking about the proper function of law, a constitutional order centered around the protection of established property rights and the promotion of commercial "intercourse"—a code word for national networks of exchange that would inevitably disrupt local patterns of regulation—would almost certainly have been unthinkable.[25] Yet it is also worth noting a second feature of Founding-era society that was arguably of equal importance in facilitating the rise of an essentially secular constitutional order: namely, the fact that the religious sphere, the natural repository of Puritan ideals, was numerically weak, institutionally divided, and increasingly liberal in its theological orientation.

Indeed, the ratio of churches to population experienced a significant decline over the course of the eighteenth century, as Mark Noll and others have demonstrated.[26] By the time of the Revolution, only 17 percent of Americans were attached to a particular religious congregation (as compared to 37 percent at the time of the Civil War), and few denominations were "adding enough new members to replace those who died."[27] Also contributing to the overall weakness of the religious sphere was the fact that the bulk of nation's religious adherents were more or less equally divided between the Congregational, Presbyterian, Anglican, and Baptist denominations (with the remaining 20 percent composed of Quakers, Methodists, various Reformed sects, and a small number of Roman Catholics).[28] To be sure, denominational diversity was hardly a new feature of the American religious landscape. Yet it is important to note that the cleavages which had long marred American Protestantism were growing more severe during the early years of the republic. In New England, the protracted conflict between the Congregationalist establishment and Baptist dissenters over issues of religious taxation and incorporation was nearing a head at precisely this point.[29] In Virginia, Baptists and Anglicans remained at war over a similar set of questions. Meanwhile, the Congregationalists of New England were beginning to experience bitter internal schisms resulting from the newfound popularity of Unitarian theology.[30] In light of these developments, it is hardly surprising to see Madison predicting in *Federalist* 10 that religious enthusiasm would not pose a serious "danger" to the "national councils" in America.[31] There were plenty of religious Americans, to be sure; but the fractured nature of American Protestantism had rendered religion politically impotent, or so it seemed in 1788.

A final feature of the Founding-era religious sphere that undoubtedly aided the institutionalization of the Federalist constitutional vision was the increasingly private orientation of American Calvinism (which is to say, the major part of American Protestantism).[32] To be sure, many Congregationalist and Presbyterian ministers, particularly in New England, continued to issue jeremiads warning of dire consequences should the nation stray from traditional standards of personal morality. But the traditional conception of public virtue—as something to be cultivated by direct involvement in public affairs—was increasingly displaced by a novel emphasis on the moral benefits of "nonpolitical organizational life." Many of the nation's Calvinist clergy, as Ruth H. Bloch has observed, came to accept that the popular virtue necessary to sustain the republic would be cultivated in families and through private educational efforts, or not at all.[33] Thus, while the decades immediately following the Founding witnessed the formation of a series of "voluntary societies" dedicated to the moral education of the lower classes, these organizations were both rigidly denominational and generally apolitical; attempts at cross-denominational cooperation failed miserably, and calls to legislate morality were generally rebuffed.[34] Among the major Protestant denominations, only a pair of non-Calvinist sects, the Quakers and the Methodists, exhibited a serious concern with personal vices such as drunkenness and gambling, and neither denomination was large enough to exert a significant influence in the political sphere.[35] Moreover, there is some evidence to suggest that even these denominations were moving in the same, generally liberal direction as their Calvinist counterparts: in 1790 the Methodists voted to permit church members to earn their livings through the "buying and selling of spirituous liquors"—a practice that had been grounds for excommunication since 1743.[36]

Religious Weakness and the Institutionalization of the Commercial Republic

In light of these general trends, it should not be surprising that an essentially secular, property-centered constitutional order managed to gain a foothold in the early republic. To gain a better understanding of precisely how this process unfolded, however, it may be helpful to briefly examine two illustrative episodes from the early history of American constitutional development. Consider, first, the institutionalization of Congress's Article I postal power, a power that managed to take root despite its obvious tendency to disrupt state and local patterns of moral regulation. The story begins in the 1790s, when Congress exercised its constitutional authority to establish a national network of post-roads. The creation of this national transportation network, which cut across countless state and local administrative boundaries, was viewed by at least some contemporaries as confirming Anti-Federalist fears of a congressional power grab. But even more disturbing was Congress's decision to require many postal employees to work on Sundays, a move that flowed naturally from Federalist concern for commercial expansion and national security.[37] As Richard R. John has written, this requirement constituted an unprecedented "invasion of the sacred," in the sense that postal employees scattered throughout the Union were forced to violate the ubiquitous state laws that prohibited labor and travel on the Sabbath.[38] On Sundays, the drivers of mail coaches, traversing the nation on newly constructed post-roads, passed through countless rural villages where literally nothing else moved.

One might expect religious Americans to protest this state of affairs, and indeed some did. For example, a significant controversy erupted in 1810 when Congress expanded the Sunday duties of postal employees by requiring that Post Offices be opened to the public on the Sabbath.[39] (Although the mail had always been sorted and transported on Sundays, Post Offices were not generally open to the public on Sundays until 1810.) But while the new law provoked vigorous and coordinated protests from Northeastern Congregationalists and Presbyterians, attempts to launch a broader, cross-denominational, and cross-sectional Sabbatarian campaign met with little success.[40] Although Baptists and Methodists were no less contemptuous of Sunday labor than Congregationalists and Presbyterians, the former sects, because of their long histories of opposition to religious establishment, were deeply suspicious of efforts to enforce religious orthodoxy by law and generally refused to join in the protest. The divide between orthodox Calvinism and the upstart sects was at this point simply too wide to bridge.

Significantly, a second round of Sabbatarian activism in the late 1820s and early 1830s did succeed in generating a degree of interdenominational cooperation.[41] But by this point the damage had been done. That is to say, the constitutionality and propriety of Sunday mail were by the late 1820s too well established to be successfully contested. State courts had plainly declared that local officials were constitutionally barred from preventing postal employees from "proceed[ing] with the mail on the Lord's day to the post office."[42] In addition, the Sabbatarian cause had by this point been tarred by its opponents, primarily merchants and religious dissenters, as a covert attempt to promote a national religious establishment—an attempt to overthrow "the spirit of the Constitution" in favor of "religious despotism," in the words of the Baptist Congressman Richard Johnson's famous 1829 committee report.[43] By the time the second round of protests had run its course, it was clear that the thin layer of national authority established by the Constitution constituted a very real limit on the moral autonomy of states and localities. As one evangelical petition lamented, the federal government had effectively "repealed" the Sabbath laws of the states, "for they are completely set aside by that part of the Post Office law . . . which renders impractical the effectual execution of any of the State laws by which a due observance of the Lord's day is enjoined."[44]

For a second illustration of how the fractured and enervated condition of American religion facilitated the rise of a commercial republic, one need only look to the famous *Dartmouth College* case, the 1819 ruling in which the Marshall Court declared that the federal Contract Clause generally barred state legislatures from interfering with corporate charters.[45] As we shall see, *Dartmouth College* would in subsequent years become a thorn in the side of the nation's evangelical reformers, as they found themselves constitutionally barred from repealing lottery grants and other "immoral" agreements between state legislatures and private parties. For this reason, it is all the more ironic that the case arose out of the bitter sectarian disputes that plagued New England in the early-nineteenth century.

On its face, the case turned on the question of whether the New Hampshire legislature possessed the authority to redraw Dartmouth College's corporate charter. And yet the controversy began as a religious power struggle between Dartmouth's president, John Wheelock, a liberal Presbyterian, and the College's orthodox Calvinist board of trustees. The case took on broader implications only after Wheelock, in an effort to rally Baptists and religious liberals on behalf of his cause, stirred up fears of an orthodox plot to establish a "sectarian despotism" in the state. Although Wheelock's activities, which angered the state's Federalist-controlled legislature, soon led to his dismissal, he was vindicated in 1816 when sympathetic Republicans won control of the legislature and the governorship on a platform that promised to wrest control of the College from the Federalists and their orthodox Calvinist allies. Soon after the election, the Republicans made good on this promise by amending Dartmouth's charter to increase the size of its board, reinstate Wheelock as president, and provide for "perfect freedom of religious opinion" within the College. At this point the original trustees filed suit, arguing that the College's charter—issued by the crown in 1769—constituted a contract, and that

any attempt to modify the charter would violate the U.S. Constitution's prohibition against laws "impairing the obligation of contracts."[46]

Dartmouth College reached the Supreme Court in 1818. And to a Federalist-dominated Court, the stakes of the dispute could not have been clearer. If
Dartmouth was a private corporation—as the Court agreed it was—then the
Republican legislature's actions could only be described as working a naked
transfer of property, as taking "away from one [party] . . . rights, property,
and franchises, and giv[ing] them to another."[47] Clearly appalled at the legislature's blatant disregard for settled property rights, Chief Justice Marshall
ensconced the principle of vested rights in the nation's fundamental law by
holding that corporate charters were indeed "contracts" within the meaning of
the Contract Clause. But while Marshall's opinion has been rightly characterized as a long-term victory for American religion—in the sense that religious
corporations were now insulated from legislative meddling—the decision also
had the ironic effect of significantly restraining the power of democratic majorities to enact broadly shared moral values into law.[48] Indeed, *Dartmouth
College* established that no consideration of public morality—not even concern
for religious liberty—could justify a state legislature's attempt to unilaterally
modify a corporate charter. The case thus provides a striking example of how
America's Protestants, in the midst of a bitter struggle over the propriety of
state regulation of religion, unwittingly facilitated the institutionalization of
a constitutional order that subordinated traditional moral and religious purposes to the worldly goal of protecting established property rights.

In sum, these episodes suggest that the religious sphere, the one area of the
polity that might be expected to resist the institutionalization of an essentially
secular vision of the American republic, was in the early-nineteenth century
unable—and in at least some cases unwilling—to do so. The framers' vision
of a commercial republic therefore became reality, as the federal government
succeeded in establishing national networks of exchange, and as state and
federal judiciaries gradually tightened their hold over the exclusively "legal"
sphere of property rights.[49] By the time American Protestantism regained a
degree of political influence in the 1830s, it was by then too late to deny that
state legislatures were significantly restricted in their ability to interfere with
established property rights or restrict the movement of goods and people in
interstate commerce. From this point forward, any effort to restore the Puritan vision of the covenanted polity through democratic channels would confront serious constitutional obstacles.

The Rise of an Evangelical Moral Order

When one considers the fractured nature of the American religious sphere during the Founding era, it is all the more remarkable that European visitors were, by the 1830s, marveling at the cultural hegemony of American Protestantism. As Alexis de Tocqueville famously observed, religion functioned as a unifying force in Jacksonian America, notwithstanding the fact that America's Christians were divided into "an innumerable multitude" of sects. To be sure, Americans held differing views on how best to "render [worship] to the Creator," but all appeared to "preach the same morality in the name of God." Indeed, so great was the influence of religion upon American mores, according to Tocqueville, that there appeared to be "no country in the world where the Christian religion" had more successfully "preserved genuine power over souls."[50]

Recent studies by sociologists and historians of religion suggest that such statements were far from hyperbole. Richard Carwardine, for example, notes that evangelical Christianity was by the 1840s "the largest, and most formidable, subculture in American society."[51] So pervasive was evangelical religion's influence in this period that scholars have often referred to the emergence of an informal Protestant "establishment."[52] The label accurately reflects the fact that American Protestants were, by the middle decades of the nineteenth century, unified by a set of broadly shared theological convictions as well as an interlocking network of ecumenical associations dedicated to the eradication of slavery, drunkenness, gambling, and other national sins. We shall see that this reorientation of the religious sphere placed American society on a collision course with the American constitutional system. But before examining the constitutional impact of moral reform, we must ask how the transformation of the religious sphere came about.

The Transformation of the Religious Sphere

When considering religion's reemergence as a significant force in American culture and politics, scholars typically begin by noting that the United States experienced a "Second Great Awakening" in the period between 1800 and 1830. The idea of a Second Great Awakening—or Great Revival, as it is also known—refers not only to the wave of popular religious revivals that swept the nation in this period, but also to a series of broader transformations within the religious sphere. For purposes of documenting religion's impact on constitutional development, it is sufficient to note here that the Revival changed American society in four distinct but interrelated respects: it significantly increased rates of church membership; transformed the reigning theological orthodoxy; spawned popular crusades dedicated to the legal enforcement of Protestant mores; and spurred significant cross-denominational cooperation among American Protestants.

The most obvious transformation was the dramatic increase in religiosity. During the Founding era, as we have seen, only a relatively small minority of Americans (about 17 percent) were attached to a particular religious congregation. By 1850, that figure had doubled to a remarkable 34 percent.[53] Moreover, in sharp contrast to the decades preceding the Revolution, the Revival era saw the number of ministers and churches increase far more rapidly than the general population—three times as fast, in the case of ministers.[54] Although scholars are divided on the question of what caused this upsurge in religiosity, there is general agreement that the collapse of the various state-level religious establishments was a major contributing factor.[55] As the sociologists Roger Finke and Rodney Stark have persuasively demonstrated, disestablishment forced the nation's myriad sects to compete on a level playing field. Accordingly, all sects found it necessary to experiment with radically new ways of recruiting adherents. Those groups whose methods and messages were best suited to the religious needs of an unsettled and rapidly expanding population generally thrived, adding adherents at a rate that far exceeded population growth, while those that resisted deviation from orthodoxy generally floundered.[56]

In denominational terms, as Finke and Stark (and others) have shown, evangelical sects like the Methodists and Baptists enjoyed several advantages in the new religious marketplace: they eschewed formal training of clergy in favor of lay preaching (and thus could produce far more ministers than their rivals); they embraced plainspoken and entertaining styles of preaching (including mass revival meetings); and they delivered a populist message that emphasized the dignity and moral responsibility of the individual believer and was therefore well-suited to "the needs of rootless egalitarian-minded men and women."[57] It should therefore come as no surprise that the period's explosive growth in church membership was heavily concentrated in the Methodist and Baptist denominations.[58] By 1850, in fact, 55 percent of the nation's religious adherents belonged to one of these two denominations (as compared to less than 20 percent at the time of the Revolution). Thus, the early nineteenth-century upsurge in religiosity is perhaps more accurately described as an upsurge in *evangelical* religiosity, as the nation's two "most militantly evangelical churches" assumed the dominant position with American Protestantism.[59]

Closely connected with the Revival-era increase in religiosity was a second major development within the religious sphere: the widespread acceptance of a new popular theology or religious worldview. Where American religious life at the time of the Founding was dominated by a relatively orthodox Calvinism, millions of Americans were by the 1830s embracing a new evangelical worldview that rejected virtually all of Calvinism's key tenets. This was true not only of those who joined the upstart evangelical sects, but also of many who remained within the traditional Calvinist strongholds of Congregationalism and Presbyterianism.[60] In other words, orthodoxy was itself pulled in an evangelical direction by the success of the upstart sects' populist message—so much so, in fact, that many of the most important prophets of the new evangelicalism, including the revivalist Charles Grandison Finney and the moral reformer Lyman Beecher, were nominal Congregationalists or Presbyterians.

The key points of contrast between orthodox Calvinism and the newly dominant evangelical worldview can by briefly summarized.[61] First, the nineteenth-century evangelicals generally rejected the doctrine of innate depravity in favor of the view that moral perfection was, with God's help, attainable in this life. No longer predisposed to sin, human beings were, in Finney's memorable formulation, "moral free agents" who possessed the capacity to choose between good (obedience to God's will) and evil (satisfaction of selfish desires).[62] Second, most nineteenth-century evangelicals abandoned the idea of a predestined "elect" in favor of the belief that all human beings might be spared eternal damnation, provided only that they voluntarily accept God's offer of salvation. As one leading evangelical pastor explained in 1827, God had not created "men on purpose to damn them," but rather "to glorify himself in their holiness and felicity; . . . and if they do not choose to be saved . . . they cannot blame him for their self-chosen condemnation."[63] Third, the nation's evangelicals tended to adopt a postmillennial eschatology, or view of the end times, which held that human agency would play a central role in preparing the world for Christ's return. Christians could no longer simply wait for divine intervention, in the form of the Second Coming, to deliver them from an inherently sinful world. Rather, as Beecher explained, it was God's will that America's Christians actively work towards the "moral renovation of the world," thereby hastening the arrival of the Millennium.[64]

This is not to suggest that the revivalists of the Second Great Awakening were the first to break with orthodox Calvinism's rather pessimistic conception of human nature. Certainly many elites had by the time of the Founding rejected the doctrine of innate depravity in favor of an Enlightenment faith in the possibility of moral progress. But the secular, Enlightenment understanding of progress which was gaining in influence at the time of the Founding held only that moral progress was possible—or at least that moral corruption could be checked—through the medium of well-designed *institutions,* or what the authors of the *Federalist Papers* called "the science of politics."[65] Most of the framers did not believe that human nature was essentially good. Rather, they believed that rational compromise and sound governing arrangements could mitigate the effects of human frailty, thus enabling citizens to live together and govern themselves in relative peace.[66] The post-Revival evangelicals, in contrast, rejected both the Enlightenment faith in institutions and the Enlightenment emphasis on rational compromise. In fact, their more radical belief in the possibility of moral perfection led them to reject any and all efforts to distinguish law from morality and thus to reject many of the constitutional compromises forged in 1787. In place of the framers' rather elitist preoccupation with institutional design, they embraced the ideal of popular sovereignty and insisted on the right of popular majorities to enact broadly shared moral values into law.[67] As Beecher informed his flock in 1826, the "science of self-government" was "the science of perfect government."[68]

For present purposes, however, the important point to note is that the evangelicals' faith in the possibility of moral perfection helped pave the way for a renewed interest in the public cultivation and legal regulation of personal morality. The temperance movement offers perhaps the most striking example of the broader phenomenon. At the time of the Founding, one would have been hard pressed to identify any prominent Americans who regarded moderate drinking as detrimental to the public welfare.[69] And although all states required liquor retailers to obtain licenses, the underlying aim of the license system was clearly social control rather than moral or spiritual perfection. (As the early American legal commentator Zephaniah Swift noted in his *System of the Laws of the State of Connecticut,* the wisest course of action with respect to liquor licensing was not to impose "severe and rigid" laws that "will be little regarded," but rather to focus on punishing only the most egregious breaches of public order.)[70] But with the discovery that human beings were capable of moral perfection, the way was opened for a radically new approach to morals regulation. For if moral perfection was not only possible but also a God-ordained duty, it followed that legal prohibition was the only morally acceptable response to vice; laws that merely *regulated* common vices like drinking and gambling, on this view, amounted to little more than official complicity in sin. Thus, Justin Edwards, chief propagandist for the American Temperance Society, declared that license laws made "the whole community . . . partakers in the guilt of [the liquor traffic]. They not only license a man to do what is wrong, but they take the price which he pays for it, and put it into the public treasury."[71]

In the early 1830s, Edwards and other temperance leaders followed this belief to its logical conclusion and endorsed the legal prohibition of alcohol, an initially controversial move that did little to stunt the movement's explosive growth. By 1833, in fact, the American Temperance Society claimed more than a million members—at a time when the total U.S. population was around twelve million—and more than six thousand local auxiliaries stretching from New England to the western frontier.[72] Even more important than the size of the ATS's membership rolls, however, was the indirect influence of its ideas. By the mid-1830s, the once-radical notion that Christians were obligated to work towards the abolition of ardent spirits had gone mainstream, as the Presbyterians, Methodists, Baptists, and many smaller Protestant denominations all adopted the ATS's official stance as their own.[73]

Demon Rum was far from the only target of evangelical ire, however. Indeed, the Revival era witnessed an equally dramatic shift in the prevailing view of other seemingly minor vices, including lottery gambling. During the Founding era, the lottery system was considered a perfectly legitimate mode of revenue generation, one used to fund the construction of countless capital-intensive projects from colleges and churches to bridges and canals.[74] In fact, most Founding-era Americans seem to have believed that the urge to gamble was inherent in human nature. On this view, lotteries provided a valuable service to the community, in the sense that they offered a safe outlet for immoral urges while also allowing the community to reap revenue from practices that would otherwise go untaxed. The influential legal commentator James Kent thus endorsed the view that lotteries were simply "a fair way" for the public "to reach into the pockets of misers, and persons disposed to dissipate their funds."[75] By the 1820s, however, both religious and secular opinion leaders had begun to characterize lottery gambling as an inherently immoral activity, and local organizations dedicated to the eradication of lotteries were springing up in Philadelphia, New York, and other urban centers.[76] Undergirding this shift in popular opinion, as Jackson Lears has written, was an evangelical "moral code" that "put human choice at the center of the spiritual order" while "demoniz[ing] magic and . . . gambling." Material success that was not the result of hard work was suddenly suspect, and institutions that held out the prospect of such success, such as the lottery, could only be described as a threat to the health of the republic.[77] Soon the religious press began to editorialize against the evils of lottery gambling, arguing that while lotteries served many useful ends, the notion that worthy projects should be financed "by legalizing the practice of gambling" was "neither logical, nor morally legitimate."[78] The nation's major Protestant denominations, which were once among the most frequent beneficiaries of lottery grants, wasted little time in adjusting to this sudden shift in public opinion. By the late 1820s, most had taken steps to formally condemn the practice of lottery gambling.[79]

As should be clear from the examples of the temperance and anti-lottery movements, the Revival-era war on vice was facilitated by a final transformative development within the religious sphere: the emergence of a genuine Protestant ecumenicalism. That is to say, from the late 1820s forward, American Protestants proved increasingly capable of transcending their establishment-era differences and cooperating on large-scale social reform projects, usually through the medium of nondenominational parachurch organizations. As Daniel Walker Howe has written, the Revival produced "an interlocking network of voluntary associations, large and small, local, national, and international, to implement its varied purposes"—purposes which ran the gamut from "antislavery to temperance, from opposing dueling to opposing Sunday mails, from the defense of the family to the overthrow of the papacy, from women's self-help support groups to the American Sunday School Union, from the American Bible Society to the National Truss Society for the Relief of the Ruptured Poor."[80] Significantly, by the 1830s, the majority of these voluntary associations or parachurch organizations were genuinely ecumenical, drawing leaders and members from across the spectrum of American Protestantism.[81] The growth of ecumenicalism, in turn, opened the doors of local Protestant congregations to the fundraising appeals of national reform organizations, allowing groups like the ATS to rival the federal government in terms of manpower and resources.[82] Indeed, the largest reform societies raised a combined total of about $2.81 million during the 1820s—a figure that very nearly equals the $3.59 million spent by the federal government on internal improvements between 1782 and 1830.[83] It is therefore no exaggeration to claim, as Noll has, that "no broad-based movement, not even the political parties, brought together so many people committed to so much social construction as did the benevolent societies" of the antebellum period.[84]

What explains this sudden upsurge in ecumenical activity? One major factor was, again, disestablishment. With the demise of the decades-long controversies surrounding religious taxation and church incorporation, Baptists, Methodists, and other traditional dissenting sects could now join in ecumenical reform projects without worrying that they were unwittingly aiding the cause of established religion.[85] In addition, it is clear that enterprising entrepreneurs, including Beecher and Finney, helped to facilitate the rise of ecumenical reform by working to smooth over lingering denominational rifts and to identify shared areas of social concern.[86] Probably an even more important factor in the consolidation of American Protestantism, however, was the sudden appearance of an identifiable outgroup: namely, the millions of Irish Catholic immigrants who arrived in the United States between 1830 and 1860. Indeed, much of the evangelical activism of the antebellum period was explicitly anti-Catholic in spirit, and even movements that usually avoided overt anti-Catholicism, like the temperance movement, clearly tapped into nativist fears of an Irish invasion.[87] Finally, it is important to note that the myriad social problems at the heart of the evangelical reform movements were not simply figments of the reformers' imaginations. Historians note that the rapid economic expansion of the early nineteenth century both reduced the cost of liquor and fed a demand for large numbers of taverns to supply a burgeoning national network of turnpikes; as a result, rates of liquor consumption—and associated social problems—increased dramatically. Accordingly, there is reason to believe that at least some of the ecumenical movements of the antebellum period were responses to genuine social maladies.[88]

Constitutional Implications

Of course, the monolithic nature of antebellum Protestantism should not be exaggerated. Ecumenical reform efforts were largely a Northern phenomenon in the antebellum period, as Southern Protestants remained deeply wary of broad social reform projects (which seemed to lead inevitably to the subject of slavery). And indeed, the slavery issue ultimately drove the Baptist,

Methodist, and Presbyterian denominations to divide into separate regional organizations in the years preceding the Civil War.[89] Yet, with these caveats duly noted, the Revival clearly left a transformed society in its awake. Two changes, in particular, played critical roles in shaping the future course of constitutional development. First, it is important to note that, although a number of the evangelical societies formed during the 1820s and 1830s disintegrated in the late antebellum period, the organizational form of the reform society lived on. From the 1820s forward, powerful parachurch organizations were, along with political parties, one of the few constants of the American political landscape.[90] And if few of the later religious reform societies could match the sheer size of the ATS, the post-Civil War parachurch organizations were nonetheless more politically savvy—and ultimately more successful in shaping policy outcomes—than their predecessors. In their respective heydays, for example, both the Women's Christian Temperance Union (WCTU) and the Anti-Saloon League (ASL) were widely regarded as the most powerful interest groups in the nation.[91]

But the most significant legacy of the Revival, from the standpoint of constitutional development, was its transformative impact on popular mores. By the mid-nineteenth century, millions of Americans were religiously committed to the abolition of slavery, drinking, and lottery gambling—activities their forebears had regarded with attitudes ranging from indifference to mild disapproval. And as mores evolved, lawmakers faced ever-greater pressure to criminalize forms of property that had traditionally enjoyed at least some degree of legal protection. In the case of lotteries, as Figure 1 makes clear, public opposition grew increasingly monolithic over the course of the nineteenth century, and lawmakers responded by experimenting with increasingly drastic forms of regulation. Although the first appeals for lottery reform were heard only in the 1820s, twelve states had by 1840 enacted statutes or constitutional amendments prohibiting the sale of lottery tickets.[92] By 1850, a majority of the states had enacted constitutional amendments banning the issuance of lottery grants and the sale of lottery tickets. By the end of the nineteenth century, the percentage of states with constitutional lottery bans would top 80 percent, and by the 1880s only a single state-authorized lottery would remain in operation.

The progress of the anti-liquor movement is hardly less striking. As late as the 1820s, the granting of liquor licenses remained a relatively routine

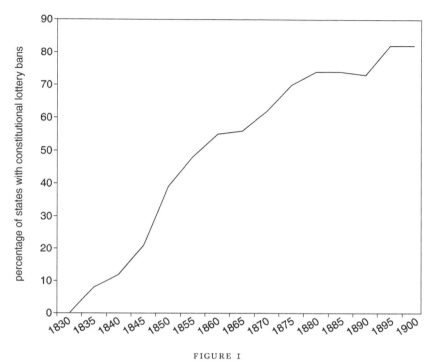

FIGURE I

Public opposition to lotteries in the nineteenth century

administrative matter, as it had been since the late colonial period. Beginning in the early 1830s, however, at the urging of the ATS and its allies, a handful of states began to experiment with local option laws, which granted local electorates the power to prohibit the granting of licenses altogether.[93] By 1847, fourteen states had enacted some form of local option, and by 1856, a full dozen states (all in the North) had taken the further step of experimenting with statewide prohibition.[94]

By the mid-nineteenth century, standards of public morality were evolving in directions that clearly threatened the core ideals of the commercial republic. The emergence of an unencumbered national market, for example, now appeared to represent a dire threat to the moral health of the citizenry. For whatever facilitated the movement of "legitimate" commercial items in the national market was sure to be equally helpful to the purveyors of liquor, lottery tickets, and other forms of vice. Thus, while evangelicals conceded that commercial expansion was increasing "national prosperity" and "social enjoyment," they decried the fact that it was also allowing unscrupulous businessmen to disseminate a "moral miasma" "over the entire land."[95] Nor were evangelicals sympathetic to the other core tenet of antebellum constitutionalism: the notion that vested property rights ought to remain insulated from legislative interference. Indeed, Beecher, Finney, and other leading evangelicals often appeared to reject outright the notion of a priori limits on the regulatory authority of the state.[96] As the temperance crusader Albert Barnes declared in 1852, it was the "inherent right" of society to protect itself against whatever vices would "corrupt or weaken it," regardless of the impact upon property:

> God never instituted a government on earth with a view to its throwing a protecting shield over vice and immorality. . . . The end of government . . . is to suppress crime; to punish wrongdoers; to remove iniquity; to promote that which is just and true. And it matters not what the evil is, nor how lucrative it may be, nor how much revenue may be derived from it, nor how many persons may have an interest in its continuance. The business of the lawgiver is to suppress it, not to protect it; to bring it as speedy an end as possible; not to become the panderer to it or the patron of it.[97]

Like the Puritans, Barnes and his theological allies demanded the absolute subordination of private right to the public good, insisting that any form of property that threatened public morality should be immediately banished "from the list of lawful articles of commerce."[98]

That the American republic could not simultaneously hold true to the ideals of the traditional order *and* purge itself of "national sins" like drunkenness and lottery gambling was becoming increasingly clear. In order to fully appreciate the impact of evangelical activism within the constitutional realm, however, we must turn now to an examination of three specific constitutional dilemmas that surfaced in the aftermath of the Revival: first, could state legislatures abolish existing lottery grants without violating the Contract Clause's prohibition against laws impairing "the obligation of contracts"? Second, could state and local officials prohibit the sale of liquor without violating the property rights of liquor manufacturers and retailers? And finally, was it possible to close the channels of interstate commerce to "immoral" forms of property without risking the collapse of the federal system? Each of these policy goals followed naturally from the newly dominant evangelical worldview, and collectively, I shall argue, they represented an existential threat to the framers' constitutional order.

Three Sites of Constitutional Conflict

Site One: Lottery Reform and the Contract Clause

The lottery was a ubiquitous feature of early American society, a generally uncontroversial mode of revenue regulation used to fund the construction of countless churches, schools, and infrastructure projects. Lotteries were, however, regulated under a legal framework that dated to the early colonial period.[99] The cornerstone of this framework was the lottery grant: a legislative act that conferred the right to raise money by means of lottery drawings. Although the projects funded by lotteries were often "public" in nature, a lottery grant usually took the form of an agreement between the state and a private individual or corporation. More specifically, a grant typically authorized some private entity—the trustees of a college, for example—to conduct lottery drawings until a given sum of money had been raised for the project in question. In exchange for permission to conduct lottery drawings, the grantee typically agreed to provide bonds and sureties; to pay out prize money in a timely fashion; to publish the results of drawings; to make regular payments to the institutional beneficiary of the grant; and to open its books to state inspectors upon request.[100] In addition, lottery grants typically conferred meaningful rights upon the grantee, including the right to designate managers and appoint agents; to contract with third-party lottery firms to conduct drawings; to pass on lottery privileges to one's survivors; and even to sell the lottery grant to another individual or firm (provided that the proceeds of the sale were applied to the original project).[101] Although state lawmakers could, if they chose, insert provisions reserving the right to modify the terms of a grant or setting an expiration date for the privileges granted, such reservations were surprisingly rare.[102]

In the years between the Founding and the onset of the Revival, most states had issued dozens—and some hundreds—of lottery grants.[103] Many of these grants were still active in the late 1820s, meaning that they had yet to raise the amount of money designated in their authorizing legislation. And in fact, as a result of complicated ordering schemes that were designed to prevent lottery operators from flooding the market with tickets from multiple projects simultaneously, many grantees were in the 1820s waiting to conduct drawings authorized several decades prior.[104] Jacksonian-era lawmakers thus found themselves confronting a backlog of lottery grants—grants made by their predecessors—at the precise moment when public opinion was moving inexorably in the direction of prohibiting lotteries. State legislatures initially responded to this shift in public opinion by vowing never to authorize new lottery grants, but such declarations did nothing to address the problem of *outstanding* grants. As petitions favoring criminalization poured into state legislatures in the 1820s and 1830s, lawmakers were eventually forced to confront the more fundamental question: could they simply renege on their predecessors' promises to lottery grantees?[105]

To the anti-lottery crusaders, at least, the answer was clear: state legislators were duty-bound to protect the public against any and all threats to public morality—and that lotteries were "wholly evil" was beyond dispute.[106] Yet the Marshall Court's landmark rulings in *Fletcher v. Peck* and the *Dartmouth College* case suggested that the rights of lottery grantees could not be dismissed so easily. Indeed, *Fletcher* and *Dartmouth College* were deeply troubling precedents for lottery opponents, for they suggested that, as a rule, any agreement between a state legislature and a private entity under which rights had "vested" was protected by the Contract Clause. The terms of the Contract Clause, according to the Marshall Court, were "general, and . . . applicable to contracts of every description."[107] Even more troubling was the fact that Marshall had in *Fletcher* explicitly rejected the suggestion that considerations of morality or "public sentiment" could be invoked to narrow the scope of the Contract Clause.[108] Confronted with a state legislature's attempt to undo a corrupt land deal carried out by an earlier legislature, Marshall had insisted that the only questions of law involved in the case were whether a valid grant had been made and whether rights had vested under that grant. If these questions were answered in the affirmative, then both the text of the Contract Clause and "general principles . . . common to our free institutions" barred the current legislature from reversing its predecessor's actions. The question of how this decision would impact the moral character of "our infant republics," Marshall insisted, was irrelevant to a proper construction of the Contract Clause.[109]

The Court's holdings in *Fletcher* and *Dartmouth College* thus appeared to leave little room for exceptions to the general rule that the Contract Clause barred legislatures from modifying or revoking their agreements with private entities, at least where property rights had vested.[110] For this reason, it is hardly surprising that attempts by Jacksonian-era legislatures to interfere with existing lottery grants met with stiff constitutional opposition. Although the first lottery-related litigation involving the Contract Clause did not reach state judiciaries until the late 1830s, the clause's troubling implications for lottery reform first surfaced in a little-remembered 1827 controversy in the state of New York. The episode began when the New York state legislature passed a statute imposing high license fees on lottery ticket vendors and requiring all vendors to post bonds and find sureties to guarantee good behavior. Religious groups, who had lobbied vigorously for stricter lottery regulation, hailed the law's passage as a great triumph over the "national vice" of lottery gambling.[111] Yet their elation was short-lived: New York's governor, DeWitt Clinton, immediately vetoed the measure on the grounds that the legislature's action violated the Contract Clause. Although Clinton deemed the anti-lottery bill "salutary, and well calculated to arrest the progress of existing evils," he nonetheless concluded that the 1827 statute was unconstitutional, since it unilaterally modified the terms of an 1822 law authorizing several educational institutions to raise funds by means of lottery drawings.[112] No doubt well aware of the *Fletcher* and *Dartmouth College* rulings, Clinton saw no way of distinguishing a lottery grant from a land grant or corporate charter. In short, a previous state legislature had proposed "a provisional grant to take effect on the occurrence of a certain event, and on the acceptance of the institutions it became absolute and executed." Rights had vested under the grant, and the state was now constitutionally barred from "re-asum[ing] or lessen[ing] the value of the thing granted." Clinton thus deemed it necessary to veto the measure in order to prevent a legal battle that "would probably terminate . . . in the highest tribunals of the country, [and] . . . last for many years."[113]

In the end, Clinton's veto ensured that no court would rule on the constitutionality of New York's anti-lottery law (though, as we shall see, dozens of such cases reached state appellate courts in subsequent decades). The New York controversy is nonetheless instructive, however, as it highlights the emerging disjunction between popular morality and entrenched constitutional ideals. Prior to the 1820s, the foundational principles of American constitutionalism were easily characterized as amoral abstractions, as the purely procedural building blocks of a constitutional republic. But with the emergence of evangelicalism as America's dominant religious persuasion, it became suddenly clear that the nation's fundamental law harbored substantive social commitments as well, in the sense that it embodied the mores of its framers and, as a result, impeded the present generation's efforts to translate a newly dominant set of mores into law. The problem was that the constitutional ideal of vested rights, while perfectly compatible with the Founding generation's relatively tolerant system of social control, was a serious obstacle to a genera-tion of Americans who sought to eradicate vice altogether. Thus, while their opponents warned against the abuse of legislative authority, anti-lottery cru-saders decried the tyranny of the past. To interpret a written constitution as a binding contract that secured the property rights of individuals against any subsequent modification was, on this view, incompatible with the very idea of self-government; it was to allow the dead hand of the Founding generation to bind the more enlightened lawmakers of the present. As one incensed an-ti-lottery activist explained in the wake of Governor Clinton's veto, the argu-ment that lawmakers were bound to honor the immoral agreements of their predecessors was akin to claiming that the Biblical King Herod was obliged to murder John the Baptist "because he had made a promise to give the damsel [Salome] whatever she asked."[114]

At first glance, it may be tempting to dismiss the constitutional contro-versy surrounding lottery repeal efforts as a relatively minor episode in the larger Jacksonian struggle against vested rights and special privilege, a strug-gle epitomized in the famous *Charles River Bridge* case.[115] But while litigation stemming from legislative efforts to modify corporate charters was certainly not rare in this period, the anti-lottery struggle actually posed a more serious threat to the traditional order than facially similar and better-known cases such as *Charles River Bridge*. In that case, the Taney Court confronted the question of whether the Massachusetts legislature's decision to charter the construction of a bridge over the Charles River violated the contractual rights of a company that had previously received a charter to construct a bridge over the same river. Because the Court upheld the validity of the second charter (much to the chagrin of Kent, Joseph Story, and other jurists who shared the Federalists' reverence for settled property rights), the case is often described as a pivotal juncture in American constitutional development; indeed, the case has long been characterized as marking the moment when the Federalist faith in the sanctity of established property rights gave way to a Jacksonian preference for "dynamic" uses of property.[116] But while the symbolic signifi-cance of *Charles River Bridge* should not be underestimated, it is important to note that the decision's core holding—that a corporate charter should not be read to *imply* a grant of exclusive rights—left the Marshall Court's concep-tual apparatus intact. Indeed, the Taney Court never seriously challenged its predecessor's conviction that rights explicitly conferred by legislative grants or corporate charters were protected from subsequent legislative interference.[117]

In contrast to the victorious party in *Charles River Bridge,* however, the nation's anti-lottery crusaders demanded the repeal of legislative grants in cases where the terms of the grants in question were unambiguous. Such an obvious break from established constitutional ideals could only be justified by an appeal to interests of a higher order, namely, the inherent right of every community to combat threats to the moral character of the citizenry.[118] The implications of the lottery struggle thus extended far beyond the narrow question of lottery grants. Indeed, the evangelical goal of eradicating the lottery business entailed the recognition of an expansive and amorphous police power capable of evolving with the moral progress of the community. Settled property rights were no more sacred than any other variety of rights, on this view, since forms and uses of property that appeared perfectly harmless in the present might be discovered to threaten the public wellbeing as future generations grew more "enlightened and virtuous."[119] Thus, where the Taney Court sought, at most, to narrow the scope of the contact clause, the anti-lottery movement demanded recognition of a glaring doctrinal exception—the right to abolish vested rights whenever necessary to protect public morals—that threatened the integrity of the larger constitutional edifice.

Site Two: Liquor Reform and the Rights of Property

The temperance movement, like the anti-lottery movement, was consistently hindered by constitutional obstacles. The chief obstacle confronting the anti-liquor movement was not the Contract Clause, however, but rather a more inchoate conviction among many jurists and liquor retailers that long-established professions and forms of property were entitled to constitutional protection, either under the due process clauses of state constitutions or in accordance with the unwritten "general principles" of republican government. The problem stemmed from the fact that the goal of liquor prohibition could only be attained by uprooting a complex system of statutory and common law rules that had remained in operation, with only minor alterations, since the early colonial period.[120] Under this inherited regulatory framework, the right to sell liquor in small quantities was limited to tavern keepers and other licensed retailers, who were required to obtain licenses on a yearly basis and to post bonds or find sureties to guarantee good behavior. County courts enjoyed wide discretion in the issuing of licenses and were expected to screen applicants (based on the recommendations of local officials) in order to ensure that only men and women of good character were permitted to dispense intoxicating beverages. License holders, in turn, were endowed with a number of quasi-official responsibilities: they were typically required to police the consumption of liquor by ensuring that no liquor was served on Sundays; that slaves, servants, and apprentices were not served without the permission of their masters; and that "common drunkards" were not served under any circumstances. In addition, most states required license holders to "keep tavern"—that is, to provide food, lodging, and entertainment for travelers. Significantly, the early licensing statutes made no attempt to control sales involving large quantities of liquor or sales made on a cash-and-carry basis; the underlying aim of the laws was not, ultimately, to minimize liquor consumption but rather to ensure that inns and taverns did not become "disorderly."[121]

To liquor opponents, the significant duties imposed by the license system suggested that liquor retailing was a quintessentially "public" profession—and thus subject to the plenary authority of state legislatures and local licensing officials. On this view, a policy of prohibition posed no serious constitutional problems: if the state enjoyed plenary authority in licensing retailers, it followed that the state also possessed the authority to *refuse* licenses—whether on a case-by-case basis or through a policy of statewide prohibition.[122] But retailers and other opponents of restrictive liquor laws could point to considerable evidence suggesting that a license conferred tangible property rights that could not be revoked at the whim of legislators or licensing officials. Indeed, available evidence indicates that although Founding-era county courts exercised plenary authority in the *issuing* of licenses, the same courts tended to regard a valid license as the private property of the license holder. In keeping with the broader routinization of morals enforcement described above, liquor licenses were by this point regularly allowed to "move with the holder to a new [location] or to be sold with an inn or store to a previously unlicensed person."[123] Indeed, the best available studies of local court records suggest that a Founding-era liquor license carried with it "a guarantee of a livelihood," in the sense that licensing officials lacked the authority "to take a license from a person" except in cases of egregious abuse.[124]

In light of these facts, it is hardly surprising that the temperance movement's first attempts at legal reform met with vigorous constitutional objections from liquor retailers who viewed restrictive liquor laws as an arbitrary interference with established property rights. We can gain a sense of the constitutional arguments available to the opponents of reform by examining briefly the controversy surrounding Massachusetts' initial, short-lived experiment with statewide liquor prohibition. The controversy began in 1838, when the state's temperance activists successfully pressured the state legislature to enact a radical new measure known as the Fifteen Gallon Law. The new law, it was hoped, would put the state's many "tippling houses" and "dram shops" out of business by prohibiting the sale of liquor in quantities smaller than fifteen gallons and by requiring that all liquor purchases be made on a cash-and-carry basis. No sooner had Governor Edward Everett signed the measure, however, than the state's liquor retailers and other opponents of prohibition launched a massive campaign to repeal the law.

The centerpiece of the repeal effort was a petition drafted by former U.S. Senator Harrison Gray Otis and signed by 4,800 Bostonians. The petitioners' specific objections to the law—twenty-four in all—can be grouped into two categories. First, Otis and his cosigners argued that the law was repugnant to specific state constitutional provisions that guaranteed the rights of property owners against arbitrary interference. In particular, they cited Article I of the Declaration of Rights: "All men are born free and equal, and have certain natural, essential, and unalienable rights; among which may be reckoned the right of enjoying and defending their lives and liberties; that of acquiring, possessing, and protecting property; in fine, that of seeking and obtaining their safety and happiness."[125] On this view, the fact that liquor had been universally recognized at the time of the state constitution's adoption "as possessing all the immunities attaching to other property" was decisive. Although it was true that the legislature possessed the power to "govern places of resort" and "preserve order," this "police" power entailed only the power "to regulate and not to prohibit."[126] The argument that the liquor trade was uniquely harmful to public health and morals was irrelevant, since the state constitution did not discriminate between "species of property." Rather, "so long as the supreme law attach[ed] to [liquor] the right of being lawfully acquired," there could be "no just distinction made as to the enjoyment and use of this right . . . which does not apply to all other property in the hands of the citizen."[127]

In addition, the petitioners argued that the Fifteen Gallon Law imposed disproportionate burdens on a particular "class" of citizens and was therefore in violation of a Massachusetts constitutional provision—as well as a broader legal/constitutional norm—which held that laws should be "equal" in their operation.[128] The purpose of a written constitution, on this view, was to prevent any one faction or "class" from using official power to oppress other segments of the community. The Fifteen Gallon Law was clearly discriminatory, according to the petitioners, because it permitted the rich to purchase as much liquor as they pleased—liquor sales in quantities greater than fifteen gallons were left unregulated—while effectively depriving the poor of the right to obtain and enjoy a form of property that was freely available to other classes of citizens.[129] Moreover, the law was discriminatory or "unequal" in the sense that it represented an attempt by one part of the community to destroy the property and livelihoods of another part.[130] If the legislature could today strip tavern keepers or grocers of their means of support, the argument went, it might one day do the same to farmers or mechanics.[131] To permit a measure such as the Fifteen Gallon Law to stand would therefore be to set the dangerous precedent that any "sect," "combination," or "party" who happened to gain "a majority in the legislature" might "prohibit and punish" whatever forms of property "they think proper to condemn."[132]

Massachusetts' brief experiment with liquor prohibition came to an abrupt end in 1840 when the state's newly elected Democratic governor successfully urged the legislature to repeal a law that was widely viewed as interfering with "individual rights, personal habits, [and] private business."[133] But while the Fifteen Gallon Law failed to produce a definitive judicial ruling on the question of a legislature's power to abolish property rights in liquor—litigation was pending at the time of the Law's repeal—the controversy nonetheless highlights the extent to which the Revival-era shift in mores worked to undermine the stability of the antebellum constitutional order. Prior to the advent of the temperance movement, the license system had for more than a century marked the generally accepted dividing line between public good and private right. Under this system, the right of local officials to suppress "disorderly" inns and taverns was beyond dispute; but so, too, was the right of the reputable tavern keeper to pursue his or her chosen profession. Constitutional conflict was rare in this period, not because Americans had yet to conceive of the idea of inviolable private rights, but rather because all parties accepted the legitimacy of rights and duties derived from the traditional regulatory framework. But when the nation's growing ranks of evangelicals called for the abolition of the license system, they were in effect advocating for the complete subordination of individual rights to a broad and dynamic power of morals police. On this view, the traditional legal status of liquor was irrelevant to the task of formulating an effective regulatory system in the present; if the licensing system had failed to protect the public from the inherent evils of the liquor traffic, it was the right of the people to institute whatever laws "the public good, and the greatest good of the greatest number, shall require."[134] The critical question, which the judiciary would soon be forced to answer, was whether a shift in mores could justify the destruction of an entire class of private property. In other words, did the legal definition of "property" evolve with the moral progress of the community, as the evangelicals believed, or did the adoption of a written constitution establish once and for all the validity of forms of property that were recognized as valid by its framers?

Site Three: The Federal System and the Interstate Traffic in Immoral Commodities

In order to appreciate the Revival's impact on American federalism, we must first recall some key features of the traditional federal system. In particular, it is important to remember that the traditional (i.e., pre-New Deal) understanding of federalism assumed a qualitative difference between state and federal power. Because the federal government was understood to possess only those powers specifically listed in the constitutional text, jurists deemed it a government of "limited" or "enumerated" powers. Thus, while the federal government was the supreme authority in the constitutional system (in the sense that a valid federal law trumped an otherwise valid state law), federal power was strictly limited to a narrow range of subjects.[135] The states, in contrast, were understood to possess "general" powers, meaning that the exercise of state power required no specific authorization from a constitutional text (though state-level legislative power was, of course, constrained by the structural provisions and rights guarantees contained in state constitutions). In this way, the traditional order theoretically preserved an important sphere of local self-government, allowing states and localities to retain a "residuary" but "inviolable" sovereignty over all subjects not specifically delegated to the national government, from the "supervision of agriculture" to the "administration of criminal and civil justice."[136]

But the location of the boundary between state and federal authority, while reasonably clear in theory, was often difficult to discern in practice. In the early decades of the nineteenth century, the federal government's commerce power, in particular, emerged as a source of controversy. That the Constitution vested the federal government with plenary authority over interstate commerce was clear. The problem, however, was that the commerce power often appeared to overlap the most important of the states' residual powers, including the "police" power, or the power to protect public health, safety, and morals.[137] Many laws, from inspection and quarantine laws to laws regulating harbor pilots, appeared to belong to both the "police" and "commerce" categories simultaneously.[138] (Quarantine laws, for example, were clearly necessary to protect public health, and yet such laws obviously impacted the flow of goods and people in interstate commerce.) Nonetheless, the integrity of the federal system depended upon the maintenance of a reasonably clear boundary between state and federal power, and nineteenth-century jurists responded by dutifully articulating a series of standards and tests designed to distinguish a valid police regulation from an unconstitutional interference with the federal commerce power (and vice versa).[139]

As we shall see, evangelical moral perfectionism worked in two distinct ways to undermine the integrity of the police/commerce distinction, the lynchpin of the traditional federal system. First, the sudden demand for liquor *prohibition* highlighted the extent to which the federal commerce power impinged upon the complex of state police regulations which governed the sale of liquor. Prior to the Revival-era shift in mores, state regulation of liquor had coexisted unproblematically with the federal commerce power for the simple reason that the states had little incentive to interfere with the interstate transportation of liquor. The goal of pre-Revival liquor regulation, after all, was social control rather than moral improvement, and the license system was more than capable of achieving this end. (There was little reason to care whether a tavern procured its liquor from domestic or out-of-state sources, so long as it was duly licensed.)[140] But when the goal of liquor regulation shifted to outright prohibition, it became suddenly clear that states and localities could not fully control their moral environments without blocking the importation of liquor. That is to say, even if a state succeeded in putting domestic manufacturers and retailers out of business, its citizens could still obtain liquor from neighboring states—and imported liquor was at least arguably entitled to constitutional protection under the Commerce Clause (as were the interstate carriers who transported it).[141]

At first glance, this problem may appear akin to the constitutional dilemmas that confronted the antebellum Court in cases involving quarantine laws and other borderline instances of state police regulation. But in reality the problem was not so much that liquor regulation fell on the border between the police and commerce powers (though it did), but rather that the anti-liquor forces aimed to eradicate the interstate traffic in a commodity that was universally recognized as a valid subject of "commerce." In other borderline cases, it was always possible for jurists to preserve the police/commerce distinction by further refining it as, for example, the Taney Court did when it drew a distinction between commercial subjects of "national" import, which were protected under the Commerce Clause, and "local" matters, such as the laws governing harbor pilots, which were better left to the states.[142] But because the temperance movement could accept only eradication of the liquor traffic, its regulatory efforts could not be accommodated so easily. Where state quarantine and inspection laws were arguably necessary to facilitate interstate commerce (though they could, of course, be used for other purposes), state prohibition laws were clearly intended to extinguish a thriving interstate traffic; and for this reason it was impossible to maintain the fiction that the "commerce" affected by restrictive liquor laws was not the sort of "commerce" that the federal Constitution was designed to protect.

From the perspective of the anti-liquor forces, then, the problem was that neither level of government appeared to possess the necessary constitutional authority to fully extinguish the liquor traffic. The states were free to regulate domestic sales and manufacture, yet any effort to block importation—by, for example, penalizing common carriers who transported liquor into a state—risked offending against the federal commerce power.[143] The federal government, in turn, possessed the authority to regulate interstate commerce, but not the authority to enact the sort of restrictive police regulations necessary to eradicate the liquor traffic. New Hampshire Senator Henry W. Blair, an ardent prohibitionist, succinctly summarized the basic dilemma in the aftermath of the Civil War:

> The police power is that under which the traffic in intoxicating drink must be controlled and prohibited, if at all—and it resides in the States. But the States and people have expressly given to the general government the right to regulate commerce with foreign nations [and] among the several States. . . . The general government recognizes and protects alcohol as property and as an article of legitimate commerce. So long as any State, domestic or foreign, continues to permit the manufacture of alcohol and the traffic therein, the general government stands pledged to exercise all its power of legislature, judicature and execution to protect and facilitate the continued infliction of the curse.[144]

The evangelical goal of annihilating the liquor traffic thus seemed to require one of two equally fundamental alterations to the federal system: either liquor, a universally recognized subject of commerce, would have to be

somehow excluded from the ambit of the Commerce Clause, or else Congress
would have to be granted the authority to enact "police" regulations so as to
aid the states in enforcing their prohibition laws. In either case, the conceptual
foundations of the federal system would be irreparably damaged.

The post-Revival movement to abolish the interstate traffic in lottery tickets posed a similar, but ultimately distinct, threat to the federal system. Most
nineteenth-century jurists excluded the lottery industry from the category of
"commerce" altogether, on the grounds that it did not involve an exchange
of tangible commodities. And for this reason, state-level efforts to police the
sale and distribution of lottery tickets were relatively uncontroversial; in fact,
lottery laws were generally viewed as a quintessential example of valid "police"
regulations (provided there was no interference with vested rights).[145] Yet, as
the anti-lottery movement gained momentum, a new constitutional dilemma
emerged: so long as the power to regulate morality resided *solely* in the states,
there was no power in the constitutional system with the authority to prevent
a handful of states from enacting laws that undermined morals enforcement
in neighboring states.[146]

By the mid-nineteenth century, all but three states—Delaware, Kentucky,
and Missouri—had succeeded in abolishing their domestic lottery industries.
The paradoxical result of this revolution in mores, however, was that the few
remaining state-authorized lotteries found themselves in an extremely com-
fortable position. Indeed, they soon discovered a ready-made market for their
tickets in states where lotteries were now prohibited by law. Not surprisingly,
lottery opponents residing in anti-lottery states regarded the emergence of
an interstate market in lottery tickets (a market facilitated by the U.S. Postal
Service) as an assault on the inherent right of every state to police its moral
environment. In 1856, the *Friends' Review* asked "upon what principle" Delaware could "be justified in granting to her own citizens the privilege of
scattering the seeds of corruption through her sister States?"[147] The *Saturday Evening Post*, in turn, accused Delaware lottery firms of sanctioning "a
common nuisance" and of "flooding" the "Northern and Middle States" with
lottery tickets and advertisements.[148] To the English journalist Edward Dicey,
who toured the United States in the mid-nineteenth century, nothing better
illustrated the peculiar nature of the American federal system than the fact
that the residents of three states were permitted to promote an "iniquitous"
business throughout the nation at a time when the other thirty-six states had
taken the "wise action" of abolishing it. "It shows the practical working of

the American Constitution," Dicey concluded, "when you consider that the United States Government has no more power to hinder [a state] from establishing lotteries than [England has] to require Belgium to suppress the gaming tables at Spa."[149]

The porous nature of the federal system thus made possible a flourishing interstate market in lottery tickets in a period when public opposition to lotteries was, at least at the elite level, nearly universal. The problem, as Dicey correctly noted, was that the only power in the constitutional system capable of curbing the interstate traffic in lottery tickets—the federal government—was widely believed to lack the constitutional authority to regulate activities, such as lotteries, which fell within the constitutional category of "police." The emergence of a vigorous anti-lottery movement therefore created an enormous incentive for Congress to use its enumerated powers—in particular, the commerce and postal powers—as a proxy for a federal police power. As we shall see in chapter 4, the demise of the police/commerce distinction, the lynchpin of the traditional federal system, was in large part the result of such efforts.

Conclusion

By the late antebellum period, American Protestantism had attained a level of integration and a unity of purpose that James Madison and other members of the Founding generation would have deemed impossible. Far from politically impotent, evangelical reformers were enjoying considerable success in rewriting the statute books of the Northern states. To be sure, their activities were largely confined to the state and local levels, so that the "national councils" were not yet in danger of being coopted for religious ends. And yet the reformers' agenda, which centered on the destruction of settled property rights and the restriction of interstate markets, was rife with broader constitutional implications. In the end, the task of negotiating the tension between post-Revival mores and entrenched constitutional commitments would fall to the judiciary, as aggrieved liquor retailers and lottery operators increasingly sought protection in the courts. In order to trace the Revival's impact on constitutional development, then, we must turn now to an examination of the body of case law arising out of the evangelical crusades against liquor and lottery gambling.

Moral Reform and Constitutional Adjudication, 1830–1854

> If these modes of accomplishing a laudable purpose, and of carrying
> into effect a good and wholesome law, cannot be pursued without a
> violation of the constitution, they cannot be pursued at all . . .
>
> —Judge Lemuel Shaw, *Fisher v. McGirr* (1854)

In 1826, Lyman Beecher delivered an influential sermon series prescribing a "course of systematic action" for combatting the "national sin" of intemperance.[1] Beecher's plan of action—which would later be published as *Six Sermons on the Nature, Occasions, Signs, Evils, and Remedy of Intemperance*—consisted of four steps. The first step would be to educate the public on the personal and social costs of the liquor traffic. Voluntary societies would be formed for this purpose: their members would "pass through the land, collect information, confer with influential individuals and bodies of men, [and] deliver addresses at popular meetings."[2] Boycotts would then be organized against merchants who refused to stop dealing in liquor. The nation's churches, in turn, would exclude from their ranks all who would not agree to abstain from the use of "ardent spirits." Finally, once the public had been "prepared for efficient cooperation," petitions would be "addressed to the legislatures of the states and to congress . . . praying for legislative interference to protect the health and morals of the nation."[3] With "the suffrage of the community" mobilized on behalf of the temperance cause, Beecher reasoned, the nation's lawmakers would have little choice but to banish liquor "from the list of lawful articles of commerce."[4] For when "public sentiment" at last began to move, "its march [would] be as resistless" as a "rock thundering down [a] precipice."[5]

Beecher's efforts to attack the demand side of the liquor traffic were, to put it mildly, less than successful. But his larger goal of promoting "efficient cooperation" among the nation's Protestants succeeded beyond anyone's wildest dreams. Over the next three decades, evangelicals crossed denominational lines, organized themselves into voluntary societies, and brought the full weight of American Protestantism to bear on the problem of intemperance—and also on a broader range of moral issues, including lotteries, slavery, and Sabbath observance. Such an outpouring of moral fervor was bound to produce a legislative response; and indeed, the reformers enjoyed a remarkable record of success in persuading lawmakers to adopt their preferred policies, particularly with respect to liquor and lottery gambling. But while Beecher correctly surmised that elected officials would be unable to resist the influence of a "roused and concentrated" evangelical population, his plan of action suffered from at least one serious defect: it failed to consider that the thriving nineteenth-century traffic in immoral commodities rested on a constitutional foundation.[6] Legislative victories, in other words, remained vulnerable to challenges in the courts. And although the force of public opinion may have been irresistible when directed at legislators, Beecher and his allies soon discovered that the judiciary was, if not impervious to public opinion, at least slower to yield its thundering force.

Although conventional wisdom holds that moral reform posed few constitutional problems outside the context of slavery, this chapter will demonstrate that prohibition and anti-lottery reformers encountered constitutional obstacles no less daunting than those that confronted their allies in the antislavery movement. Indeed, as liquor retailers and lottery operators turned to litigation as their primary means of resisting reform, the resulting cases placed nineteenth-century judges on the horns of a dilemma, forcing them to choose between fealty to the constitutional ideals of the framers, on the one hand, and post-Revival mores, on the other. Careful examination of the resulting body of case law reveals that some of the period's innovative morals laws survived judicial scrutiny, while others were invalidated on constitutional grounds. Nonetheless, a clearly discernible trend is evident in the antebellum judiciary's response to evangelical reform: the more authority reformers sought to displace, the more they found themselves mired in constitutional controversy.

Stated otherwise, the cases examined below do not suggest a bias for or against morals regulation per se, but rather a bias in favor of existing forms of property and traditional regulatory frameworks. On rare occasions, antebellum judges' pervasive concern with the "rule of law" worked in the evangelicals' favor, particularly in cases where reformers sought to strengthen existing regulatory frameworks instead of uprooting them altogether. More often, however, the judiciary's status quo bias favored the "immoral" individuals who claimed that constitutionally protected rights would be destroyed by radical reform. Many antebellum judges seem to have believed—correctly, as it turned out—that to accommodate the demands of the prohibitionists and anti-lottery crusaders would be to invite a never-ending series of exceptions to the constitutional principles of the Founding generation. The evangelical notion of a dynamic and unbounded police power, on this view, was nothing short of a slippery slope to "legislative despotism" or "pure democracy."

Liquor Licenses, Lottery Contracts, and Vested Rights

As a point of departure, let us begin by contrasting the judiciary's response to a pair of evangelical-inspired reforms implemented in the period around 1840. Consider, first, the innovation known as the "no-license" campaign. Invented by temperance advocates in Massachusetts, the no-license campaign aimed to impose de facto prohibition on a given town or county by electing local officials who had previously pledged to deny all requests for retail liquor licenses. Successful no-license campaigns in several Massachusetts counties in the mid-1830s produced a flood of litigation, as aggrieved liquor retailers took to the courts to challenge the constitutionality of the tactic.

The no-license debate first reached the state's Supreme Judicial Court in the 1837 case of *Commonwealth v. Blackington.* The defendant in the case, a liquor dealer who had the bad fortune to reside in a no-license county, argued that the county commissioners' decision not to grant any licenses for the year 1836 amounted to a violation of specific rights guaranteed in the state's constitution, including the right "of acquiring, possessing, and protecting property." But the Supreme Judicial Court was not persuaded. Writing for the Court, Chief Justice Lemuel Shaw dismissed the dealer's objection for the simple reason that the licensing system in place in 1836 was, in its principal features, identical to the system that had been in place since the early colonial period. As Shaw explained, the liquor license laws "in nearly the same form in which they are now found, were commenced soon after the Colony of Massachusetts was founded." And although the idea of using the license power to bring about a de facto prohibition regime was unprecedented, the no-license campaign had in no way interfered with the operation of the traditional license system. And indeed, from a legal standpoint, Blackington's case was no different from the "numerous prosecutions" of unlicensed retailers which had taken place in the "nearly sixty years that the [state] constitution has been in operation." The claim that a licensing official's refusal to grant a license to a particular retailer amounted to a violation of the state constitution, Shaw concluded, could only be described as "remarkable."[7]

Based on Shaw's blunt rejection of the retailer's constitutional objections, one may be tempted to conclude that antebellum judges reflexively subordinated private rights to the protection of public morals. There are at least two reasons to doubt this conclusion, however. First, it is important to remember that the *Blackington* litigation involved an alleged conflict between the rights of two individuals: the liquor retailer and the licensing official. Technically speaking, both men were officers of the state, in the sense that they were charged with performing specific public duties and could be held criminally liable for failing to perform them.[8] Because the licensing official's position within the official hierarchy was superior to that of the retailer or tavernkeeper, it is hardly surprising that Shaw sided with the licensing official in *Blackington*. Significantly, however, other judicial rulings handed down in the same period make clear that antebellum judges did not regard the licensing official's power to destroy existing property rights as plenary or unlimited. In a ruling issued a few years after *Blackingon,* for example, the noted North Carolina jurist Thomas Ruffin held that a blanket denial of license applications amounted to an abuse of authority for which local licensing officials could be indicted.[9] The appropriate remedy for an aggrieved retailer, then, was not to challenge the licensing official directly, but rather to seek an indictment from a higher official.[10]

But there is an even more important reason to doubt the claim that decisions such as *Blackington* are indicative of a wider judicial hostility towards the constitutional claims of "immoral" individuals. When we examine roughly contemporaneous cases involving the anti-lottery movement, it is apparent that judges did not hesitate to set aside innovative morals laws whenever reformers threatened to disrupt existing patterns of authority. The most serious constitutional question arising from the movement to abolish lotteries, as we have seen, was whether a state's attempt to revoke or alter the terms of a lottery grant amounted to a violation of the Contract Clause. This question, which was not directly addressed by the U.S. Supreme Court until 1880, was first presented to a state court in the 1842 Delaware case of *State v. Phalen and Paine.* The case involved an 1841 anti-lottery law that required the state's lottery operators to pay high license fees and make additional payments to their institutional beneficiaries.[11] The large lottery company of Phalen and

Company, which was operating a lottery under a contract negotiated with the original grantees in 1839, refused to make the additional payments and was subsequently sued by the state.

In arguments before the Delaware Court of Errors and Appeals, counsel for the state attempted to shift the focus from the Contract Clause to the broader subject of the nature and purposes of constitutional government. A decision in favor of the lottery firm, the state argued, would have disastrous consequences for public morals, leaving the people of Delaware "liable to the greatest evils." For if all lottery grants were insulated from subsequent repeal or modification, then even the most unscrupulous lottery operators would enjoy the privilege of "doing mischief indefinitely" and without fear of "further legislation or control."[12] In response, counsel for Phalen and Company pointed out that the company had paid the original grantees $10,000 for the right to operate the lottery in question (and to retain the bulk of the profits). The company had entered into this contract with the understanding that the terms of the grant were fixed. Any attempt by the legislature to unilaterally alter the rules governing the drawings therefore amounted to an unconstitutional interference with contractual rights. Accordingly, the firm implored the Court to uphold the sacred principle of the inviolability of contracts and to ignore the state's appeal to the doctrine of "public morals"—"a doctrine that has no application in free governments, acting under a written constitution; a doctrine which is the favorite resort of tyranny, and the admission of which as a ground of legal judgment would be more dangerous than any evil it could possibly correct."[13]

Based on the conventional, moralistic depiction of the antebellum judiciary, one might expect the Delaware Court to reject out of hand the notion that the mere private rights of an individual or corporation should be permitted to interfere with the community's right to rid itself of a great moral evil. In reality, however, the Court took precisely the opposite position, effectively endorsing the lottery firm's claim that "the high principle of the inviolability of contracts was more important to civil government than any question of the immorality of lotteries."[14] Fixing on the fact that the original lottery grant had explicitly conferred the right to negotiate a contract with third-party lottery managers, the justices determined that the legislature had made the original grantees its agents, authorizing them "to make a contract with others for a valuable consideration, which would be binding on the State." Thus, while the legislature would have been free to "modify or change" the terms of the grant prior to 1839, the contract "between the managers and [Phalen and Company]" had "conferred new rights and imposed new obligations."[15] Like the Georgia landowners at the heart of the *Fletcher v. Peck* controversy, the lottery firm had paid good money for property (a lottery grant) with the understanding that the sale was final and not contingent upon the will of the legislature.[16] The Delaware justices thus concluded that, because the U.S. Constitution barred "all legislative action . . . impairing the obligation of contracts," the state legislature had "no right to violate" the 1839 agreement negotiated by its agent nor to "revoke or modify the contract as to impair its obligation."[17]

Anti-lottery crusaders were dealt a second blow in 1845 when Missouri's highest court handed down a ruling that followed the basic outlines of *State v. Phalen and Paine*. In 1842, the Missouri legislature had enacted an anti-lottery statute prohibiting both the drawing of lotteries and the sale of tickets within the state. In 1845, when an agent of the St. Louis Hospital Lottery was charged with illegally selling tickets, he pointed out that his employers had obtained the rights to conduct the lottery through a third-party contract entered into prior to the passage of the 1842 anti-lottery act. Based on this fact, the agent argued that the act under which he had been arrested was in violation of the federal Contract Clause. In *State v. Hawthorn*, the Missouri Supreme Court endorsed the agent's claim. Although the Court declared itself reluctant to interfere with an "act whose obvious tendency is to suppress an evil and promote public and private morals," its members ultimately encountered "no difficulty" in reaching the conclusion that the contract under which the lottery agent was operating was "as much obligatory upon the state as upon the other contracting party."[18] As in the Delaware case, the terms of the Missouri grant explicitly authorized the grantees to contract with third-party lottery operators; and from the moment the grantees had exercised this right, the Court reasoned, the legislature's hands were tied. In short, both the Contract Clause and unwritten principles of "reason and justice" barred the legislature from attempting to "rescind . . . alter, or impair" the terms of its original agreement once third-party rights had vested.[19]

As late as the Civil War era, long after public opinion had turned solidly against the lottery industry, state appellate courts continued to rebuff attempts to alter the terms of lottery grants under which third-party rights had vested. By the time Kentucky's highest court decided the 1859 lottery grant case of *Gregory's Executrix v. Trustees of Shelby College*, for example, more than half of the states had enacted constitutional lottery bans, and all but three had managed to retire their existing lottery grants.[20] Naturally enough, the author of the *Gregory's Executrix* opinion thought it advisable to nod in the direction of public opinion and affirm that the lottery was a "demoralizing" business that "exercis[ed] a pernicious influence over the ignorant and cred-ulous part of the community." But in the end, the Kentucky court refused to budge from the established view that the contractual rights of lottery op-erators were entitled to the same degree of constitutional protection as any other form of property. Citing *Fletcher v. Peck* and *Dartmouth College*, they deemed it "obviously unjust" for the state to attempt to revoke or alter any "rights that ha[d] been acquired . . . upon the faith" of a decades-old lottery grant. The state's newly enacted lottery ban was therefore "unconstitutional and inoperative," at least to the extent that it interfered with any rights that had "vested" under existing grants.[21]

In the absence of guidance from the U.S. Supreme Court, these early rul-ings from the high courts of Delaware, Missouri, and Kentucky set a prec-edent that was followed by state and lower federal tribunals, almost without exception, though the 1870s.[22] Of course, the problem of vested rights was hardly an insurmountable obstacle for anti-lottery reformers. As public op-position to lotteries solidified, most legislatures simply ceased the practice of issuing lottery grants.[23] The gradual expiration of existing grants, coupled with the sharp decline in the authorization of new grants, meant that only a few authorized lotteries were still operating at the time of the Civil War.[24] For now, however, the important point to note is that while the judiciary's sympa-thy for lottery operators may at first seem difficult to square with its apparent indifference to the plight of liquor retailers, the rulings in the "no-license" and lottery cases are in fact easily reconciled: in both cases, antebellum judges displayed a clear preference for settled property rights and traditional patterns of authority. To the extent that antebellum evangelicals were content to work within the confines of existing regulatory frameworks, they therefore had little reason to fear that state appellate courts would seriously impede their efforts. And yet, because they believed that God had ordered the eradication, rather than regulation, of immoral forms of property, reformers were rarely content with such half-measures. To respect the authority of liquor licensing officials or state-sanctioned lottery operators was, after all, to abandon the God-ordained pursuit of moral perfection.

"The Wholesome Restraints of the Law":
Local Option and the Non-Delegation Principle

When the "no-license" campaigns of the 1830s failed to eradicate the liquor traffic, anti-liquor crusaders next turned to a reform known as the "local option" law. As the name suggests, local option laws permitted the voters of a given town or county to conduct an annual vote on the question of whether local licensing officials should be permitted to issue licenses during the coming year.[25] Unlike the "no-license" reform, which ultimately rested on the voluntary pledge of a licensing official, the local option system entailed a fundamental reorganization of authority. Specifically, it attempted to wrest the licensing power from local officials and vest it directly in local electorates; and this move, according to several state appellate courts, was fundamentally at odds with the spirit of constitutional government.

For state legislators—Whigs and Democrats alike—the local option was an ideal policy. It removed a highly divisive question from state politics, leaving the fanatical "drys" and their "wet" opponents to fight things out at the local level.[26] Yet, precisely because it passed the buck to local electorates, local option arguably ran afoul of the venerable common-law maxim *delegata potestas non potest delegari* (delegated powers cannot be further delegated). The origins of this maxim can be traced (at least) to Locke's *Second Treatise*, which listed four fundamental "bounds" that "the consent of society" and "the law of God and nature" had placed upon the legislative power. The last of these bounds was the principle of non-delegation: "The legislative cannot transfer the power of making laws to any other hands; for it being but a delegated power from the people, they who have it cannot pass it over to others."[27] Applied to the constitutional governments of the American states, Locke's non-delegation principle called into question a state legislature's power to make a criminal offense conditional on the votes of local electorates. As the influential nineteenth-century legal commentator Thomas Cooley explained (with a footnote to Locke), it was a "settled maxim" of "constitutional law . . . that the power conferred upon the legislature to make laws cannot be delegated . . . nor can [the legislature] substitute the judgment, wisdom, and patriotism of any other body for those to which alone the people have seen fit to confide this sovereign trust."[28]

Predictably, the wave of local option laws enacted by the Northern states in the 1840s and early 1850s produced an abundance of litigation, as liquor retailers took to the courts to challenge the constitutionality of a policy that (they argued) transferred "legislative power" to local electorates. The resulting test cases provided a forum for a vigorous debate on the nature and purposes of constitutional government. On one side, counsel for the states leaned heavily on the argument that the powers of state legislatures were plenary or "general" in nature, unlike the strictly "enumerated" powers of the federal government. On this view, state legislatures possessed "the right to regulate the internal police of the state, and to pass all laws necessary to the good order and government of the same." Given that liquor was "known . . . to promote intemperance and impoverish the state, to disturb the public peace and greatly to multiply evils and crimes," it followed that a legislature could adopt whatever policy it believed would best protect the community from these evils.[29] On the other side, the retailers pressed the *delegata potestas* maxim, arguing that the legislative power was "a trust to be executed with judgment and discretion, [which] cannot be delegated to any other body . . . or persons."[30] The legislative power, according to the retailers, existed "as a unit, to be applied to all the people alike who are under the same sovereignty."[31] To hold otherwise was to deprive citizens of their right "to the protection of the whole legislative body," thus leaving them "to the tender mercies of [their] particular neighborhoods."[32]

The first local option test case to reach a state's highest court was the Delaware case of *Rice v. Foster*, decided in June 1847.[33] Given that state judges in this period allegedly operated within the context of a state constitutional tradition that prioritized "shared moral principles" and the "shaping of citizen character," one might naturally expect the Delaware Court of Errors and Appeals to make short work of the constitutional objections of the state's liquor retailers.[34] And yet, in *Rice v. Foster*, we again see a state appellate court expressing sympathy for a "minority" whose rights had been "trampled" upon by a "vindictive, arbitrary, and excited" majority.[35] Significantly, Judge James Booth, who authored the Court's opinion, began by flatly denying the state's assertion that the legislature was empowered to pass whatever laws it deemed "beneficial to the community." In reality, the state constitution established clear "limits to the exercise of legislative power, beyond which it cannot constitutionally pass."[36] The most glaring fallacy in the state's argument, according to Booth, was the assertion that the constitutional form of government adopted at the state level was fundamentally different from that adopted at the national level. It was true, of course, that the powers of the state legislatures were somewhat broader than the powers of Congress. But the nature and purposes of constitutional government were in both cases the same: namely, to subject the "popular rights" of the majority to the "the wholesome restraints of the law."[37] The task of a judge in a case involving grave constitutional questions was not to gauge the popular will, but rather to safeguard the institutional arrangements that prevented a republican government from devolving into despotism:

> The framers of the Constitution of the United States, and of the first constitution of this State, were men of wisdom, experience, disinterested patriotism, and versed in the science of government. They had been taught by the lessons of history, that equal and indeed greater dangers resulted from a pure democracy, than from an absolute monarchy. Each leads to despotism. Wherever the power of making laws, which is the supreme power in a State, has been exercised directly by the people under any system of polity, and not by representation, civil liberty has been overthrown. Popular rights and universal suffrage, the favorite theme of every demagogue, afford, without constitutional control or a restraining power, no security to the rights of individuals, or to the permanent peace and safety of society.[38]

Hewing closely to the logic of Locke's *Second Treatise*, Booth deemed it a fundamental principle of "republican government" that "the power of making laws," once delegated, could not be "transferred . . . to any other body or persons; not even to the whole people of the State; and still less to the people of a county."[39] To subject citizens to the authority of a lawmaking power to which they had not consented "would be an infraction of the constitution, and a dissolution of the government."[40] Booth thus declared it the Court's solemn duty to render "null and void" a law that was "repugnant to the principles, spirit, and true intent and meaning of the constitution of this State."[41]

Lest the Delaware Court's ruling be dismissed as idiosyncratic, it is important to note that local option met an identical fate in the neighboring state of Pennsylvania.[42] Pennsylvania's local option law, enacted in the summer of 1846, reached the state Supreme Court in the 1847 case of *Parker v. Commonwealth*. In an opinion that closely tracked (and repeatedly cited) *Rice v. Foster*, the Pennsylvania justices followed their Delaware counterparts in rejecting the claim that the state legislature possessed a plenary or general power of morals police. According to Judge Thomas S. Bell, the government of Pennsylvania was inherently a "government of limited authority." The fact that the legislature's powers were not strictly "enumerated" was irrelevant, since the ends of constitutional government were everywhere the same: to establish "a marked distinction between the indefinite and unlimited power of the community, considered as a whole, and [the] definite and limited power of the legislature."[43] Like his counterparts who were simultaneously invalidating anti-lottery laws on Contract Clause grounds, Bell viewed the local option movement as a dangerous innovation upon the constitutional principles of the framers—one that threatened to erase the distinction between representative government and pure democracy. Indeed, Bell's rigid adherence to the *delegata potestas* maxim was motivated, at least in part, by the Madisonian fear that too much democracy would inevitably culminate in the annihilation of private rights, as self-interested factions battled to seize power for the sole purpose of confiscating what rightfully belonged to others.[44] By placing lawmaking authority directly in the hands of local electorates, in other words, local option practically invited the "the majority" to "trampl[e] on the rights of the minority"—precisely the sort of abuse that "Mr. Madison" and the other framers had sought to prevent.[45] The liquor dealers of Allegheny County, like all of the states' citizens, were constitutionally entitled to the protection afforded by representative institutions and a legislative branch consisting of "two [chambers] designed to hold each other in check." Any law that dispensed with these protections or otherwise subjected the state's citizens to the whims of "irresponsible and fluctuating majorities," Bell concluded, amounted to an unconstitutional "usurpation" of the people's sovereignty.[46]

To be sure, not all of the local option laws enacted in the 1840s were declared unconstitutional.[47] Yet it is a striking fact that antebellum liquor retailers prevailed in five of six state appellate cases in which they pressed the *delegata potestas* objection. (In addition to their Delaware and Pennsylvania triumphs, the retailers won decisions declaring local option unconstitutional in Indiana, Iowa, and Texas.[48]) Only in Vermont did a state's highest court reject the non-delegation principle, and even then the Court was careful to distinguish that state's local option law from the apparently similar laws enacted in Pennsylvania and Delaware.[49] Taken collectively, then, the local option cases of the 1840s and early 1850s offer further confirmation of the antebellum judiciary's tendency to resist sweeping reorganizations of governmental authority, even in cases where the existence of a threat to public safety and morals was acknowledged.[50] The fact that judicial opposition was more vigorous in the case of local option, relative to no-license, followed naturally from the more radical nature of the proposed reform. In the words of Judge Booth, local option attempted to uproot a regulatory framework that had remained in operation from "a very early period in the history of our colonial government."[51] Worse, it did so in a manner—that is, by delegating legislative authority to local electorates—that threatened to undermine the institutional checks and balances that formed the very foundation of constitutional government.

"Legislation Cannot Change the Nature of Things": The Judiciary and Maine Law Prohibition, 1851–1854

As the shift from no-license to local option laws suggests, the anti-liquor forces were by the late 1840s inching closer to the view that the entire licensing system was corrupt and ought to be replaced with a policy of statewide prohibition. The temperance movement took this final, decisive step in the early 1850s when it embraced a highly contentious reform known as the Maine Law—a form of statewide prohibition that was adopted in about a dozen states between 1851 and 1856. Originally drafted by the state of Maine's leading temperance crusader, Neal Dow, the Maine Law abandoned any pretense of preserving the traditional licensing system and instead banned the manufacture and sale of intoxicating liquors altogether.[52] This sweeping prohibition was enforced by a provision allowing any three registered voters claiming knowledge of liquor illegally kept for sale as a beverage to demand the issuance of a search warrant. Any liquor discovered in the subsequent search was subject to summary destruction, unless the owner came forward to prove before a magistrate that the liquor had been legally imported or acquired for mechanical or medicinal purposes from a bonded agent.[53] The owners of the illegal liquor, if they could be identified, were subject to stiff fines and/or jail time. In addition, the laws typically contained provisions that voided debts and contracts involving liquor and barred the owners of seized liquor from bringing suit against the officers or other individuals who had seized their property. Taken collectively, these various provisions amounted to a declaration that liquor was no longer to be considered a valid form of property, but rather a public nuisance on the order of diseased goods or obscene prints.[54]

The Maine Law forced judges to grapple with the constitutional limits of the police power in a way that no previous regulatory innovation had done. As Thomas Cooley would write in 1868, there was in the history of American law no "more striking" example of an attempt to eradicate an entire class of private property.[55] Indeed, the law not only destroyed the value of a common and traditionally valid commodity (the traditional licensing system, after all, had left bulk sales of liquor unregulated), but also permitted its summary abatement through procedures normally reserved for a small class of inherently "noxious" items. Further complicating matters was the fact that the law permitted private ownership of liquor for medicinal or mechanical purposes, meaning that the question of whether or not a given store of liquor constituted a public nuisance depended entirely upon a magistrate's judgment about what the owner intended to do with his or her property. Finally, the law placed the burden of proof squarely upon the property owner, who was required to establish that the liquor in question had *not* been intended for use as a beverage.

Perhaps not surprisingly, the Maine Law had a polarizing effect on the state judiciary: some state appellate courts upheld the law as a valid exercise of the police power; others invalidated it for contravening the constitutional rights of property owners. Given the wide range of judicial responses engendered by the Maine Law, one might well despair of drawing any systematic conclusions about the nature of antebellum constitutionalism from these cases. And yet, a careful examination of the chronology of state judicial rulings reveals that the judiciary, in keeping with its deep-rooted commitment to the protection of settled property rights, *initially* greeted the Maine Law with near-universal condemnation. Indeed, nearly every state appellate decision involving the Maine Law handed down between 1851 and 1854 resulted in the invalidation of one or more of the law's most important enforcement provisions. Not until the late 1850s, as we shall see in the next chapter, did judges begin to treat liquor as an exceptional form of property that could, in some cases, be excluded from the ambit of constitutional protection.

The original Maine Law, enacted in 1851, was in effect for less than a year when the Supreme Judicial Court of Maine struck down one of the law's most potent enforcement provisions—the ban on suits against officers who seized illegal stores of liquor. The ruling came in the case of *Preston v. Drew*, an action of replevin for the recovery of eight barrels of rum seized by a justice of the peace.[56] Chief Justice Ether Shepley, in his opinion for the Court, began by acknowledging that the state legislature possessed the abstract power to "determine that articles injurious to the public health or morals, shall not constitute property, within its jurisdiction." Shepley used the rest of his opinion, however, to make clear that this theoretical power of morals police was in practice subject to strict constitutional limitations. Among these limitations was a state constitutional provision guaranteeing to "every person" the right to "have remedy by due course of law" for every "injury done him in his person, reputation, property, or immunities."[57] The key question, then, was whether liquor amounted to a form of "property" within the meaning of the state constitution; if so, then the Maine Law would appear to conflict with the property owner's constitutional right to a remedy at law. In *Preston*, the state attempted to meet this objection by arguing that liquor was no more deserving of constitutional protection than diseased goods, obscene prints, and other traditional public nuisances. Justice Shepley disagreed:

> It is, however, insisted . . . that a person, by the common law, can no more acquire property in spirituous and intoxicating liquors, than he can in obscene publications and prints. There is a clear and marked distinction between them. Such liquors may be applied to useful purposes. This is admitted in the Act. . . . It is their misuse or abuse alone which occasions the mischief. Obscene publications and prints are in their very nature corrupting, and productive only of evil. They are incapable of any use which is not corrupting and injurious to the moral sense.[58]

Shepley thus drew a key distinction between liquor, which was capable of harmless and even productive uses, and obscene items, which were not. In so doing, he bluntly rejected one of the key arguments in the evangelical arsenal, namely, that liquor, because of its harmful tendencies, properly belonged in the legal category of "nuisance" rather than "property." And so long as liquor remained a valid form of property in the state of Maine—even if only for mechanical and medicinal purposes—it followed that liquor owners were entitled to their day in court.[59]

Temperance advocates would be dealt three additional blows from the judiciary during the early 1850s, and in each case the adverse ruling followed the basic logic of the Maine Court's opinion in *Preston v. Drew*. First, the New Hampshire Supreme Court, in November 1852, stalled the prohibition movement in that state by handing down an advisory opinion that identified no less than eight constitutional violations in the Maine Law. Chief among the Court's complaints was the fact that the state legislature, in its haste to divest liquor retailers of traditional constitutional guarantees such as the right to a jury trial and the right to bring suit for damages, had forgotten that "liquors are property" and that legislation "cannot change the nature of things."[60] Then, in the very same month, U.S. Supreme Court Justice Benjamin Curtis issued a circuit court opinion striking down the major enforcement provisions of Rhode Island's recently enacted Maine Law.[61] In *Greene v. Briggs*, Curtis ruled that the Maine Law was in conflict with the "law of the land" clause of the Rhode Island constitution, as well as state constitutional provisions guaranteeing criminal defendants the right to a jury trial and the right to confront their accusers. Like the Maine and New Hampshire Courts, Curtis could not overlook the fact that "spirituous or intoxicating liquors are still property," notwithstanding the Rhode Island legislature's attempt to transform them into a nuisance *per se.*[62] And so long as liquors remained property, it followed that a law authorizing their summary destruction amounted to "an arbitrary and unconstitutional exertion of the legislative power."[63]

The fourth major anti-Maine Law decision of the early 1850s came from a seemingly unlikely source: Chief Justice Lemuel Shaw of Massachusetts. In the case of *Fisher v. McGirr*—yet another suit brought by a liquor owner against the officers who had seized his property—Shaw ruled that Massachusetts' newly enacted Maine Law was incompatible with key civil liberties guaranteed in the state constitution, including the right to a jury trial, the right to be free from unreasonable searches and seizures, the right to confront one's accusers, and the right to bring suit in a court of law.[64] At first glance, this holding may appear difficult to square with Shaw's 1837 ruling in *Blackington v. Commonwealth*. In that case, as we have seen, Shaw had handed the temperance forces a major victory by upholding the constitutionality of the "no-license" effort. Moreover, in the intervening years, Shaw had authored an opinion in *Commonwealth v. Alger* that would come to be viewed as the classic American statement of the police power doctrine, an opinion declaring that all "[r]ights of property . . . are subject to such reasonable limitations in their enjoyment, as shall prevent them from being injurious, and to such reasonable restraints and regulations established by law, as the legislature . . . may think necessary and expedient."[65]

How can Shaw's earlier opinions recognizing an expansive police power be reconciled with his 1854 ruling that the Maine Law represented an unconstitutional interference with individual rights? One possible response is that Shaw's police power rulings are in fact irreconcilable.[66] But a more likely explanation is that Shaw, like other jurists of his era, harbored deep reservations about a reform that appeared to contravene the constitutional commitments of the Founding generation. For, despite some claims to the contrary, the Maine Law was hardly identical to the traditional common law abatement procedures that routinely passed constitutional muster in antebellum courts.[67] The key distinction, as Shaw made clear in his *Fisher* opinion, was that the sorts of items traditionally destroyed through proceedings *in rem* were either illegal to hold as property for any purpose (as in the case of obscene books or prints), or else deemed nuisances based on a simple and indisputable set of facts (as when a store of gunpowder was discovered in a populous area). The Maine Law, on the other hand, "fully recognize[d]" liquor as "lawful property," but declared that it could be seized and destroyed, not based on any simple set of facts, but based on the owner's intent to sell it as a beverage.[68] And the question of *intent*, according to Shaw, was one that could only be settled through a proceeding that was consistent with the state constitution's criminal procedure guarantees.[69] Shaw's *Fisher* opinion was thus hardly a radical departure from his earlier police power opinions; like other jurists of his era, Shaw simply believed that the theoretically unlimited police power was, in practice, subject to a set of well-defined boundaries established by common law and tradition (and often codified in state constitutions). In Shaw's words, the people of Massachusetts had the "right to require of their lawgivers . . . an exact and constant observance" of those "homely and familiar maxims" that functioned "to preserve the advantages of liberty, and [to] maintain a free government."[70]

In all, four state appellate courts and one federal circuit court passed judgment on the substantive provisions of the Maine Law in the period between 1851 and 1854.[71] Significantly, these four tribunals handed down nearly identical decisions eviscerating the law's most important enforcement provisions. To be sure, none of these decisions declared that a policy of prohibiting liquor sales was inherently unconstitutional or impossible to implement in a way that did not violate key constitutional commitments. But without question, the judicial consensus in the early 1850s held that because liquor—unlike diseased goods, counterfeiters' tools, or obscene prints—had been recognized as a valid form of property from time immemorial, and because it was undeniably capable of beneficial uses, a law that stripped liquor owners of basic procedural protections could only be characterized as an "arbitrary" invasion of private rights.[72]

Liquor Regulation and the Commerce Power: The *License Cases*

Challenging innovative morals laws in the courts was clearly a winning strategy for liquor retailers, lottery operators, and other opponents of evangelical reform. Yet it is important to note that antebellum evangelicals were able to point to at least one significant constitutional victory in the period under consideration. This, at least, is how the reformers themselves interpreted the *License Cases,* the rather convoluted 1847 decision in which the Taney Court upheld a series of liquor license laws against a Commerce Clause challenge.[73] And indeed, this is how the decision is usually interpreted today.[74] Yet, upon close inspection, the *License Cases* were far from a clear-cut victory for the prohibitionists. In fact, the decision did nothing so much as illustrate the constitutionally problematic nature of a movement whose ultimate aim was the eradication of a traditionally valid commodity.

The origins of the *License Cases* can be traced to the enactment of the first local option laws in the late 1830s. One way in which retailers attempted to block the spread of local option was to claim that an outright denial of liquor licenses amounted to an interference with Congress's exclusive authority over foreign and interstate commerce. In support of this claim, retailers typically cited two pieces of evidence. First, in the 1827 case of *Brown v. Maryland,* the Supreme Court had held that the Commerce Clause protected importers of foreign goods from state-level taxation so long as the imported goods remained in their "original package."[75] Justice Marshall's *Brown* opinion also suggested in dicta that the "original package" doctrine would protect goods imported from a sister state.[76] Based on these facts, liquor retailers argued that the Commerce Clause guaranteed the right of importers not only to buy and sell goods across state lines, but also to *resell* them in the domestic market, so long as they remained in their original packages. In addition, liquor retailers were well aware that Congress had frequently imposed duties on liquor imported from foreign countries. And for this reason, it could be argued that Congress had occupied the regulatory field with respect to liquor, thus nullifying restrictive state liquor laws—at least in the case of imported liquor. As the opponents of Massachusetts' Fifteen Gallon Law put the point in their 1838 petition to the state legislature, the "paramount laws of Congress" had authorized "the importation of [liquor]," and "therefore no State can prevent such importation and incorporation into the mass of property."[77]

In 1847, three cases involving Commerce Clause challenges to restrictive liquor laws reached the U.S. Supreme Court. Decided jointly as the *License Cases,* the cases challenged the liquor laws of Rhode Island, New Hampshire, and Massachusetts, respectively. (Local option laws were in effect in New Hampshire and Massachusetts, while Rhode Island required licenses for all liquor sales in quantities of less than ten gallons.) On a doctrinal level, the cases confronted the Court with a serious dilemma. It was clear that distilled liquors were, in Justice Taney's words, "universally admitted to be subjects of ownership and property, and are therefore subjects of exchange, barter, and traffic, like any other commodity in which a right of property exists."[78] But if liquor was a legitimate subject of commerce, how could local option laws—which clearly affected sales of imported liquor—be reconciled with the federal commerce power? In the Massachusetts and Rhode Island cases, the justices were saved by the fact that the liquor in question had not been in its "original package," and thus did not fall within the doctrine laid down by Marshall in *Brown.* The New Hampshire case, however, involved a barrel of gin imported from a sister state and resold in its original container. The case thus forced the justices to confront directly the question whether state license laws, to the extent that they interfered with the sale of imported liquor, conflicted with the federal commerce power.

Coming at the precise moment when the nation was awakening to the constitutional dimensions of the slavery controversy, the *License Cases* were rife with broader political implications.[79] It is therefore not surprising that the justices approached the case with extreme caution, with six of the seven participating justices authoring separate opinions.[80] Yet beneath this veneer of doctrinal conflict, five of the six *License Cases* opinions were undergirded by a shared conviction that local option laws were *not* incompatible with the Commerce Clause since, from a federalism perspective, they differed little from the traditional license laws which predated the adoption of the Constitution.[81] That is to say, like Lemuel Shaw in the early no-license cases, the Court concluded that states and localities had enjoyed plenary authority in the granting of licenses since the early colonial period; and although licensing authorities were now granting fewer licenses, this fact did nothing to alter the constitutionality of the underlying power. Thus, Justice Woodbury emphasized that local option laws were, from a federalism standpoint, neither "novel nor extraordinary." Rather, they were substantially identical to "the policy of most of the old states, as well before as since the constitution was adopted."[82] Justice McClean, while acknowledging that "a great moral reform" had recently extended liquor regulation "beyond its former limit," nonetheless concluded that the new laws were no more invasive of federal authority than the traditional license laws that had been in force "since the adoption of the Constitution."[83] Justice Catron, in turn, argued that "long usage, general acquiescence, and the absence of complaint" with respect to state license laws should be taken as evidence of their constitutionality.[84]

And yet it is important to note that the justices were not interested in antiquity for its own sake. Rather, the Court's primary interest was in delineating a workable boundary between the police and commerce powers, and deference to the authority of local licensing officials facilitated this process, in the sense that it represented a stable and widely accepted division of authority. But while the decision was indeed a victory for the temperance forces, the victory was in some sense pyrrhic, since the constitutionality of state-level liquor regulation now rested at least in part on its conventional nature. The decision gave no guarantee that more radical measures would be sustained, and indeed several of the justices were clearly haunted by the specter of statewide prohibition, which they saw looming on the horizon. In fact, four of the justices who participated in the *License Cases* offered explicit warnings that any state law interfering with the sale of foreign liquor in its original package would be invalidated on Commerce Clause grounds.[85] In addition, three of the justices were careful to link the license laws' constitutionality to the fact that they did not operate on importers directly. No state, in other words, was attempting to physically disrupt the flow of imported liquor across its borders, and for this reason, as Justice Woodbury pointed out, the laws did not constitute a serious threat to the national market; indeed, "importations" still went on "abundantly into each of [the] states" in question.[86] Of course, there was every reason to believe that the prohibitionists' ultimate aim was to block all importation of liquor into dry areas, thus destroying the interstate market in liquor. The Court was able to evade this ominous possibility with the reply that, as Justice McLean put it, it was "enough to say . . . that the legislature has not done what is supposed by the plaintiff's counsel it might do."[87]

As the remarks of Woodbury and McClean suggest, the justices were struggling to define a workable test that would ensure the constitutionality of essential police measures—license laws, quarantine laws, inspection laws—without permitting states to threaten the integrity of the national market. Woodbury hinted at the Court's ultimate solution when he argued that the category of interstate commerce should be divided into separate "local" and "national" spheres. This would allow the states to assume responsibility over matters that could be more efficiently managed at the local level while simultaneously preserving the federal government's exclusive authority over matters of national import.[88] Woodbury's proposed distinction, which was ultimately endorsed by a majority of the Court in the 1851 case of *Cooley v. Board of Wardens,* spelled further trouble for the temperance movement, since it implied that the commerce power could preempt police measures, even in the absence of a specific conflict with federal legislation, whenever state laws disrupted the uniformity required for the efficient functioning of the national market.[89]

The *Cooley* Test's implications for liquor regulation would not become clear until the aftermath of the Civil War, however. For now, the important point to note is that the temperance movement, as it edged closer to its ultimate goal of prohibition, found itself impaired not only by the property rights provisions of the state and federal constitutions, but also by the general structure of the federal system. As even the relatively friendly *License Cases* ruling made clear, any effort to eradicate the foreign and interstate trade in a traditionally valid commodity risked transcending the limits of the states' police powers. Thus, even as they publicly celebrated the *License Cases* as a great legal triumph, reformers were forced to redraw state-level liquor laws to avoid even the appearance of a conflict with the federal commerce power. Virtually every Maine Law enacted in the 1850s contained a clause declaring that the law should "not be deemed . . . to apply to the importer of foreign intoxicating liquors . . . imported under the authority of the laws of the United States"—a provision plainly intended to placate the four justices who had warned against interfering with foreign liquor in its original package.[90] In addition, although several antebellum prohibition laws imposed penalties on common carriers that transported liquor, most were careful to distinguish between intra- and interstate carriers. In fact, of all the Maine Laws enacted in the 1850s, it is striking that only four attempted in any way to address the problem of liquor imported from out of state. Of the states that *did* take steps to block the flow of out-of-state liquor, one (New York) required that shipments of liquor be clearly marked as such; another (Maine) imposed a twenty-four-hour time limit on common carriers transporting liquor across the state; and a third (Massachusetts) imposed penalties on common carriers who had "reasonable cause" cause to believe that they were transporting illegal shipments of liquor.[91] These provisions, because they imposed relatively minor burdens on carriers, were easily analogized to inspection laws, quarantine laws, and other traditional public health and safety measures. Significantly, only one state, Iowa, imposed a blanket prohibition on out-of-state shipments of liquor, making common carriers and their agents criminally liable for any unauthorized liquor found in their possession.[92] This ban on interstate shipments was never challenged in federal court, however, as the Iowa Supreme Court effectively nullified the provision in 1857.[93]

The *License Cases* thus left the prohibition movement in a state of limbo. That there was nothing inherently problematic about restrictive liquor laws, from a federalism standpoint, was now clear. But equally clear was the fact that any effort to implement "bone dry" prohibition regimes at the state level—for example, by banning importation from abroad or from sister states—would raise grave constitutional questions with respect to the relationship between the states' police powers and the federal commerce power. In order to eradicate the hated liquor traffic, it would be necessary for evangelical reformers not only to uproot settled property rights, but also to fundamentally alter the nature of the federal system.

Conclusion

The story of the judicial encounter with anti-liquor and anti-lottery laws in the years between 1830 and 1854, then, is neither a story of unqualified support nor of unbroken opposition. As we have seen, the claim that judges in this period reflexively subordinated private rights to the protection of public morals simply does not hold water. But neither would it be accurate to characterize antebellum judges as unthinking opponents of moral reform. Rather, if judges displayed a systematic bias in this period, it was in favor of property rights and patterns of authority that existed under the traditional, colonial-era regulatory framework. Far from defending the community's right to translate its evolving moral values into law, the judiciary remained faithful to the traditional view that the underlying purpose of a written constitution was to protect private rights from the ever-present danger of self-interested or shortsighted democratic majorities. Yet, if the edifice of the commercial republic had yet to crack, it was clearly under strain. Its integrity now depended on the judiciary's willingness to defy a public that was increasingly unified in the belief that it was not only possible but also morally necessary to eradicate liquor, lotteries, and other forms of vice. And although the judiciary remained remarkably monolithic in the Jacksonian period, it was perhaps only inevitable that fissures would appear in the late 1850s when the prohibition question moved, briefly, into the spotlight of national politics.

{ 3 }

The Triumph of Evangelical
Public Morality in the States

*The privilege to do wrong cannot . . . be . . . purchased and fastened,
like the shirt of Nessus, upon the community, without any
power of getting rid of it.*
—Judge Ephraim Peyton, *Moore v. The State* (1873)

In early 1855, Vermont Chief Justice Isaac Redfield authored an opinion declaring that the enforcement provisions of the state's recently enacted prohibition law were "at variance with the very first principles of constitutional
liberty." Although Redfield, a jurist who is today remembered as a proponent
of an expansive police power, affirmed the legislature's power to declare any
form of property to be "contraband" and "unworthy [of] the protection of the
law," he nonetheless insisted that this power was in practice limited by the
constitutional rights of property owners and criminal defendants.[1] Redfield
thus deemed his state's prohibition law unconstitutional, on the grounds that
permitting the summary abatement of property in liquor would be "altogether
without parallel . . . in the history of jurisprudence in free states."[2]

In light of *Fisher v. McGirr* and the other Maine Law rulings discussed in
the previous chapter, there is little in Redfield's opinion that is new or surprising—except, that is, for the fact that Vermont's Chief Justice was writing
in dissent. Indeed, much to Redfield's dismay, a majority of his colleagues had
endorsed the constitutionality of the Maine Law's enforcement provisions,
thus making the Vermont Supreme Court the first tribunal to uphold the
law in its entirety. Why had Redfield's colleagues failed to perceive that the
Maine Law had abrogated "the liberties of a free state"? Here, Redfield could
only point suggestively in the direction of an answer by noting that such an
invasion of individual liberties would "never have been attempted" by the legislature, nor upheld by the judiciary, "upon any other subject."[3]

Without reading too much into a brief aside, it seems fair to speculate that
Redfield was subtly accusing both the legislature and his judicial colleagues

of sacrificing constitutional principle on the altar of public opinion. The mid-1850s marked the undisputed high point of the antebellum prohibition movement, as seven states and one territory enacted Maine Laws in 1854 and 1855. The sudden popularity of prohibition in the Northern states undoubtedly created strong incentives for the judiciary to reconsider its initial hostility towards the Maine Law. And to Redfield, at least, it was clear that many judges were permitting their sympathy for a "good cause" to override their fealty to the constitutional commitments of the Founding generation.[4]

This chapter will argue that Redfield's intuition was largely correct. Beginning in the mid-1850s, state courts responded to the growing power of the temperance movement by adopting a vastly expanded view of the police power in cases involving threats to public morality. Where most jurists had previously insisted on the inviolability of constitutional rights provisions, even in cases involving acknowledged threats to public morals, many state judges now adopted a more flexible understanding of constitutional guarantees. In fact, some judges now suggested that, at least in cases involving the liquor and lottery industries, the rights and duties of citizens should be understood to evolve in tandem with the moral progress of the wider community. This shift to a dynamic understanding of the social compact, while at this point limited to a narrow range of cases, marks a critical juncture in American constitutional development. For the first time, dozens of state-level jurists accepted that evolving mores could in at least some cases justify the destruction of settled property rights; and this admission, as we shall see in subsequent chapters, would soon produce calls for a more flexible understanding of the constitutional enterprise in cases far removed from the subject of morals regulation. In order to understand *why* judges ultimately acquiesced in the destruction of newly immoral forms of property, however, we must briefly examine the political landscape of the mid-1850s. The shift in judicial attitudes described above can only be fully understood, I argue, when viewed in the context of the partisan realignment that began in 1853 and 1854—a development that greatly increased the salience of the liquor question in Northern state politics.

Partisan Realignment and the Liquor Question

A glance at Table 1 reveals that a remarkable shift in judicial attitudes towards the Maine Law took place in the period after 1854. More specifically, the table reflects a sudden polarization of judicial opinion. The first five appellate courts to consider the Maine Law's constitutionality, as we have seen, handed down nearly identical opinions invalidating the law's enforcement provisions. Remarkably, there were no dissenters from these early Maine Law rulings. Beginning in 1855, however, dissent became the norm in cases involving liquor prohibition; indeed the first five opinions handed down in the period after *Fisher v. McGirr* issued from sharply divided tribunals. A careful examination of Table 1 reveals, moreover, that judicial attitudes towards prohibition were becoming polarized in a second sense—that is, not only within particular tribunals, but also across states. The pre-1854 rulings, because they focused largely on issues of procedural due process, left open the possibility of a middle ground between the traditional license system and the draconian Maine Law procedure. This possibility largely evaporated after 1854, as state judiciaries divided into two clearly demarcated camps: five courts upheld the Maine Law in its entirety, on the grounds that the state's power of morals police was effectively plenary, while two invalidated the law, not on procedural due process grounds, but based on the much broader claim that any legislative act that destroyed the value or vendibility of property legally acquired under existing law required compensation to the property owner.

The Maine Law's polarizing effect on the antebellum judiciary has, of course, been noted before. In the existing scholarship, one set of Maine Law decisions (usually the group upholding the law) is typically described as reflecting the "true" or "original" strand of American constitutionalism, while the opposing decisions are dismissed as curious outliers.[5] When we turn our attention to the chronology of events, however, a different picture emerges. The fact that the judiciary, after an initial period of unanimity, splintered badly in 1855 suggests that we are witnessing an important turning point in American constitutional development. More specifically, it is striking that of the eight Maine Law rulings handed down after 1854, five upheld the law in its entirety with barely a word of concern about the formerly problematic enforcement provisions. Indeed, the obvious winners in the post-1854 period were the prohibitionists, as several state judiciaries for the first time clearly subordinated settled property rights to the enforcement of the new, post-Revival public morality.

But why did the state judiciary, after decades of stubborn resistance, begin to accommodate a reconstructed moral order in the mid-1850s? The fact that the critical shift occurred around the year 1855 strongly suggests that the collapse of the Jacksonian party system was an important factor in the judiciary's

TABLE I

Appellate Rulings on the Constitutionality of the Maine Law, 1852–1858*

Year	State	Case	Result	Dissent?
1852	Maine	*Preston v. Drew*	Enforcement Provisions Void	No
1852	New Hampshire	Advisory Opinion	Enforcement Provisions Void	No
1852	Rhode Island (Fed.)	*Greene v. Briggs*	Enforcement Provisions Void	No
1854	Massachusetts	*Fisher v. McGirr*	Enforcement Provisions Void	No
1854	Rhode Island (State)**	*State v. Snow*	Enforcement Provisions Void	No
1855	Vermont	*Lincoln v. Smith*	Upheld	Yes
1855	Indiana	*Beebe v. The State*	Void in Entirety	Yes (Party-line)
1855	Iowa	*Santo v. State*	Upheld	Yes
1856	Michigan	*People v. Gallagher; Hibbard v. The People*	Enforcement Provisions Void	Yes
1856	New York	*Wynehamer v. The People; The People v. Toynbee*	Void in Entirety	Yes (Party-line)
1856	Connecticut	*State v. Wheeler; State v. Brennan's Liquors*	Upheld	No
1858	Rhode Island***	*State v. Paul*	Upheld	No
1858	Delaware	*State v. Allmond*	Upheld	No

*Where a tribunal handed down multiple rulings on the constitutionality of the Maine Law, I have included only the case of first impression, except in cases where the law was substantially revised (as was the case in Rhode Island).

**Rhode Island's original Maine Law was declared unconstitutional in the 1852 federal case of *Greene v. Briggs*. Following the enactment of minor revisions in 1853, the law was again found unconstitutional, this time by the state Supreme Court in *State v. Snow*.

***Following the state Supreme Court's 1854 *State v. Snow* ruling, the Rhode Island legislature again enacted a series of minor revisions to the state's prohibition law. Significantly, the new law left intact a number of controversial provisions, including the requirement that owners of forfeited liquor post a $100 bond before they would be permitted to appeal from the judgment of a magistrate (and receive a jury trial).

reconsideration of the Maine Law. During the 1830s and 1840s the nation's two major political parties, much to the chagrin of temperance advocates, obstinately refused to stake out clear positions with respect to the liquor question. Although the Whigs were generally viewed as slightly more favorable to the cause—owing to the Democratic party's perceived affiliation with "wet" elements, including immigrants and Catholics—liquor was a crosscutting issue that both major parties did their best to downplay.[6] This situation changed abruptly in 1854 and 1855, when the loose coalition of anti-slavery, temperance, and nativist elements that would eventually coalesce into the Republican party began to replace the Whigs as the Democrats' major opposition in the Northern states. Unlike the two established parties, the nascent Republican party initially had little to lose by wholeheartedly endorsing the Maine Law, as party leaders believed that most anti-slavery voters were also foes of the liquor traffic.[7] The Republicans' embrace of prohibition, not surprisingly, produced a corresponding adjustment in their competitors' electoral calculations. Because most temperance supporters gravitated towards the upstart Republicans (or their chief competitors, the nativist Know Nothings), Democrats no longer had reason to fear that a vigorous anti-Maine Law stance would result in intraparty strife. Moreover, in those states where the Whigs clung to power through 1854 and 1855, they did so only by capitulating to the demands of the upstart factions—demands that included an unambiguous endorsement of the Maine Law.[8] For present purposes, then, the most important result of the mid-1850s realignment is the fact that the major political parties for the first time adopted clear stances on the Maine Law and its constitutionality.[9]

Although it is perhaps impossible to *prove* that partisan realignment directly impacted judicial-decision making with respect to prohibition, there is a great deal of circumstantial evidence suggesting that post-1854 Maine Law decisions were highly partisan affairs. It is important to remember that most state appellate judges in this period were either popularly elected or elected by state legislatures to relatively brief terms, meaning that they were hardly immune to the pressures of public opinion and party affiliation. Naturally enough, many judges in states dominated by fusionist or Republican elements suddenly adopted an expansive view of the state's police powers in cases involving liquor. The justices of the Vermont Supreme Court, for example, handed down their pro-Maine Law ruling shortly after being elected to one-year terms by a pro-temperance, fusionist state legislature.[10] The justices of the Iowa Supreme Court, who issued the nation's second unequivocal endorsement of prohibition, were elected in 1855 by the same Whig-Free Soil legislative coalition that enacted the state's Maine Law.[11] In all, four of the five pro-Maine Law decisions handed down in 1855 or later came from states— Vermont, Iowa, Connecticut, and Rhode Island—that were by now firmly in the fusionist or Republican camps.[12]

In states where the Democrats remained powerful, in contrast, post-realignment Maine Laws encountered serious problems in the courts. In New York, where statewide prohibition was enacted in 1854 and again in 1855 (after the first law was vetoed by the state's Democratic governor), it is no exaggeration to say that the liquor question dominated state judicial elections during the 1850s.[13] In 1856, when the Maine Law test case of *Wynehamer v. The People* finally reached the state's popularly elected high court, the justices divided along party lines, with a bare majority declaring the law unconstitutional.[14] In fact, the *Wynehamer* majority went far beyond earlier anti-Maine Law rulings, holding that the due process clause of the state constitution barred the legislature from destroying even the value or vendibility of liquor acquired prior to the law's enactment.[15]

The Maine Law met a similar fate in Indiana, where the state's highest court invalidated the law on a party-line vote in the November 1855 case of *Beebe v. The State*. In this instance, a direct link to party politics is easily established: Justice Samuel Perkins, the author of the Court's opinion, was the publisher of a Democratic newspaper whose editorials regularly denounced the Maine Law as unconstitutional. So anxious was Perkins to invalidate the law, in fact, that he effectively nullified it in the summer of 1855 by issuing writs of *habeas corpus* on behalf of individuals convicted of selling liquor.[16] When the law finally reached the state Supreme Court, Perkins authored an opinion that was no less sweeping than *Wynehamer*. The state legislature, he declared, was bound not only by the specific, textually enshrined rights provisions of the state constitution, but also by a vaguely defined "right of property" that barred the legislature from interfering with any form property lawfully acquired under existing laws. Indeed, in an opinion that reads much like the Maine Law plank of a contemporaneous Democratic party platform, Perkins attacked the "paternalistic" philosophy of the prohibitionists—a philosophy derived from the "absolute" governments of Europe, where "the people had no rights except what the government . . . graciously saw fit to confer on them," and where it was the state's "duty, like a father towards his children, to command whatever it deemed expedient for the public good, without first . . . consulting the public, or recognizing in its members any individual rights."[17]

In the existing literature, the anti-Maine Law decisions of the New York and Indiana Courts, with their expansive conception of property rights, are regularly dismissed as beyond the mainstream of antebellum legal thought.[18] And indeed, when compared to the early liquor cases discussed in the previous chapter, there can be no doubt that *Wynehamer* and *Beebe* articulate a far broader—and less textually grounded—understanding of the rights of property owners. A point that is almost entirely overlooked in the existing literature, however, is the extent to which the *pro*-Maine Law decisions of the late 1850s were themselves undergirded by a radically new constitutional philosophy—one that, for the first time, unambiguously subordinated the rights of property owners to an expansive and amorphous power of morals police.

"With This Question We Have Nothing to Do": The Post-Realignment State Judiciary and the Maine Law

The task confronting pro-Maine Law jurists in the post-realignment period was to explain why a law that appeared, on its face, to conflict with the specific, textually enshrined rights of property owners and criminal defendants was not, in fact, unconstitutional. And to be sure, antebellum constitutional law was not without useful precedents for such an endeavor. Since the 1830s, prohibitionists had defended the constitutionality of restrictive liquor laws by citing state-level decisions in which the police power—or its close cousin, the power of nuisance abatement—had been successfully employed to destroy diseased goods, fire hazards, gambling instruments, and other threats to public health and morals.[19] That such precedents confirmed a legislature's power to transform a traditionally valid form of property into a nuisance *per se* was far from obvious, however. In fact, while the major antebellum jurists regularly acknowledged that the state could, in some instances, destroy property through summary proceedings and without compensating the owner, they consistently characterized this power as consisting of a series of narrow, common-law-based exceptions to the general rule of inviolable property rights.[20] And although it is true that some state judiciaries began to embrace a broader view of the police power in the 1840s and 1850s, not even the doctrine's most ardent proponents were willing to endorse the idea of an unbounded police power that would be effectively detached from custom and precedent.[21] Lemuel Shaw, for example, famously endorsed the destruction of private property (a wharf) so as to keep Boston Harbor free from obstructions—a power well established in English common law—but refused to sanction a liquor prohibition law that dispensed with the constitutional rights of property owners and criminal defendants.[22]

In short, the Maine Law differed radically from existing police powers precedents in that it was not a response to an imminent physical threat, such as fire or epidemic; asserted a power that was not clearly recognized in the common law; and subjected property to summary abatement in an instance when no specific injury or malicious use of property was alleged. In order to ground the law's constitutionality, it would be necessary to develop a novel understanding of the constitutional enterprise, one that unambiguously subordinated private rights to the protection of public morality. We can begin to see the emergence of such a philosophy in *Lincoln v. Smith*, the case that sparked Isaac Redfield's spirited dissent.[23]

The litigation that would eventually bring the Maine Law before Vermont's highest court originated in 1854 when a constable seized and destroyed a barrel of rum owned by one Russell Lincoln. Like the plaintiff in *Fisher v. McGirr* and the other Maine Law cases discussed in the previous chapter, Lincoln brought suit against the constable who had seized his liquor, alleging trespass, breaking and entering, assault and battery, and false imprisonment.[24] When Lincoln was awarded damages at the trial stage, the constable appealed the verdict on the ground that the Maine Law barred suits against officers who seized or destroyed liquor in accordance with its provisions.[25] In early 1855, a majority of the Court issued an opinion that not only reversed the trial court's verdict, but also offered an unequivocal endorsement of the Maine Law's constitutionality. Ignoring the half-dozen anti–Maine Law rulings handed down during the previous two years (which were widely available[26]), Judge Milo Bennett rested his holding on the claim that the Maine Law's enforcement provisions, while "somewhat loosely drawn," were in effect no different from the *in rem* proceedings used to abate traditional public nuisances:

> Nuisances may be abated in the most summary manner; dogs found chasing sheep may be shot down; bucks running at large within a given period, without the marks of the initials of the owner's name, may become the property of the captor; and race horses may be declared forfeited; gambling implements may be destroyed; lottery tickets and obscene prints may be prohibited, and under the quarantine laws, the health officer of a city, to prevent the spread of infection or contagion, may destroy bedding or clothing, or any part of the cargo of a vessel, subject to quarantine, and which "he may deem infected." Gunpowder kept in improper places, may be seized and confiscated; and the exercise of these powers, is a power of prevention, highly conservative in its character, and essential to the well being of the body politic, and ought not to be characterized as arbitrary or despotic. . . . The power to seize and confiscate private property for the violation of municipal laws, and as a means of preventing infractions thereof, has long been exercised by the general government; and I am not aware that the existence of that power has ever been denied; and it is a familiar principle that the long exercise of a power by a government, without objection, furnishes the strongest if not conclusive evidence that it was rightfully exercised.[27]

At first glance, this passage appears to offer strong support for the argument that American law has *always* acknowledged the state's essentially unlimited power to seize and destroy forms of property deemed injurious to public health or morals. Upon close inspection, however, it is clear that Bennett's opinion marks a radical departure from the traditional understanding of the police power. As we have seen, the early Maine Law opinions of Shaw, Curtis, and Shepley begin with a simple question: does liquor constitute a form of "property" within the meaning of the state constitution? After this question is answered in the affirmative, the opinions proceed to ask whether the law's enforcement provisions are consistent with the constitutional rights of property owners and criminal defendants. Although these opinions often include dicta pointing to an expansive conception of the police power, this language is always accompanied by the caveat that this *abstract* power is in practice subject to a series of common law and constitutional limitations.

Justice Bennett's *Lincoln* opinion, in contrast, proceeds in a completely different manner. Bennett begins his discussion of the Maine Law's constitutionality with the familiar observation that individuals forfeit some portion of their "natural rights" upon entering into civil society:

> But it is said, that the right of private property is founded in the laws of nature, and that a statute taking away the use and disposal of a man's own acquiring, is in violation of his own natural right of property. To this we answer: when men enter into the social compact, they give up a part of their natural rights, and consent that they shall be so far restrained in the enjoyment of them by the laws of society, as is necessary and expedient for the general advantage.[28]

Although the idea of the social compact was, of course, a commonplace of nineteenth-century constitutional thought, Bennett's use of the idea was innovative in one critical respect. By beginning with the observation that all natural rights are subject to limitations imposed by the community, and by characterizing property rights as "natural rights," Bennett effectively reversed the logic of earlier Maine Law decisions: now it was the abstract right of the *individual*—and not the police power of the state—that was subject to practical limitations. Bennett's litany of traditional public nuisances—gunpowder, diseased goods, gambling instruments, obscene prints—was not intended as a list of exceptions to the otherwise sacrosanct rights of the property owner; it was intended, rather, to provide support for the idea of an expansive and amorphous power of morals police. Thus, while Bennett dutifully listed the various provisions of the state's bill of rights with which the Maine Law was said to conflict—the right of property owners to a remedy at law; the right of "acquiring, possessing, and protecting property"; the right to be free from unreasonable searches and seizures—these he dismissed as merely describing "the natural rights of persons *before* entering into the social compact."[29] Just as the individual's natural right to life was circumscribed by "the law punishing murder with death," the natural rights of property owners were subject always to "the conservative powers of government." Indeed, no provision of the state's constitution "should be so construed as to trammel upon the legislature in passing such laws as they shall deem the public good requires."[30]

The critical test for whether a given use of the police power was justified, in Bennett's formulation, was not whether it was consistent with the traditional rights of property owners and criminal defendants, but whether the "evil" in question was sufficiently serious to warrant the destruction of private property. Judged by this standard, there could be no doubt that the Maine Law represented an appropriate use of the state's power of morals police:

> If it be granted, that the use of intoxicating liquors as a drink is worse than useless, and intemperance a legitimate consequence of such use, and that intemperance is an evil, injurious to health and sound morals, and productive of pauperism and crime; it seems to us, that a law designed to prevent such consequences must clearly fall within the class of laws, denominated police regulations.[31]

The other Maine Law rulings of the late 1850s, with the exception of the two that declared the law unconstitutional, employ the same three-step argument: the "natural" rights of property owners are subject to limitation upon entering civil society; one such limitation, as demonstrated by the abatement of traditional nuisances, is that property injurious to the public health and morals may be destroyed; therefore liquor, which is clearly a "moral contagion," is subject to summary abatement at the discretion of the lawmaking power.[32] Significantly, the early Maine Law decisions handed down by Shaw, Curtis, Shepley, and the New Hampshire Supreme Court are devoid of the language of natural rights. The sudden appearance of natural rights language in the Maine Law opinions of the mid-1850s may be explained by the fact that liquor retailers had, since the early 1830s, responded to temperance reforms by asserting the idea of a "natural" right to possess, manufacture, and sell any form of property, including liquor; and it is clear that many retailers raised natural rights arguments in cases involving the Maine Law. At the same time, however, it is striking that the paradoxical result of introducing natural rights language into judicial rulings on the Maine Law was often to restrict the concrete, constitutional rights of property owners. Put a different way, judges in pro-Maine Law decisions, by hammering on the widely accepted point that all natural rights were subject to practical limitation, managed to elide the critical question of whether the Maine Law had not violated specific *constitutional* rights.

Consider, for example, the Rhode Island Supreme Court's 1858 opinion in *State v. Paul*.[33] The case involved a Providence man who, after being convicted by a trial court of selling liquor without a license and keeping a "grog shop," appealed his conviction on the grounds that the Maine Law had created a type of legal proceeding that was both unknown to the common law and in conflict with rights guaranteed in the state and federal constitutions. In his opinion for the Court, Justice Samuel Ames flatly denied that the novelty of the Maine Law's enforcement provisions had any bearing on the question of their constitutionality. Again, the idea of a dynamic social compact provided the theoretical basis for the Court's argument: "The argument here proceeds upon the false assumption, that rights of property are absolute and unqualified, and not restricted, as they necessarily must be, *by the greater right of the community*, to have them so exercised within it as to be compatible with its well-being."[34] After establishing that the natural rights of individual property owners were subject to practical limitations imposed by the community, Ames proceeded to make clear that the traditional common-law nuisances represented only one small facet of the state's power in this area. In other words, like the Vermont Court in *Lincoln*, Ames used the existence of the traditional, closely bounded power of nuisance abatement to infer the existence of a much broader power of morals police:

> Our regulations of internal police and of trade, adapted by positive law to our condition, and changed by it according to our changing circumstances, are designed in great part to control the use of property to such modes as are consistent with the health and morals of the community. . . . That [grog shops] do, in general tend to corrupt the morals and destroy the health of those attracted to them by their appetites . . . is, as a matter of fact, perfectly notorious. . . . The best mode of dealing with these places, for the purpose of preventing such evils . . . is indeed a problem difficult to solve, and concerning which the wisest and the best may well entertain widely different opinions. *With this question, sitting here, we have nothing to do, for the very reason, that it is entrusted by the constitution to the lawmaking power alone to answer it, by legislation practically adapted to that end.*[35]

For Ames, the "fact" of liquor's injurious impact on the community effectively
ends the constitutional inquiry; an evil of such massive proportions must
be addressed by the legislative power though whatever laws or procedures it
deems well "adapted to that end."

The Connecticut Supreme Court's opinion in the 1856 case of *State v.
Brennan's Liquors* provides a final example of the basic trend. In appealing his
conviction on charges of possessing liquor "with the intent to sell," the defendant in *Brennan's Liquors* laid out the usual list of constitutional objects to
the Maine Law: the law conferred excessive authority on justices of the peace;
the warrant failed to state the name of a specific person suspected of violating
the law; and the right to a jury trial was made to depend upon an individual's
posting bond and finding sureties.[36] Connecticut Chief Justice Henry Matson
Waite, in his opinion for the Court, met these objections with a quotation
from a seemingly unlikely source: Lemuel Shaw's *Fisher v. McGirr* opinion.
Neglecting to mention that Shaw had *struck down* the Massachusetts' prohibition law's enforcement provisions, Waite highlighted Shaw's dictum "that
it is competent for the legislature to declare the possession of certain articles
of property, either absolutely or when held in particular places, and under
particular circumstances, to be unlawful, because they would be injurious,
dangerous or noxious, and . . . to provide for the abatement of the nuisance,
and the punishment of the offender, by the seizure and confiscation of the
property . . . or destruction of the noxious articles."[37] In *Fisher*, of course,
Shaw had followed this description of the state's abstract power of morals
police with a thorough discussion of the practical limitations imposed by the
state constitution. Waite, in contrast, jumped straight to the "fact" of liquor's
detrimental impact on the community:

> The object of the legislature in passing [the Maine Law], was to aid in
> the suppression of intemperance, pauperism, and crime; evils which impose
> very heavy and onerous burdens upon the public. The expenses attending
> the prosecution of crime, the support of criminals, and the maintenance
> of paupers are very great; and no one can doubt but that, to a very great
> extent they have been caused by the multitude of tippling shops with which
> our community has been heretofore infested. *The measures best calculated to
> prevent those evils, and preserve a healthy tone of morals in the community, are
> subjects proper for the consideration of the legislature. Courts of justice have noth-
> ing to do with them.* . . . [38]

For Lemuel Shaw, the magnitude of the "liquor evil" was irrelevant to the question of the Maine Law's constitutionality because the lawmaking power, even in its role as guardian of public morality, was bound to conform to the criminal procedure provisions of the state constitution. For Waite, in contrast, the fact of liquor's injurious effects—effects that are arguably even more severe than those accompanying traditional public nuisances—gives rise to an effectively unlimited power of morals police.

To reiterate, it is not simply because they upheld the Maine Law's constitutionality that the opinions of Bennett, Harrington, Ames, and Waite mark a critical turning point in American constitutional development. Rather, it is because they define the state's power of morals police so expansively as to subordinate even the specific, textually enshrined rights provisions contained in their respective state constitutions. Adopting a view long trumpeted by the nation's evangelical reformers, these antebellum jurists rejected the traditional, static conception of the social compact according to which the primary function of a written constitution was to insulate preexisting property rights from the whims of fluctuating democratic majorities. In its place, they proposed a dynamic understanding of constitutionalism in which the rights and duties of citizens evolved to keep pace with the moral progress of the larger community. It mattered little, on this view, that liquor was regarded as a valid and generally harmless form of property at the time that most state constitutions were adopted. Although the framers had been largely unaware of liquor's corrosive effect on society, the preponderance of evidence now suggested that Demon Rum was "destructive alike to the body and soul."[39] And, in the words of Judge Waite, "acts considered lawful at common law" might be prohibited "by statute" whenever necessary to ensure "the preservation of public morals."[40]

In effect, this way of framing the issue inverted the traditional relationship between the constitutional rights of property owners and the state's power of nuisance abatement. Instead of asking whether the Maine Law's enforcement provisions were compatible with the traditional rights of property owners, judges now asked whether the "natural" or "abstract" rights of property were compatible with the pressing policy goal of curbing the liquor traffic. Reversing Lemuel Shaw's dictum that the worthy goals of the prohibitionists would be achieved by constitutional means or not at all, the new constitutional philosophy ridiculed the notion that "the arm of . . . government is too feeble and too short to relieve itself against the evils of intemperance."[41]

The Lottery Revival and the Emergence
of the Inalienable Police Power

From the 1840s through the Civil War period, state courts were virtually unanimous in holding that the Contract Clause barred a state legislature from interfering with a lottery grant when doing so would impair vested rights. The opportunity for a judicial reconsideration of this issue arose in the 1870s, however, as several Southern state legislatures attempted to abolish lotteries authorized by their Reconstruction-era predecessors. (The years immediately following the Civil War witnessed a brief resurgence of state-authorized lotteries, as cash-strapped Southern legislatures turned to lottery grants as a means of generating revenue.[42]) As public opposition to lotteries solidified, it was perhaps only inevitable that some state tribunal would depart from existing precedent and, in 1873, the Reconstruction-era Supreme Court of Mississippi—a court composed entirely of Republican appointees—became the first tribunal to break with the dominant understanding of the Contract Clause.

The lottery in question was operated by the Mississippi Agricultural, Educational, and Manufacturing Aid Society, which had been granted a twenty-five year charter by the Mississippi legislature in 1867. The charter provided that the Society, in exchange for the right to raise money by lottery, would pay the state an initial incorporation fee, plus annual payments of $1,000 and a percentage of ticket revenue. A mere two years after the Society's incorporation, however, the state adopted a new constitution that explicitly prohibited both lottery drawings and the sale of lottery tickets. The legislature subsequently enforced this constitutional prohibition with a criminal statute. No doubt believing that its activities were protected by the Contract Clause, the Society continued to conduct drawings, and in 1872 one of its agents was arrested on charges of selling lottery tickets.

In the resulting case of *Moore v. The State,* Judges Ephraim Peyton and H.F. Simrall flatly denied that a lottery grantee could claim protection under the federal Contract Clause.[43] Peyton, remarkably, began his opinion by asserting that "after an exhaustive search into the authorities upon this subject," he had been unable to find a single case "where a charter granted to deal in lotteries for a series of years has been . . . protected under the Federal constitution from the future legislation of the state."[44] Lacking, or so he said, the guidance of precedent, Peyton simply asserted that that the Contract Clause of the federal

Constitution did not apply to legislative grants that were later discovered to endanger public morality—a claim he bolstered with an analogy:

> Suppose the legislature of 1867 . . . had granted to said corporation, for a bonus of $5,000, the privilege of keeping a common gaming-house . . . for the period of twenty-five years; can it, with any shadow of reason, be contended that the bonus can give to such pernicious privilege the sanctity of a contract which would be shielded by the constitution of the United States against any subsequent legislation in the state? And yet there is very little difference in their demoralizing tendencies. The privilege to do wrong cannot . . . be thus purchased and fastened, like the shirt of Nessus, upon the community, without any power of getting rid of it for a quarter of a century. Such a doctrine would deprive the state of the power to right herself by repealing any reckless legislation whose certain tendency is to corrupt the fountain of public morals.[45]

In likening the Aid Society lottery to a state-licensed gambling den, Peyton was making the perfectly valid point that a Contract Clause which granted ironclad protection to corporate charters would deprive the state's citizens of the ability to undo the misguided or corrupt actions of their representatives. (Counsel for the state had made the same point in oral arguments, only substituting the more colorful idea of a state-licensed "school for prostitution" for that of a state-licensed gambling den.) This was, of course, the same dilemma that had confronted the Marshall Court in *Fletcher v. Peck*. But where Marshall had unflinchingly subordinated considerations of public morality to settled property rights, Peyton, after a perfunctory citation of the *Dartmouth College Case*, did precisely the opposite.[46] (Tellingly, the more relevant *Fletcher* precedent is nowhere to be found in the Mississippi Court's opinion.) Judge Simrall, in a separate concurring opinion, likewise ignored the relevant precedents, opting instead to highlight the practical consequences of a rigid interpretation of the Contract Clause:

> It is . . . essential to the safety of the public that the law-making department should have full authority to regulate and abate all evil practices and vices that are hurtful to society. If the legislature may grant a lottery franchise for one generation, it may do so for two or more, or for an indefinite term of years. If it should turn out, in after experience, that its effects in the community were to encourage idleness and recklessness, to beget the disposition to live by the chances of gaming rather than the pursuits of industry to encourage, in the young and inexperienced, vicious instead of virtuous

habits, it would be a matter of regret to all who cherished the public good that there was no remedy for the improvident and inconsiderate act of the legislature that authorized it.[47]

The Mississippi Court thus articulated, for the first time, the doctrine that the state's police power with respect to lottery gambling was "inalienable," and thus not subordinate to the contractual rights of lottery grantees or operators.[48] Although neither Peyton nor Simrall cited the prohibition cases of the late 1850s in support of this doctrine, the logical structure of their opinions closely tracked the pro-Maine Law rulings discussed above. Citing a host of common law nuisances—including gambling dens, fire hazards, and stagnant bodies of water—the Mississippi justices concluded that rights of property and contract were never truly "absolute," since all individual rights were subordinate to the police power of the state.[49] Moreover, because the ultimate purpose of the social compact was to "protect the virtue and morals of the whole community," it followed that the state's power of morals police was inherently dynamic. Property rights "granted for a use harmless and innocent at the time" could be revoked if "experience shall show that the use is prejudicial to the public." In such a case, "private right must yield to the public good."[50] Thus, although the terms of the Society's lottery grant were unambiguous, and although the grantees had clearly paid a significant sum for their lottery privileges, the Mississippi Court denied that the grant amounted to a binding contract within the meaning of the Contract Clause. In matters of "vital importance to the welfare of the state," the Court declared, no legislature possessed the power to bind its successors.[51]

Perhaps conscious of the fact that existing case law offered little support for the idea of an inalienable police power, the Court bolstered its holding with reference to a series of antebellum Contract Clause cases in which courts had refused to recognize implied exemptions in corporate charters.[52] One of these was the Taney Court's famous *Charles River Bridge* ruling, which had held that a legislature's decision to charter the construction of a bridge over the Charles River did not violate the contractual rights of a company that had previously received a charter to construct a bridge over the same river.[53] Another was *Thorpe v. Rutland and Burlington Railroad*, in which Isaac Redfield and the Vermont Supreme Court had upheld a law requiring a railroad to construct cattle guards, notwithstanding the fact that the company's corporate charter contained no mention of this duty.[54] That the Mississippi Court would cite these landmarks of antebellum Contract Clause jurisprudence was perhaps inevitable; both cases had indeed subordinated the private rights of corporate charter holders to the police powers of the state. Yet, upon close inspection, the Mississippi Court's decision to rest its ruling on *Charles River* and *Thorpe* only highlighted the radical nature of its doctrinal departure. For while these decisions had merely rebuffed attempts to read *implied* exemptions into corporate charters, the Mississippi Court was endorsing the destruction of corporate rights in a case where the terms of the charter were unambiguous. Thus, in contrast to *Charles River* and *Thorpe*, the *Moore* decision flatly rejected a key tenet of the traditional order: the notion that legislatures, like individual citizens, were bound by the terms of their own agreements.

Conclusion

State judicial attitudes towards liquor and lottery reform underwent a decisive shift in the period between the mid-1850s and the mid-1870s. In the case of liquor, this shift is likely attributable to the collapse of the Jacksonian party system and the resulting increase in the political clout of the temperance movement. Links to political pressure are less clear in the case of the Mississippi Supreme Court's groundbreaking ruling that lottery grants were not entitled to constitutional protection under the Contract Clause. And yet the Mississippi Court's anomalous decision can be seen as further evidence that mid-nineteenth-century judges were well aware of the emerging tension between post-Revival mores, on the one hand, and entrenched constitutional commitments, on the other. Even as most state courts continued to affirm that the constitutionally protected status of lottery grants was "so long and so well established that it hardly needs the citation of authorities," pressure was clearly building for a reconsideration of the Marshall Court's unyielding interpretation of the Contract Clause.[55]

For the time being—that is, in the 1870s—the doctrinal shifts described in this chapter likely appeared to hold little significance for the larger course of constitutional development. There is little evidence that state-level jurists aimed at anything more than the accommodation of a pair of broadly popular reforms; and indeed, they almost certainly had no intention of weakening due process or Contract Clause protections as applied to other, more reputable forms of property. As we shall see in chapter 4, however, these seemingly narrow doctrinal exceptions were not easily confined to the subjects of liquor and lottery regulation. In fact, upon finding their cause blocked at the state level, liquor retailers and lottery operators simply turned to the federal judiciary. As a result, the late-nineteenth-century Supreme Court was forced to grapple with the question that its counterparts at the state level had for the most part avoided: if evolving mores could justify an abandonment of entrenched constitutional commitments in the case of liquor and lotteries, why not in the case of other newly discovered social ills? And if the police power was inherently dynamic—as the liquor and lottery cases seemed to suggest—what was to become of the fixed and unchanging jurisdictional boundaries that were the hallmark of the American constitutional order?

The Triumph of Evangelical Public Morality in the Supreme Court

> We should hesitate long before adjudging that an evil of such appalling character, carried on through interstate commerce, cannot be met and crushed by the only power competent to that end.
>
> —Justice John Marshall Harlan, *Champion v. Ames* (1903)

The Civil War and Reconstruction years were trying times for evangelical reformers, notwithstanding their constitutional victories in the state courts. By the late 1860s, most of the twelve Maine Law states had abandoned the experiment with statewide prohibition and returned to some form of local option. What was worse, the lottery industry, which had been all but extinct in 1861, returned from the grave, as several cash-strapped state legislatures authorized new lottery grants for the first time in a generation. But the moral declension of the war years did not, in the end, reflect a fundamental shift in social mores. Indeed, the emergence in the 1880s of a new generation of religiously affiliated reform organizations ensured that liquor and lottery regulation would remain at the center of national political discourse through the early twentieth century.

At the vanguard of the postwar reform movement was the Women's Christian Temperance Union (WCTU), led by the indefatigable Frances Willard. At its height in the 1890s, the WCTU boasted a quarter of a million members and a formidable legislative department that successfully lobbied for the enactment of state and federal laws targeting liquor, gambling, sexual immorality, and other vices.[1] (Perhaps even more formidable was the WCTU's Department of Scientific Instruction, which oversaw temperance instruction in the nation's public schools—instruction that was by 1901 mandatory in all forty-eight states and in federal territories.[2]) Also during this period, the Prohibition Party, the first political party dedicated to the eradication of the liquor traffic, developed into a national force that garnered as many as 300,000 votes in presidential elections—more than enough to command the attention of the major parties in an era of closely contested races.[3] Finally, the Anti-Saloon League (ASL), although not founded until 1893, quickly developed a national lobbying apparatus that was unrivaled in its era. Fueled by the financial backing of thousands of local evangelical congregations, the group successfully tightened liquor restrictions at the state level before turning its attention to the enactment of a national prohibition amendment.[4] The ASL, which almost single-handedly spearheaded the adoption of the Eighteenth Amendment, was so skilled at the art of legislative arm-twisting, in fact, that an early political scientist coined the term "pressure politics" to describe the group's tactics.[5]

The organizational successes of the 1880s and 1890s led many evangelicals to conclude that the nation was on the brink of a major political realignment. Just as slavery had destroyed the Jacksonian party system, the argument went, the liquor question would soon dissolve Gilded Age party loyalties, thus paving the way for evangelicals to unite under the banner of a new national party.[6] But if the reformers ultimately failed to supplant the existing party system, they nonetheless succeeded in building considerable bipartisan and cross-sectional support for innovative forms of morals regulation. At the state level, prohibition supporters began a successful—if grindingly slow—push for the adoption of constitutional prohibition amendments. (Having watched as the gains of the 1850s were erased during the war years, movement leaders resolved to henceforth embed their principles in the fundamental law of the states, where they would be more difficult to overturn.) And at the national level, reformers lobbied for federal laws to stem the flow of immoral goods in interstate commerce and through the mails. Although some of these reforms were initially opposed by Southern Democrats, moral reform ultimately proved as popular in the South as elsewhere.[7] As a result, much of the evangelical legislative agenda sailed through Congress with little or no opposition—a remarkable fact, given that these measures extended the reach of congressional power into areas that had long been regarded as the exclusive province of the states.

As legal challenges to innovative morals laws filtered through the judicial system, judges were once again caught between contemporary mores and Founding-era constitutional principles. Indeed, the reemergence of evangelical reform confronted the justices of the Supreme Court with much the same dilemma that had earlier confounded their state-level colleagues. That is to say, they recognized that the constitutional order rested on a series of static and allegedly natural categorical distinctions; any suggestion that the meanings of concepts such as "police" and "commerce" were not, in fact, fixed and unchanging would likely reverberate through the entire system, encouraging demands for the judicial accommodation of other types of "social" legislation, from railroad rate regulations to restrictions on child labor. And yet, like their counterparts at the state level, the justices ultimately acquiesced in efforts to eradicate the great national sins of liquor and lottery gambling. As we shall see, the Court attempted—to a much greater extent than had the state judiciaries—to minimize the doctrinal impact of liquor and lottery reform. But in the end all efforts to cabin the newly expanded police powers of the state and federal governments met with failure. Precisely as many antebellum jurists had predicted, the admission that the constitutional principles of the framers could, in at least some cases, be modified to accommodate the mores of later generations did considerable damage to the traditional order's legitimacy. For if social change was sufficient to justify the abandonment of entrenched constitutional commitments in one case, why not in all?

Few scholars, it should be noted, have perceived any larger significance in the postwar Supreme Court's liquor and lottery rulings. In fact, conventional wisdom holds that these decisions had little impact beyond their immediate doctrinal contexts, since nineteenth-century legal thought was both highly compartmentalized and permeated by Victorian moral sensibilities. On this view, the vast majority of judges—and Americans, for that matter—were simply blind to the irony of a constitutional jurisprudence that rigidly enforced property protections and federalism constraints in the industrial realm while affording legislators near-total control over personal morality.[8] But when one traces the path of doctrinal evolution within the three "sites" of constitutional development sketched in chapter 1, it is apparent that the conventional wisdom on this point is mistaken. In fact, we shall see that at each of the three points where post-Revival mores intersected with traditional constitutional ideals—in the jurisprudence of the Contract Clause, due process, and the Commerce Clause—the Court's accommodation of moral reform gave rise to embarrassing doctrinal tensions that were widely noticed by contemporary observers. Far from being blind to the broader implications of the Court's deferential morals rulings, commentators immediately recognized that the justices had paved the way for a potentially open-ended expansion of state and federal regulatory authority. And although the Court responded to such

criticism by reasserting the importance of traditional constitutional constraints in the economic sphere, its doctrinal maneuvering merely highlighted
the tension between two seemingly incompatible lines of precedent—one insisting on rigid fidelity to the principles of the framers, the other acknowledging that regulatory authority might be expanded indefinitely when necessary
to address pressing social ills.

Site One: Lottery Reform and the Contract Clause

As late as the mid-1870s, it remained a bedrock principle of American constitutional law that agreements between legislatures and private entities
were contracts within the meaning of the Contract Clause. To be sure, state
legislatures invented creative ways of limiting the impact of the *Dartmouth
College* doctrine; but in cases where the terms of a grant or charter were
explicit, rights that had vested under such contracts remained more or less
inviolable.[9] Thus, Justice Noah Swayne used his majority opinion in the 1877
case of *Farrington v. Tennessee* to reaffirm the familiar antebellum belief that
permitting even a single exception to the general principle of the inviolability of contracts would undermine the stability of the constitutional edifice.
The key passage of Swayne's opinion, which invoked the Contract Clause to
block a state's attempt to alter the rate of taxation specified in a corporate
charter, closely tracked the logic of the Marshall Court's landmark Contract
Clause decisions:

> A compact lies at the foundation of all national life. Contracts mark the
> progress of communities in civilization and prosperity. They guard as far
> as is possible against the fluctuations of human affairs. They seek to give
> stability to the present and certainty to the future. . . . They are the springs
> of business, trade, and commerce. Without them, society could not go on.
> Spotless faith in their fulfillment honors alike communities and individu-
> als. Where this is wanting in the body politic, the process of descent has
> begun and a lower plane will be speedily reached. . . . The Constitution
> of the United States wisely protects this interest, public and private, from
> invasion by state laws. . . . This limitation no member of the Union can
> overpass. It is one of the most important functions of this tribunal to apply
> and enforce it upon all proper occasions.[10]

In the very year that the *Farrington* decision was handed down, however,
the Court began to waver. In fact, one can trace the beginning of the Contract

Clause's decline to a trio of cases argued in the late 1870s—two involving lotteries and one involving liquor—in which certain justices began to flirt with the idea that the police power, unlike the taxing power, should be deemed "inalienable." The first decision in which this idea is clearly expressed is *Boyd v. Alabama,* an 1877 case involving the state of Alabama's effort to repeal a lottery grant it had issued in 1868.[11] In *Boyd,* Justice Field upheld the state's recently enacted anti-lottery law, but only on the grounds that the 1868 lottery grant had been in violation of the state constitution. There had never been a valid contract, in other words, and the lottery operator therefore lacked standing to bring suit under the Contract Clause. Field might well have ended his opinion at this point. Instead, he concluded the opinion with a bit of dictum declaring that the Court was "not prepared to admit that it is competent for one legislature, by any contract with an individual, to restrain the power of a subsequent legislature to legislate for the public welfare, and to that end to suppress any and all practices tending to corrupt the public morals."[12] The following year, in *Beer Company v. Massachusetts,* the Court heard a similar Contract Clause challenge to a Massachusetts liquor prohibition law.[13] Here, Justice Bradley denied that the state's prohibition statute had violated the vested rights of a brewery incorporated prior to the enactment of the statute. The holding was not based explicitly on the idea of an inalienable police power, however, but on the narrower point that the company's charter had contained a clause reserving the legislature's right of repeal. Still, like Field, Justice Bradley gratuitously attached dictum to his opinion stating that a "legislature cannot, by any contract, divest itself of the power to provide" for "the preservation of good order and the public morals."[14]

Finally, in early 1880, the Court handed down a decision that employed the inalienable police power doctrine as the sole justification for rejecting a Contract Clause challenge. In *Stone v. Mississippi,* a case involving the same lottery grant at issue in *Moore v. The State,* the justices confronted the question of whether a state could constitutionally criminalize lotteries shortly after granting a corporation the right to conduct drawings for a twenty-five year period. Writing for the Court, Chief Justice Morrison Waite—whose father had endorsed the Maine Law's constitutionality in the case of *Brennan's Liquors*—found that what appeared to be a blatant interference with the contractual rights of the grantee was in fact only a routine exercise of the state's inalienable power to regulate public morality. Although the language of the lottery grant was unambiguous, Waite nonetheless declared that all governments possessed the inherent right to suppress immoral activities "at their discretion"—and that lotteries were "demoralizing in their effects" was a question that did not "admit of doubt."[15] Essentially reversing the logic of earlier state-level decisions involving lottery grants and the Contract Clause, Waite laid down as a principle of constitutional law the assertion that no state "can bargain away the public health or the public morals."[16]

The *Stone* decision thus carved a glaring "police power" exception from the first pillar of the traditional order, the Contract Clause. As we shall see, the Court soon wandered into a doctrinal morass as it attempted to confine the sweeping implications of its *Stone* ruling. But before we examine the Court's efforts in this regard, it is worth asking: why did the Court, in the late 1870s, suddenly endorse the inalienable police power doctrine that so many previous courts had rejected, a doctrine that many antebellum jurists had viewed as a dire threat to constitutional government? To the extent that scholars have examined this question, their answers have focused almost exclusively on the evolution of judicial ideology in the period following the Civil War. It is well known, for example, that Stephen Field, Thomas Cooley, and other major jurists of the postwar period shared a Jacksonian distaste for monopolies and were for this reason eager to scale back the "special" corporate privileges that had long been protected under *Dartmouth College*.[17] A second, closely related ideological explanation focuses on the adoption of the Fourteenth Amendment and the rise of economic due process. Here, the argument is that jurists in the mold of Field and Cooley viewed due process as a better vehicle than the Contract Clause for protecting economic rights. Where the Contract Clause was primarily useful in protecting the vested rights of specially chartered corporations, due process was a more flexible instrument that could be used to protect individuals from almost any type of regulation that appeared to interfere with fundamental rights, including the right to enter into contracts or engage in a particular trade.[18] But if accounts centered on ideological change are useful in understanding the gradual weakening of the Contract Clause over time, they are less helpful in explaining the doctrinal incoherence that followed in the wake of the *Stone* ruling. The fact that the Court continued to vigorously protect corporate charter exemptions in many cases—including cases involving public utility monopolies—while abandoning them in others suggests that something more than an ideological aversion to monopolies was at work in these decisions.

The Interstate Lottery Traffic and the
Invention of the Inalienable Police Power

When we situate the Court's late 1870s Contract Clause rulings in a broader historical context, it appears far more likely that the Court's adoption of the inalienable police power doctrine was a response to a concrete policy problem: namely, the rise of large lottery corporations that earned their profits through illegal out-of-state sales. By the mid-1870s, the Louisiana Lottery Company, in particular, had established itself as a national symbol of vice and corruption. Granted a twenty-five-year charter in 1869, the company quickly capitalized on the pent-up demand for lottery tickets in states where lotteries were prohibited by law, earning as much as $30 million per year from illegal out-of-state sales.[19] (By 1879, the company was billing itself as the "Last Legal Lottery in America.") Not surprisingly, lawmakers in states where lotteries were prohibited were outraged at the company's interstate activity, and in 1872 Congress enacted postal regulations designed to prevent the company from distributing its wares through the mail. Postal regulations had little effect on the Lottery's business, however, as Lottery officials simply shifted to distributing materials through front companies and traveling agents.[20] A particularly notorious incident occurred in 1879 when Anthony Comstock, newly appointed special agent for the Post Office, staged a series of high profile raids in which dozens of Louisiana Lottery agents were arrested for illegally selling tickets in New York City. Comstock's investigation of company records revealed that the New York City agents were taking in as much as $175,000 a month from a city specially selected for its "rich, liberal, and changing population."[21] Later that year, and perhaps in response to Comstock's findings, Congress ordered its own investigation into the interstate lottery business.[22]

But for all the public outrage at the Louisiana Lottery's brazen defiance of state laws in New York and elsewhere, the fact remained that, under existing constitutional doctrine, only the state of Louisiana could put the company out of business. So long as the company held a valid charter from the Louisiana legislature, other states or federal postal inspectors could arrest the company's traveling agents, but they could not reach the company itself. The nation therefore watched with great interest in 1879 when a reform-minded Louisiana legislature voted to revoke the Lottery's charter.[23] The repeal vote was particularly noteworthy because the nation's only other authorized lottery had been brought to a close the previous year in Kentucky.[24] With the abolition of the Louisiana Lottery, it appeared that the longstanding evangelical dream of a lottery-free America had at last been realized.

And yet the victory was short-lived. Company officials immediately challenged Louisiana's lottery ban in federal court, where Judge Edward Coke Billings granted their request for injunctive relief. Billings, not surprisingly, was widely denounced as a shill for the lottery interests.[25] But his opinion was entirely consistent with existing precedent. Drawing on the settled conviction that rights vested under lottery grants were entitled to constitutional protection—and sounding much like Justice Swayne in the Supreme Court's recent *Farrington* decision—Billings flatly rejected Louisiana's contention that a state could not alienate its police power:

> Where rights have become vested, I know of no distinction which would allow states to recede from contracts, or avoid contracts which they have made, more than can individuals. States at all times can and should make advances to higher and still higher ground, with the view of protecting public and private morals. But they owe a duty, not only founded in natural justice but happily enforced by the supreme power of the Constitution of the United States, in all their advances to recognize and protect rights which have become vested and obligations to which they have lent their own sanction.[26]

Given the timing of events, there can be no doubt that the widely covered Louisiana repeal drama weighed heavily on the minds of the Supreme Court justices in October 1879, when they heard oral arguments in *Stone*. Indeed, far from an abstract doctrinal exercise, the practical stakes of the *Stone* litigation could not have been clearer. To overturn the Mississippi legislature's revocation of a lottery grant on Contract Clause grounds would mean that Judge Billings's ruling on the Louisiana Lottery would remain good law. As a result, the most notoriously corrupt corporation in America—a corporation which peddled a product that the vast majority of Americans deemed immoral and which earned the bulk of its revenue from illegal out-of-state sales—would enjoy perfect immunity from state regulation for another fifteen years. That the Court was aware of this possibility is clear from Waite's opinion. Noting that there was "now scarcely a state in the Union where lotteries are tolerated," the Chief Justice reasoned that the "will of the people" concerning the lottery business had been "authoritatively expressed."[27] In addition, Waite made special note of Congress's efforts to combat the interstate traffic in lottery tickets, indicating the Court's awareness that the existence of even a single state-authorized lottery could undermine morals enforcement in the rest of the nation.[28] Finally, Waite described lotteries as an inherently corrupt and "demoralizing" industry that tended to "disturb the checks and balances of a well-ordered community"—a likely reference to the Louisiana Lottery's penchant for bribing state and federal officials.[29] Given that state and federal lawmakers were now unified in their opposition to the lottery industry, Waite seemed to be saying, the only thing standing between the American people and the eradication of a great national vice was the traditional reading of the Contract Clause. At this point, the Court faced a decision: it could either remain faithful to existing precedent or embrace the novel idea that the police power was an "inalienable" power that trumped even the most explicit provisions of corporate charters. The most likely explanation for why the Court chose the latter course is that the alternative, allowing the Louisiana Lottery to remain in the national spotlight for another fifteen years while sheltered from regulation by the federal judiciary, was simply too horrible to contemplate.

From the perspective of constitutional development, however, the larger significance of *Stone* lies in the fact that the decision introduced a doctrinal exception to a foundational constitutional norm—the inviolability of contracts—that could not be cabined without undermining the legitimacy of the norm itself. Put simply, an exception holding that the police power trumped the rights of individuals who had entered into agreements with the state was more than broad enough to eviscerate the central holding of *Dartmouth College*. And yet, because the Court had no intention of erasing the Contract Clause from the Constitution, it was almost immediately forced into the uncomfortable position of explaining why some rights conferred in corporate charters should remain inviolable while others—such as the right to conduct a lottery—were now subject to revocation at the pleasure of the state.

The Inalienable Police Power and the Erosion of the Contract Clause

Although a full review of the Waite and Fuller Courts' Contract Clause jurisprudence is beyond the scope of this chapter, we can gain a sense of how *Stone* worked to undermine the traditional constitutional order by briefly examining three illustrative sets of decisions. Consider, first, the Court's post-*Stone* rulings in cases involving efforts to repeal or modify the tax provisions of

corporate charters. (Such cases arose frequently in the 1880s and 1890s, as
state legislatures and municipalities attempted to undo the tax breaks that
their predecessors, in an effort to stimulate economic growth and infrastructure development, had granted to various corporations.[30]) Based on the underlying logic of *Stone*, one would expect the Court to extend the inalienable
power doctrine to include the taxing power as well as the police power—
thus permitting state lawmakers to renege on tax breaks promised by their
predecessors. After all, the power to tax, like the police power, was widely
considered to be an inherent attribute of sovereignty: all governments were
assumed to possess this power, since without the ability to raise revenue it
would be impossible to provide for the basic needs of society.[31] Moreover,
these inherent powers were clearly interrelated, in the sense that a state which
had alienated its powers of revenue generation would clearly lack the ability to
enforce police regulations. Yet, perhaps because the justices sensed the need
to preserve the *Dartmouth College* doctrine against further erosion, the Court
never budged on the question of the alienability of the taxing power. Indeed,
in the 1880s alone it handed down eight decisions rebuffing attempts by states
or municipalities to interfere with the tax provisions of corporate charters.[32]
Although no doubt intended to preserve the vital core of the Contract Clause,
the Court's refusal to modify its stance on the taxing power had the paradoxical effect of further eroding the legitimacy of this pillar of the traditional
order. As a writer in the *American Law Register* complained in 1887, it seemed
a curious doctrine to "say that the state cannot part with its inherent police
power, yet it may tie up its revenues—part with them, barter them away for
a consideration which brings no money, so that it will have no money with
which to enforce what would be under such circumstances a *barren* police
power."[33] The early political scientist John Burgess echoed the point four years
later in his treatise on constitutional law: "I must say that I do not comprehend the reasoning which, upon general principles, concedes the power to a
commonwealth to create a right to an exemption from one of its governmental
powers and not from another; nor is any there any such distinction between
the powers in question as to justify such discrimination."[34]

  A second problem that surfaced in the immediate aftermath of *Stone* was
that even if one limited the inalienable power doctrine to the police power,
there was no way of determining with logical precision how far this exception ought to extend. After all, virtually any legislative act that modified the
terms of a corporate charter could be justified on the grounds of protecting the

public health, safety, or morals. Certainly, there were some cases in which the inalienable police power doctrine suggested a clear result, as when the Court invoked the doctrine in *Butchers' Union Slaughterhouse Co. v. Crescent City Co.* (1884) to reject a Contract Clause challenge to a law abolishing a state-sponsored slaughterhouse monopoly.[35] (Slaughterhouses, the Court reasoned, represented a clear threat to public health, and for this reason no lawmaking body could alienate its power to regulate the industry.) The very next year, however, the Court endorsed a largely identical challenge to a law revoking the monopoly privileges of a pair of public utility providers. Perhaps sensing the need to construct another firewall to contain the effects of *Stone,* Justice Harlan held in *New Orleans Gas Co. v. Louisiana Gas Co.* and *New Orleans Water Works Co. v. Rivers* that a pair of charters granting the exclusive right to provide gas and water to the city of New Orleans were not covered under the inalienable police power doctrine.[36] Rejecting the state's argument that the provision of gas and water was no less threatening to the public welfare than slaughterhouses or lotteries, Harlan advanced the dubious proposition that the private rights destroyed in *Stone* and *Butchers' Union,* unlike the rights at stake in the public utility cases, had belonged to industries that "in whatever manner conducted, were detrimental to the public health or the public morals." In the case of inherently dangerous industries, Harlan reasoned, the Contract Clause did not prevent "the withdrawal of [rights granted in charters], or the granting of [such rights] to others." The provision of gas and water, in contrast, "far from affecting the public injuriously, [had] become one of the most important agencies of civilization, for the promotion of the public convenience and the public safety." Harlan thus found that a charter granting exclusive privileges in the provision of gas and water was "none the less a contract because the . . . distribution" of these substances "when not subjected to proper supervision, may possibly work injury to the public."[37] In addition, Harlan flatly rejected the state's argument that the introduction of competition in the provision of public utilities constituted a valid exercise of the police power, in the sense that monopolies were inherently threatening to the public welfare. The question of the propriety of monopoly grants, Harlan concluded, was unrelated "to the preservation of the public health, or the promotion of the public safety," and was therefore outside the scope of the inalienable police power doctrine.[38]

The Court's rulings in *New Orleans Gas* and *New Orleans Water Works* thus established yet another seemingly arbitrary limitation on the doctrine announced in *Stone:* public utilities were "franchise[s] belonging to the government . . . to be granted . . . on what terms it pleases."[39] The protection afforded corporate rights under the Contract Clause now appeared to depend on the Court's subjective judgment about the inherent danger or utility of particular industries, as well as the motives underlying particular attempts to modify corporate charter provisions. Even more troubling, however, was the fact that the Court failed to strictly observe its own doctrinal firewalls. Having declared in *New Orleans Gas* and *New Orleans Water Works* that efforts to curb monopolies did not constitute "police" measures within the meaning of the police power exception, the Court seemingly reversed course in *Pearsall v. Great Northern Railway Co.*, a case involving a railroad whose charter granted it the right to consolidate with any parallel road.[40] When the state of Minnesota, citing the dangers of corporate consolidation, attempted to modify this provision, the company objected on the grounds that the right was explicitly granted in its charter and therefore protected under the Contract Clause. Writing for the Court, and over the dissent of Field and Brewer, Justice Brown refused to protect the railroad's right to consolidate. Noting "the popular prejudice against monopolies" which had recently "found expression in innumerable acts of legislation," Brown deemed it "competent for the legislature, out of due regard for the public welfare, to declare that [a corporate charter] should not be used for the purpose of stifling competition and building up monopolies."[41] *Pearsall* demonstrated the inherently problematic nature of the Court's efforts to cabin the police power exception. For as contemporary commentators immediately recognized, there existed no objective standard for determining what types of charter modifications belonged within the scope of the exception. Writing in the *American Law Review*, Alfred Russell noted in the year of the *Pearsall* decision that it was "quite apparent . . . that the court will always nominally adhere to the doctrine of the [*Dartmouth College*] case, and yet that they will not apply it to cases . . . where the result would be unreasonable from the point of view of the general public."[42]

Finally, it is important to note that the implications of the inalienable police power doctrine were not easily confined to corporate charters. Now that the Court had decided that the police power could, in at least some instances, trump rights guaranteed in public contracts, there was no logical reason why the same power should not trump rights guaranteed in *private* contracts. The underlying rationale for the *Stone* decision, after all, was that the state had a permanent and affirmative *duty* to protect the wellbeing of the public. And if the prior agreements of public officials could not relieve the state of this duty, then how could the prior agreements of mere private citizens do so?

The Court was ultimately forced to confront this question in the 1905 case of *Manigault v. Springs*.[43] The case involved a private contract in which neighboring landowners had agreed to leave a navigable creek unobstructed. Shortly after the contract was formalized, the state of South Carolina enacted legislation authorizing one of the parties to construct a dam on the creek, ostensibly for the purpose of promoting public health. Not surprisingly, the other party objected that the state's action had interfered with private contractual obligations, thereby violating the Contract Clause. Writing for a unanimous Court, however, Justice Henry Billings Brown held that, in light of the Court's recent decisions, there could be no logical basis for permitting private contractual obligations to trump the state's police powers. Significantly, Brown cited the "familiar" example of prohibitory liquor and lottery laws to demonstrate that the states' authority to abolish contractual rights in the name of the police power was no longer open to question:

> It is the settled law of this Court that the interdiction of statutes impairing the obligation of contracts does not prevent the state from exercising such powers as are vested in it for the promotion of the common weal, or are necessary for the general good of the public, though contracts previously entered into between individuals may thereby be affected. . . . Familiar instances of this are where parties enter into contracts, perfectly lawful at the time, *to sell liquor, operate a brewery or distillery, or carry on a lottery,* all of which are subject to impairment by a change of policy on the part of the state prohibiting the establishment or continuance of such traffic—in other words, that parties, by entering into contracts, may not estop the legislature from enacting laws intended for the public good.[44]

With this admission, the Court all but demolished the distinction between public and private contracts, one of the last remaining doctrinal firewalls that might theoretically have contained the spread of the *Stone* doctrine and preserved some sphere of contractual rights against regulatory invasion. For while the Marshall Court's finding that corporate charters constituted contracts within the meaning of the Contract Clause had always been a source of controversy in American constitutional thought, the traditional fallback position for those who desired a weaker Contract Clause was to argue that the clause's guarantees ought to apply only to legislative acts that interfered with private contracts (with the paradigmatic case being debtor relief laws).[45] *Manigault* foreclosed this possibility by making clear that rights arising from public and private contracts rested on the same increasingly insecure footing.

We will have occasion to examine the final stages of the Contract Clause's demise in the next chapter. For now, the important point to note is that, although the Contract Clause clung to life until the 1930s, the Court's adoption of the inalienable police power doctrine in *Stone* began a process of decay that was already far advanced by the turn of the century.[46] Indeed, what remained of the clause at this point can perhaps best be described as a series of logically unrelated firewalls. Charter provisions involving taxation remained secure, as did those guaranteeing the monopoly privileges of public utilities. But there was no logical reason why these particular doctrinal firewalls, any more than the distinction between public and private contracts, should be permitted to resist the ineluctable advance of the police power. As more than one antebellum jurist had predicted, the Court's decision in *Stone* to sacrifice principle to expediency had opened the door to a never-ending procession of exceptions to the traditional ideal of the sanctity of contracts. If the Court was willing to set aside a clear contractual obligation to accommodate shifting mores in the case of lotteries, it was unclear how it could logically refuse to do the same in any case where the wellbeing of the community appeared to demand the destruction of private rights.[47]

Site Two: Liquor Prohibition and Economic Due Process

At the federal level, the debate over the constitutionality of liquor prohibition began in earnest following the adoption of the Fourteenth Amendment in 1868. The centerpiece of the Reconstruction amendments, the Fourteenth prohibited states from infringing the "privileges and immunities" of American citizens; from depriving "any person of life, liberty, or property, without due process of law"; or from denying to any person "the equal protection of the laws." For present purposes, the Amendment's most important practical effect was to call into question the constitutionality of a host of state-level police regulations that arguably interfered with vested property rights or other economic liberties. For, while most postwar jurists agreed that the Amendment was intended to provide *some* protection to property and economic rights, there was no immediate consensus on precisely which rights were protected or how these rights could be reconciled with the states' traditionally broad police powers. Moreover, in an age of rapid industrialization, the task of defining the precise scope of the Amendment's guarantees was complicated by the emergence of new and innovative forms of industrial regulation, from wage and hours laws, to railroad rate regulations, to antitrust measures.[48] The challenge confronting the postwar Court, then, was to somehow mark the boundary between public power and private right; that is, to provide a jurisprudential framework capable of distinguishing a valid exercise of the police power from an unconstitutional deprivation of liberty or property.

To date, scholars have generally described liquor prohibition as among the least controversial forms of regulation to reach the Court in the wake of the Fourteenth Amendment's adoption. According to one school of thought, prohibition was an easy case for the simple reason that the states had always enjoyed the power to abate unlicensed taverns as public nuisances. The deep historical roots of liquor regulation, in other words, provided judges with a convenient way of distinguishing prohibition from more innovative forms of "social" legislation—such as rate regulations and labor measures—that were simultaneously being challenged on due process grounds.[49] Alternatively, other scholars have argued that post-Civil War jurists looked favorably on prohibition measures because such laws could not reasonably be described as discriminatory. Most postwar decisions that invalidated legislation on economic due process grounds, on this view, stemmed from the judiciary's aversion to "class legislation," or laws that arbitrarily bestowed special benefits (or imposed special burdens) on particular groups or social classes.[50] Prohibition laws were not open to charges of arbitrariness, the argument goes, because all citizens were equally barred from engaging in the buying, selling, or manufacturing of liquor.[51]

As we shall see, the reigning conventional wisdom vastly underestimates the degree of controversy and contingency that surrounded liquor litigation in the two decades preceding the Court's definitive ruling in *Mugler v. Kansas* (1887). In reality, it was far from clear to postwar jurists how prohibition, which entailed the uncompensated destruction of millions of dollars' worth of private property, could be reconciled with any meaningful conception of economic liberty. Many jurists clearly believed that a police power broad enough to permit the uncompensated destruction of a traditionally valid commodity like liquor ought logically to encompass the regulation of employment conditions, railroad rates, or virtually any other form of economic activity. Thus, if the judiciary intended to use the Fourteenth Amendment to rein in state-level industrial regulation, logical consistency seemed to require the establishment of similar limits on the states' liquor prohibition regimes. In *Mugler*, the Court indeed managed to sever the question of prohibition's constitutionality from the broader constitutional questions surrounding industrial regulation, but only at the cost of further destabilizing the traditional order.

The Case of First Impression: Reexamining Bartemeyer v. Iowa

Bartemeyer v. Iowa (1874), the first significant liquor case to reach the Supreme Court following the adoption of the Fourteenth Amendment, provides an excellent illustration of the sense of uncertainty that surrounded liquor litigation in the postwar period.[52] *Bartemeyer* was argued at the same time as—and somewhat overshadowed by—the landmark *Slaughterhouse Cases*, and a few words on *Slaughterhouse* are therefore necessary to place the liquor decision in its proper context. In *Slaughterhouse*, the Court had divided 5–4 on the constitutionality of a Louisiana law that confined the slaughtering and processing of livestock to a single, privately operated facility.[53] All four of the dissenters in *Slaughterhouse* signed onto an opinion by Justice Field which argued that the Fourteenth Amendment should be understood to bar the establishment of state-sanctioned monopolies in the "ordinary trades or callings of life."[54] Writing for the majority, however, Justice Samuel Miller declared that the Amendment had not been intended to confer new substantive economic rights, but merely to provide for federal enforcement of those rights traditionally recognized in state law. The power to regulate slaughterhouses in the interest of public health, according to Miller, had been exercised at the state level since the inception of the Union—it was clearly recognized in the earliest treatises on American law, including Kent's *Commentaries*—and for this reason the right to operate a slaughterhouse could not be regarded as one of the "privileges and immunities" of citizenship.[55] In addition, Miller disputed the dissenters' assertion that the Louisiana law had deprived the state's butchers of the ability to pursue their chosen profession. Although it was true that the statute had restricted a dangerous profession to a single, easily supervised location, the law also declared that anyone who wanted to butcher animals at the facility could do so upon payment of a small fee. Therefore, Miller concluded, the law did "not . . . prevent the butcher from doing his own slaughtering."[56]

But if *Slaughterhouse* was a difficult case, *Bartemeyer* is usually described as presenting few conceptual difficulties. The case involved an Iowa liquor retailer who argued that his state's prohibition law had both deprived him of property without due process and violated the "privileges and immunities" of citizenship.[57] Writing for a unanimous Court, Justice Miller again refused to employ the Fourteenth Amendment to invalidate a state police measure. Bartemeyer's due process claim failed, according to Miller, because the defendant had not established that he had owned any liquor prior the enactment of prohibition.[58] The claim that the right to sell liquor was one of the "privileges and immunities" of citizenship similarly failed, since, as in *Slaughterhouse,* the regulatory power in question long predated the enactment of "the recent amendments"[59] Significantly, Justices Bradley and Field, the most vociferous of the *Slaughterhouse* dissenters, authored separate concurring opinions expressing the view that the Iowa prohibition law was a valid "police" measure and not in conflict with the Fourteenth Amendment.[60]

Given the unanimity of the ruling—and the supportive concurring opinions of Bradley and Field—it is not surprising that *Bartemeyer* is regularly invoked to illustrate the postwar judiciary's solicitude for liquor regulation.[61] A close reading of the three *Bartemeyer* opinions tells a different story, however. Consider, first, Justice Miller's majority opinion. Although it is true that Miller rejected the "privileges and immunities" argument outright, it is important to note that he refused to similarly dismiss Bartemeyer's due process challenge. Indeed, although the point was technically moot, Miller declared that the uncompensated destruction of property rights in liquor raised "very grave" constitutional questions:

> But if it were true and it was fairly presented to us that the defendant was the owner of the glass of intoxicating liquor which he sold . . . at the time that the State of Iowa first imposed an absolute prohibition on the sale of such liquors, then we concede that two very grave questions would arise, namely whether this would be a statute depriving him of his property without due process of law and secondly whether, if it were so, it would be so far a violation of the Fourteenth Amendment in that regard as would call for judicial action by this Court?[62]

Although Miller declined to give a definitive answer on the due process implications of prohibition, the fact that he acknowledged the seriousness of Bartemeyer's constitutional objections is significant. In *Slaughterhouse,* Miller had flatly denied that the state's creation of a virtual monopoly in the slaughterhouse business raised *any* due process issues, declaring that "no construction" of due process he "had ever seen" would deny a state the power to confine dangerous trades to particular locations or licensed practitioners.[63] But in *Bartemeyer,* Miller frankly acknowledged that Iowa's prohibition law might well have deprived liquor retailers of property in violation of the Fourteenth Amendment. The most significant difference between the two cases appears to have been the extent of the alleged interference with established property rights. For where the Louisiana slaughterhouse law had, in Miller's view, merely confined a potentially dangerous trade to a single, easily supervised location, Iowa's prohibition law had gone further, literally abolishing the market in a traditionally lawful commodity, and thereby rendering valueless millions of dollars' worth of private property. The claim that Iowa's retailers had been "deprived" of their property was therefore hardly outlandish.[64]

To be sure, Miller might have dealt with the Iowa prohibition law by drawing on the state-level Maine Law rulings of the late 1850s, many of which had managed to reconcile prohibition with due process or "law of the land" clauses. But these rulings were increasingly problematic in light of recent doctrinal trends. For example, in *Pumpelly v. Green Bay* (1871), the Court had rejected the argument that the "takings" clauses of the state and federal constitutions required compensation to property owners only in cases involving a physical seizure of property. Indeed, Justice Miller's majority opinion in *Pumpelly* had held that any governmental action—in this case the construction of a dam that flooded neighboring property—that destroyed the value or impaired the use of property might constitute a "taking" for public use.[65] As Miller explained, "[i]t would be a very curious and unsatisfactory result, if . . . the government . . . can destroy [property's] value entirely, can inflict irreparable and permanent injury . . . without making any compensation, because, in the narrowest sense . . . it is not *taken* for the public use."[66] That Miller refused to simply reject the defendant's due process claim outright in *Bartemeyer* may well be explained by the fact that he had so recently given a ringing endorsement to the idea that citizens who saw even the *value* of their property destroyed by government action were entitled compensation.[67]

Significantly, Justices Field and Bradley, in their separate concurring opinions, readily confirmed what Miller had only implied: that the only way of reconciling liquor prohibition with the Fourteenth Amendment was to treat prohibition like a "taking" and compensate liquor owners for their losses. Thus, while it is true that Bradley deemed the Iowa law a valid police measure, he nonetheless insisted that even valid police measures required compensation whenever they destroyed "vested rights of property." Private rights could

certainly be abolished when they stood "in the way of the public good," Bradley reasoned, but only by "awarding compensation to the [property] owner."[68]
Field likewise drew a sharp distinction between police *regulations,* which did
not require compensation to property owners, and outright *prohibitions* on
particular forms of property, which did. Although he had "no doubt" of the
states' power "to regulate the sale of intoxicating liquors," this power did not
extend to "the destruction of the right of property in them." "The right of
property in an article," Field concluded, "involves the power to sell and dispose
of such article as well as to use and enjoy it. Any act which declares that the
owner shall neither sell it nor dispose of it, nor use and enjoy it, confiscates it,
depriving him of his property without due process of law. Against such arbitrary legislation by any State the fourteenth amendment affords protection."[69]

A careful reading of the Court's first post-Fourteenth Amendment encounter with liquor prohibition suggests that the justices saw no plausible
way—short of compensating liquor owners—of reconciling prohibition with
a meaningful conception of economic due process. The purely formal distinction between the police power and eminent domain, which would characterize later liquor decisions, is nowhere to be found in *Bartemeyer.* Indeed,
far from declaring that liquor laws, as valid police measures, were necessarily
compatible with the constitutional guarantee of due process, the Court leaned
toward the more intuitive conclusion that the uncompensated destruction of
property rights in liquor amounted to a deprivation of property within the
meaning of the Fourteenth Amendment.

Prohibition and Economic Due Process
in the Lower Federal Courts

The *Bartemeyer* decision left the prohibition movement in a state of limbo.
The latter half of the 1870s witnessed relatively little constitutional litigation
on the liquor question, however, since most states were in the midst of repealing or loosening the restrictive liquor laws of the 1850s.[70] The questions
raised in *Bartemeyer* therefore remained unaddressed until the early 1880s,
when the adoption of the nation's first constitutional liquor bans—in Kansas
and Iowa—simultaneously reenergized the movement and sparked a revival
of the legal battle over prohibition's constitutionality. By this point, however,
the legal environment had begun to evolve in ways that did not bode well for
the nation's anti-liquor crusaders. Two trends, both of which can be traced to
the wave of industrial regulation then sweeping the nation, are particularly

worthy of note. First, state courts were, by the 1880s, beginning to use the constitutional guarantee of due process to invalidate police regulations that were believed to lack a valid "public purpose."[71] Police regulations, on this view, could not impose special burdens on particular groups or industries, except in cases where established precedent dictated special treatment or where the wellbeing of the entire community was at stake. Where these conditions did not hold, a law that singled out a particular group or industry for special treatment could only be denounced as "class legislation."[72] Second, courts had by this point moved further in the direction of recognizing a "de-physicalized" conception of property. That is to say, judges were increasingly willing to accept that the line between regulation and confiscation was not defined by the presence or absence of physical seizure. By 1884, for example, the Supreme Court had declared in dictum that a state law which set maximum railroad rates at an unreasonably low level would amount to a "deprivation" of property within the meaning of the Fourteenth Amendment.[73] And in one particularly influential case, decided in 1885, the New York Court of Appeals ruled that a law which banned the manufacture of cigars in residential apartments had violated the due process rights of cigar-makers.[74] Echoing the contemporaneous arguments of dry-state brewers and distillers—and citing the antebellum prohibition case of *Wynehamer v. The People*—the New York Court declared that *In re Jacobs* "any law which destroys [property] or its value, or takes away any of its essential attributes" required compensation to property owners.[75] To be sure, judges in this period did not question that the state could, in certain instances, protect the public good through laws that destroyed the value of property or placed limits on its use. But many did insist that a legislature's decision to impose novel restrictions on traditionally lawful trades or forms of property required compensation in order to be compatible with the guarantee of due process.[76]

American law was therefore trending in the direction of an expanded conception of economic due process at the precise moment when many states were beginning to experiment with constitutional amendments that criminalized a range of economic activities relating to the manufacture and sale of liquor. To the modern observer, the potential for conflict between these trends is readily apparent. The critical question, however, is whether late-nineteenth-century jurists believed that the movement to check the expansion of the police power in the industrial sphere had any bearing on contemporaneous developments in the regulation of liquor. Evidence that late-nineteenth-century jurists were not blind to the due process ramifications of prohibition can be seen in the period's major legal treatises, including Christopher Tiedeman's influential *Treatise on the Limitations of Police Power in the United States* (1886). Although Tiedeman conceded the constitutionality of license laws and laws that prohibited liquor sales to minors and alcoholics, he nonetheless insisted that, in the absence of compensation to property owners, outright prohibition exceeded the scope of the police power. The primary problem with prohibition, according to Tiedeman, was that it invoked the police power to abolish a traditionally lawful form of property that was not "necessarily" or "essentially" injurious to the public." Indeed, "thousands" of Americans viewed liquor as either "harmless" or "positively beneficial," and for a narrow majority to "compel" the destruction of property in liquor was therefore tantamount to class legislation. After all, a legislature that could abolish property rights in liquor could just as easily "pass a law prohibiting the eating of hot bread because the majority of the people believe it to be injurious to the health."[77]

Even more revealing, however, is the lower federal judiciary's response to the new wave of prohibition laws. In the mid-1880s, the nation's brewers and distillers launched a series of test cases challenging the constitutionality of the Kansas and Iowa prohibition amendments—and were rewarded with a series of favorable lower federal court rulings.[78] In 1885, the first lower federal court to hear a due process challenge to the Kansas prohibition law invalidated the law's enforcement provisions.[79] The following year, in *State v. Walruff* (1886), the same lower federal court ruled that a total ban on the sale and manufacture of liquor required compensation to brewery owners whose property was rendered valueless by the act.[80]

The federal court's opinion in *Walruff,* which was authored by future Supreme Court Justice David J. Brewer, is worth examining in some detail, as it dwells at length on the relationship between liquor prohibition and the emerging trends in the jurisprudence of economic due process. The case involved a Lawrence, Kansas, brewer who had invested $50,000 in a brewery that in the aftermath of prohibition was appraised at a mere $5,000. In response to Walruff's claim that this governmentally imposed loss of value was a violation of due process, the state argued that it had not "deprived" the defendant of tangible property, but had merely "restrict[ed]" the uses to which his property could be devoted. Judge Brewer, however, rejected the attempted distinction between regulation and confiscation. In light of the Supreme Court's ruling in *Pumpelly v. Green Bay Co.,* Brewer could see no way of distinguishing liquor prohibition, as applied to established brewers, from governmental acts that flooded private property or seized farmland for purposes of railroad construction.[81] Although it was technically true that Walruff remained free to use his brewery for any lawful purpose, the more pertinent fact was that "the use which is of special value" had been taken "from [the defendant] for the benefit of the public."[82] The constitutional norm of due process protected both "the title and the right to use," Brewer reasoned, and "when the right to use in a given way is vested in a citizen, it cannot be taken from him for the public good without compensation."[83]

The most noteworthy feature of Brewer's *Walruff* opinion, however, was the judge's insistence that the uncompensated abatement of an established brewery constituted a form of class legislation. Although Brewer was devoutly religious and personally supportive of evangelical reform efforts, he could not help but view statewide prohibition as a paradigmatic case of majority tyranny.[84] There was no denying that prohibition singled out a particular class of law-abiding property owners and effectively abolished their means of livelihood. And if the police power could be used to destroy one traditionally lawful form of economic activity merely because a majority had come to regard it as offensive, Brewer reasoned, it could similarly be used to destroy *any* form of economic activity:

> Were similar action taken by the state in respect to other industries, I can but think the vigor of constitutional guaranties would seem clearer. . . . Suppose the legislature should determine that the best interests of the state would be promoted by stopping the growing of wheat, and increasing the crop of corn, and to that end should prohibit the milling of flour, must the owners, without compensation, abandon their milling and sacrifice their investment? Does not natural justice, as well as constitutional guaranty, compel compensation as a condition to such sacrifice? Yet who can state what the law will recognize as a legal distinction between those cases and this.[85]

A police power that was not firmly anchored to custom or precedent, in other words, would likely open the door to a never-ending series of "arbitrary" interferences with liberty and property. Thus, while Brewer did not dispute the legislature's right to abolish traditionally lawful commodities or professions in the name of public health or morality, he reasoned that the state had a duty to "pay the value of the property destroyed" whenever it invoked the police power to prohibit traditionally lawful economic activities.[86]

This conclusion was backed by the added weight of two additional federal decisions handed down later in 1886. First, in *Kessinger v. Hinkhouse,* a federal judge invalidated Iowa's newly enacted prohibition law and extended Brewer's reasoning to cover liquor retailers as well as manufacturers.[87] It had been "lawful to sell wine, ale, and beer in Iowa" prior to the adoption of the state's prohibition law, the judge reasoned, and for this reason "a party investing money in these things had a clear legal vested right of property in them." Any law that "prohibit[ed] the sale" of liquor was "an invasion of the petitioner's right of property" and required compensation.[88] The *Walruff* holding was likewise endorsed in *Ex Parte Yung Jon,* a federal case involving a Fourteenth Amendment challenge to an Oregon law criminalizing the sale of opium.[89] Although the judge in *Ex Parte Yung Jon* ultimately upheld Oregon's opium ban, he grounded his decision on the fact that the recreational use of opium, unlike the recreational use of liquor, had no "place in the experience or habits of the people of this country, save among a few aliens." The right to sell opium for nonmedicinal purposes could be destroyed without compensation to property owners because this "right" had never been recognized in American law or custom. In contrast, "the people of this country have been accustomed to the manufacture and use of [liquor and tobacco], and they are produced and possessed under the common and long-standing impression that they are legitimate articles of property, which the owner is entitled to dispose of without any unusual restraint." Any law abolishing the right to sell or manufacture liquor thus required "compensation to the owners for the loss occasioned thereby."[90]

The Mugler Court's Dilemma and the Origins of Doctrinal Decay

Having reviewed the federal judiciary's response to prohibition in the period between 1868 and 1886, we can begin to appreciate the nature of the dilemma that confronted the U.S. Supreme Court in the 1887 case of *Mugler v. Kansas* when, for the first time since *Bartemeyer,* the justices found themselves confronted with a due process challenge to a state prohibition law. The central question in *Mugler* roughly paralleled the question presented in *Bartemeyer:* did the uncompensated destruction of an established brewer's right to sell or manufacture liquor violate the Fourteenth Amendment guarantee of due process? (In *Mulger,* the brewing industry was careful to select a test case involving a Kansas brewer who was clearly in business prior to that state's adoption of prohibition.)[91] Yet much had changed in the thirteen years since the

Court had last heard a significant prohibition case. For starters, a movement that had appeared moribund in the early 1870s was again a national force. A decision mandating compensation for established brewers, distillers, and retailers would therefore place the Court squarely in the path of a formidable popular crusade. Nor would the impact of such a decision have been confined to the prohibition states. By the mid-1880s, state court decisions had erased any remaining questions about the constitutionality of local option laws, and portions of twenty-one states were now officially dry as the result of local action. For this reason, a decision holding that liquor owners in dry areas were entitled to compensation would wreak havoc on liquor regulation, not only in Kansas and Iowa, but also throughout much of the nation.[92]

On the other hand, a decision endorsing the uncompensated destruction of property in liquor would arguably reduce the economic rights embodied in the Fourteenth Amendment to parchment barriers. And while such a decision might have been feasible in 1874, a growing body of case law had, by the mid-1880s, firmly established that the norm of due process imposed meaningful limits on the states' police powers. Indeed, as legislatures responded to the rise of a new industrial economy by enacting innovative police measures that were unknown to the common law, many jurists now concluded that only vigorous enforcement of constitutional norms that prohibited class legislation and limited interference with established economic concerns could save the republic from the rise of a dynamic and amorphous police power.[93] Not surprisingly, Joseph Choate and George Vest, the eminent attorneys hired by the brewing industry to argue *Mugler*, built their case squarely on the connection between liquor prohibition and industrial regulation. Citing *Jacobs* and *Pumpelly*, Choate declared that, if state prohibition laws were upheld, there would soon be no legal barriers left to prevent states from "strik[ing] down innocent occupations," "invad[ing] private property," or otherwise going "beyond the utmost verge of constitutional power."[94]

This, then, was the crux of the dilemma confronting the Court in *Mugler*: to uphold the Kansas prohibition law would be to risk eviscerating the constitutional norm of due process; to invalidate the law would be to side with the purveyors of vice and against a post-Revival public morality which viewed liquor as the single greatest threat to the moral health of the republic. Writing for a majority of eight, Justice John Marshall Harlan took what must have seemed the safer course and upheld the Kansas law in its entirety. The center-piece of Harlan's opinion was a rigid formal distinction between takings or appropriations of property for public use, which interfered with the rights of *innocent* property owners, and police regulations, which applied only to inherently *noxious* uses of property. Valid police measures, according to Harlan, were by definition exempt from Fourteenth Amendment scrutiny and thus, unlike eminent domain seizures, did not require compensation to property owners. In Harlan's words, the use of the police power to prevent citizens from "inflict[ing] injury on the community" though "a noxious use of their property" was "very different" from "taking property for public use, or from depriving a person of his property without due process of law. In the one case, a nuisance only is abated; in the other, unoffending property is taken away from an innocent owner."[95] The responsibility of determining whether a specific governmental act should be classed as a police regulation or a taking, Harlan insisted, belonged to the judiciary. Where a purported police measure had no "real or substantial relation" to the ends of "protect[ing] the public health, the public morals, or the public safety," it would be the "solemn duty" of the Court to declare that the state had "transcended the limits of its authority."[96] Applying this empirical test to the case at bar, Harlan concluded that a total ban on the sale and manufacture of liquor—an inherently harmful form of property—was well within the bounds of the police power:

> There is no justification for holding that the State, under the guise of police regulations, is here aiming to deprive the citizen of his constitutional rights; for we cannot shut out of view the fact, within the knowledge of all, that the public health, the public morals, and the public safety, may be endangered by the general use of intoxicating drinks; nor the fact, established by statistics accessible to every one, that the idleness, disorder, pauperism, and crime existing in the country are, in some degree at least, traceable to this evil. If, therefore, a state deems the absolute prohibition of the manufacture and sale of intoxicating liquors . . . to be necessary to the peace and security of society, the courts cannot, without usurping legislative functions, override the will of the people.[97]

The genius of Harlan's *Mugler* opinion lay in the fact that it defined the police power broadly enough to establish the constitutionality of liquor prohibition while at the same time leaving the door open to future constitutional challenges to industrial regulation. By declaring the manufacture and sale of liquor to be inherently "noxious" uses of property, in other words, Harlan successfully severed the liquor question from the myriad other innovative police measures that were beginning to inundate the nation's courts. Yet this move was also fraught with difficulty. For while few would quibble with the claim that liquor contributed to the social ills of crime and poverty, there was no such consensus on the fact that liquor was an *inherently* "noxious" form of property on the order of diseased goods or poisons. In fact, as Justice Field pointed out in dissent, it was clear that liquor was *not* inherently noxious, since Kansas' own prohibition law contained exceptions for medicinal and scientific use. And where a form of property was only provisionally dangerous, Field asked, was the state not obligated to show that this particular defendant had somehow endangered the health or wellbeing of the community? No doubt marveling at how far the *Mugler* majority had traveled from the principles sketched in *Bartemeyer* and later applied in the lower federal courts, Field declared that the state of Kansas had clearly "crossed the line which separates regulation from confiscation."[98]

That Justice Field was the Court's most ardent defender of property rights should of course be pointed out. Indeed, it would be tempting to dismiss Field's views on prohibition as outside the mainstream of late-nineteenth-century legal thought, were it not for the fact that so many contemporary commentators raised precisely the same objections to the *Mugler* majority's opinion.[99] In a *Harvard Law Review* article published in 1889, for example, Everett Abbott dismissed Harlan's rigid distinction between the police and eminent domain powers as "not . . . founded on any principle of sound justice." In the absence of any showing that liquor was inherently harmful to society, or that a specific brewer had used his property in a noxious manner, there could be no way of distinguishing a prohibition law from a taking of private property for public use: "In [both] these cases property has been taken for the public good, and the mode of the taking would seem to be immaterial. The owner has been guilty of no legal wrong, and his property should not be confiscated. The community should pay for the benefit it has received at his expense."[100] J.I. Clark Hare's 1889 treatise on *American Constitutional Law* echoed the charge. Where past police power rulings had been grounded in "the common law" and "the common experience of life and trade," the Court's recent decisions on liquor prohibition had entered the realm of "arbitrary" legislation. Unlike "poisonous drugs" or "merchandise laden with infection," there existed no firm public consensus on the question of whether liquor was "hurtful . . . when used moderation." For this reason, Hare concluded, the Court had erred when it permitted state legislatures to prohibit the sale or manufacture of liquor without first "compensating the parties who have expended money or labor on the faith of the pre-existing law."[101] Perhaps the most prescient critique of the decision came from W. Frederic Foster, writing in the *Yale Law Journal*. Although it was no doubt true, Foster wrote, that the police power could sanction the destruction of innocent forms of property, it was essential that this awesome power remain closely yoked to tradition and precedent—otherwise there would be no way of distinguishing a valid police measure from an "arbitrary" destruction of property. The *Mugler* majority's mistake was that it had allowed the police power to escape the bounds of precedent, and without specifying an objective standard of public harm that might serve as an alternative means of preventing unwarranted interferences with private rights:

> It is submitted that [*Mugler*] differ[s] in principle from . . . earlier decisions in that the injury to the public, by which the exercise of the Police Power is justified, is one more of opinion than fact. . . . All opinions would agree in principle that the indiscriminate slaughter of animals might be gravely prejudicial to the health, or the unrestricted sale of peculiarly inflammable oils dangerous to the safety of the community, as might be also the injudicious exercise of a calling which might threaten fire. . . . But when these plain principles, founded on states of fact which command universal assent, are passed, and the heated and hazy realm of opinion is entered upon, the conditions are changed. Instead of the exercise by the State of a salutary protective power, whose sphere and limits are understood and acquiesced in by all, there is substituted the spasmodic activity of a fluctuating public opinion. If the final word as to what is or what is not within the scope of the Police Power be left to a legislative majority, all security to the citizen is gone; all he has, all he does, would be subject to the veto or the regulation of the omnipotent half plus one.[102]

Harlan and the *Mugler* majority had thus highlighted the very tension they were attempting to resolve. They had declared that economic activities related to the sale and production of liquor were inherently noxious and therefore not subject to due process review. But as contemporary commentators were quick to note, the "fact" of liquor's inherently harmful nature was far from universally accepted. To many, the decision looked more like a pragmatic attempt to accommodate public animosity towards the liquor traffic than a principled application of constitutional doctrine. In the words of Christopher Tiedeman, "public opinion" had been "so greatly influenced by the excitement of temperance agitators" that the courts had been "forced" to recognize the "validity of [prohibition] laws, notwithstanding the violation of . . . fundamental principles of constitutional interpretation."[103] Conservative commentators feared that the *Mugler* decision would inevitably lead to increased state supervision of business and industry—a fear that proved groundless, at least in the short run. But, in a larger sense, *Mugler* had indeed damaged the foundations of the old order. For whenever the Court employed its new empirical test to invalidate industrial or economic regulations, the charges of judicial activism and class bias that greeted these decisions gained credibility from the justices' deferential response to prohibition. As we shall see in chapter 5, it became increasingly difficult, after the *Mugler* decision, for the justices to explain why *any* police measure backed by a democratic majority should be subjected to constitutional limitation.

Site Three: Moral Reform and the Federal System

The Court's rulings in *Stone* and *Mugler* effectively eliminated two of the three constitutional obstacles—the contract and due process clauses—that had previously threatened to halt the advance of evangelical reform. But as late as the late 1880s, one serious constitutional obstacle remained: the federal system. We have seen that the federal system frustrated evangelical reform in two distinct but related ways. First, the fact that the power to regulate interstate commerce was vested in the *national* government meant that any *state* effort to block the importation of "immoral" commodities, including liquor, was inherently suspect (although the precise location of the boundary between the federal commerce power and the state police power was not always clear, as demonstrated by the Court's convoluted ruling in the *License Cases*). Second, the fact that congressional regulatory authority was limited to those powers specifically enumerated in Article I of the Constitution—a list that did not include the police power—meant that the federal government was barred from directly combating moral threats like liquor and lotteries. So long as these foundational tenets of American federalism—that is, the unencumbered national market and the national government of strictly enumerated powers—remained intact, the evangelical goal of eradicating vice would remain out of reach. For so long as any state permitted liquor production, then liquor producers would theoretically enjoy the constitutional right of shipping their wares throughout the nation. Similarly, so long as at least one state-authorized lottery remained in operation, then enforcement of lottery bans would be frustrated by a steady stream of out-of-state tickets.

The evangelical dream of a liquor- and lottery-free America thus required a blurring of the boundary between "commerce" and "police": either the states would have to be permitted to interfere with the interstate movement of commodities, or else the federal government would have to perform "police" functions that had traditionally been exercised at the state level. And while such a blurring had seemed feasible in the aftermath of the *License Cases*, when several members of the Court had endorsed the idea of a "concurrent" commerce power, this possibility appeared to evaporate in the postwar period. Indeed, one of the most notable developments in the jurisprudence of the Waite and Fuller Courts was a move to formalize the separation of regulatory authority that had been suggested—but not clearly delineated—by the early Commerce Clause rulings of the Marshall Court.[104] Beginning in the 1870s, the Court repeatedly invoked the ideal of the unencumbered national market to invalidate a variety of state laws that threatened to impede interstate transactions or the movement of goods across state lines. The doctrinal vehicle for this effort was the "dormant" Commerce Clause. Given that the framers' goal in formulating the Commerce Clause had been to ensure "the freest interchange of commodities among the people of the different States," the justices reasoned that the clause must be read to preempt state regulations of interstate commerce even in cases where no conflict with federal law was alleged—that is, when the commerce power remained in its "dormant" state.[105] To be sure, the Court recognized that, as a practical matter, the dormant Commerce Clause could not preempt *all* state regulation of interstate commerce; a corollary known as the *Cooley* Test—after the 1851 case of *Cooley v. Board of Wardens*—therefore authorized state regulation of "local" matters, such as harbor pilots and quarantines, that could be more efficiently managed at the lower levels of government.[106] But in cases where a lack of uniformity would significantly burden interstate commerce, the Court repeatedly held that state laws were preempted by the dormant commerce power. To name but a few examples, laws taxing out-of-state peddlers, regulating the rates charged by interstate carriers, and establishing state-level telegraph monopolies all were voided on the theory that their enforcement hindered the flow of goods and information across state lines.[107] Needless to say, these rulings did not bode well for the prohibition movement, which was at the time struggling to stem the flow of out-of-state liquor into dry states.[108]

But neither could moral reformers turn to the federal government for help in enforcing state-level morals laws, since any attempt by Congress to exercise "police" functions would arguably exceed the scope of the federal government's enumerated powers. Indeed, for all its economic nationalism, the postwar Court was equally diligent in ensuring that Congress did not use the commerce power as a pretext for the exercise of "police" powers not granted in the Constitution.[109] In *U.S. v. Dewitt* (1870), for example, the Court unanimously struck down a federal law banning the sale of illuminating oils that ignited at less than 110 degrees Fahrenheit. Here, the Court concluded that the law in question was unrelated to the movement of goods or people in interstate commerce; rather, it was "a police regulation, relating exclusively to the internal trade of the states."[110] Similarly, in the *Trade-Mark Cases* (1879), the Court unanimously invalidated a federal law establishing a national system for the registering of trademarks on the grounds that the power in question was not explicitly enumerated in the Constitution; and even if such a power were implied in the Commerce Clause, Congress could not thereby regulate wholly intrastate businesses and transactions.[111] Finally, in *U.S. v. E.C. Knight Company* (1895), the Court blocked the federal government's attempt to enforce the Sherman Antitrust Act against the American Sugar Refining Company, which had secured a virtual monopoly on the production of refined sugar. Although the Court, in an 8–1 decision, acknowledged the "evils" that resulted "from the restraint of trade," it nonetheless insisted that the phrase "interstate commerce" comprehended only the transportation or exchange of commodities. The regulation of "production" or "manufacturing," on the other hand, was a state police power that had never been surrendered to the federal government. As Chief Justice Fuller explained, "police" and "commerce" were natural categories, rooted in the attributes of particular subjects of regulation. It was "vital" that the "delimitation between" these powers "should always be recognized and observed," lest the nation's "dual form of government" collapse.[112]

The post-Civil War Court thus established a reasonably coherent set of formal categories to govern the allocation of regulatory authority between the states and the federal government.[113] That this body of jurisprudence remained relatively stable over a period of several decades, as Barry Cushman has written, "testifies to the degree to which the balance it struck between state and federal regulatory competence satisfied Americans of the era."[114] But as even this brief survey should make clear, the integrity of the entire system depended in large part upon the justices' ability to give precise and empirically plausible definitions to the terms "commerce" and "police." For the Court's federalism jurisprudence to retain legitimacy, it had to be abundantly clear to jurists, lawmakers, and the public alike which subjects of regulation belonged in the national sphere of interstate commerce and which in the local sphere of police. So long as this was the case, the federal structure would appear to rest on the natural attributes of particular subjects of regulation and not on the subjective judgments of particular jurists or lawmakers. To be sure, there were borderline cases; but disagreements at the margins did little damage to the integrity of the overall system so long as the term "interstate commerce" retained a fixed core of meaning.[115] What the system could *not* likely withstand was any suggestion that the definitions of "commerce" and "police" were not fixed and inherent in the subjects of regulation themselves. If a subject were to appear to move between these categories at the will of lawmakers or jurists, then the objectivity of the Court's categories—and, by extension, the legitimacy of the entire federal system—would be called into question.

The Wilson Act and the Blurring of the Police-Commerce Distinction

As in the case of the Contract Clause and Fourteenth Amendment due process, the first significant fissures in the edifice of dual federalism can be seen in cases involving liquor and lotteries. In fact, the Court's response to morals laws which threatened to erase the police-commerce distinction followed a familiar three-stage pattern of judicial resistance, followed by accommodation, and—ultimately—doctrinal incoherence. In the case of liquor, this process began with *Bowman v. Chicago and Northwestern Railway Co.* (1888), a case arising out of prohibition Iowa's efforts to block the flow of liquor from the neighboring "wet" state of Illinois. Although Iowa had experimented with prohibition intermittently since the 1850s, its enforcement efforts were undermined by the fact that the state shared a 200-mile border with the nation's leading producer of distilled liquor. In the mid-1880s, after more modest attempts to discourage importation had failed, the state legislature took the drastic step of imposing criminal penalties on any common carrier that transported liquor into the state.[116] Iowa's importation ban, because it acted on shippers directly, represented a more fundamental challenge to the ideal of the unencumbered national market than had the local option laws at issue in the 1847 *License Cases*. Indeed, the importation ban, which could only be enforced by inspecting the contents of train cars as they entered the state, was patently at odds with previous postwar Commerce Clause decisions holding that interstate carriers were entitled to "[u]niformity in the regulations by which [they are] governed from one end to the other of [their] routes."[117] Significantly, even many leaders of the prohibition movement conceded that an outright ban on importation would violate the Constitution.[118]

The Supreme Court's decision in *Bowman* proved them right. Although Justice Stanley Matthews's majority opinion conceded that the liquor traffic contributed to various "physical and moral evils," he nonetheless insisted that the framers' "great object" in vesting Congress with the commerce power had been "to secure uniformity of commercial regulations, and thus put an end to restrictive and hostile dominations by one State against the products of other states."[119] Iowa's importation ban, while no doubt well intentioned, was precisely the sort of state regulation that the framers had intended the Commerce Clause to prevent. For if the states were permitted "to exclude . . . articles of commerce because in their judgment the articles may be injurious to their interests or policy," they would almost certainly use this power to "establish a system of duties as hostile to free commerce among the states as any that existed previous to the adoption of the constitution."[120] Two years later, in *Leisy v. Hardin,* the Court expanded on its *Bowman* ruling by holding that the ideal of the unencumbered national market protected not only the right to import liquor but also the original importer's right to sell it—at least so long as the liquor remained in its "original package."[121] *Bowman* and *Leisy* thus cleared up any remaining confusion from the forty-year-old *License Cases.* Henceforth, the states' police power could reach imported liquor only *after* it had left interstate commerce and become "mingled with the common mass of property," either through resale or the breaking of the original package into smaller units.[122]

But if the Court hoped that its *Bowman* and *Leisy* rulings would settle the importation question, they in fact had the opposite effect. Indeed, the national leaders of the prohibition movement immediately took to the press to equate the Court's importation rulings to the infamous *Dred Scott* decision: where *Dred* had denied the rights of citizenship to African Americans, *Bowman* and *Leisy* had similarly declared that the prohibition states had "no rights which the United States is bound to respect."[123] Subsequent events appeared to bear out this interpretation of the decisions, as dry states and counties soon found themselves inundated with imported liquor. Indeed, many dry areas bordered on lawlessness as liquor retailers enthusiastically exercised their newly discovered constitutional rights, only to be arrested by local officials who refused to recognize the Supreme Court's "original package" doctrine.[124] A commentator in the popular dry periodical *The Chautauquan* described the chaotic aftermath of the *Bowman* and *Leisy* decision in vivid terms:

> These decisions are a stunning blow to the cause of temperance. . . . Newspapers are now teeming with accounts of saloons established where before they were unknown. To Leechburg, Pennsylvania, where no license has been granted, a Cincinnati brewing company has shipped carloads of beer . . . for sale in original packages. . . . It said beer is now shipped into Maine and sold with an impunity hitherto unknown. In Marshalltown, Iowa, the "original package" business is budding to bloom in the receipt of carloads of beer from St. Louis packed in bottles wrapped individually at the factory. . . . So, too, in Kansas and many other states the "original package" houses are starting up in many of the towns. . . . The manufacturers of glass have encountered a sudden demand for bottles far beyond [their] power to supply. . . . Scores if not hundreds of liquor sellers are now under arrest for violations of law, who have entered the plea, already trite, of "original package."[125]

The "original package wars" of 1890 posed a serious dilemma for the Republican party, which controlled both houses of Congress and the White House. Although the Republicans were widely viewed as the more prohibition-friendly of the two major parties, party leaders were nonetheless wary of openly embracing a policy that remained controversial in many parts of the country.[126] In the end, the party dealt with the controversy by closing ranks in support of a measure known as the Wilson Act.[127] Introduced by Iowa Senator James Wilson, the measure declared that intoxicating liquors "shall upon arrival [in a state] . . . be subject to the operation and effect of the laws of such state . . . in the exercise of its police powers."[128] By permitting each state to set its own policy with respect to importation, party leaders hoped to appease prohibition radicals in states such as Kansas and Iowa, but without unnecessarily alienating voters in other states who were less inclined to support the dry cause. There was also some reason to believe that the Court would endorse this solution to the importation dilemma, since Chief Justice Fuller had included dicta in his *Leisy* opinion suggesting that Congress might use its commerce power to authorize state importation restrictions.[129] But the legislation also posed obvious constitutional problems, for the Court had declared on numerous occasions that the underlying purpose of the Commerce Clause was to ensure that the buying, selling, and transportation of goods across state lines would be governed by uniform national standards. And if the Wilson Act guaranteed anything, it was that interstate shippers would henceforth be subject to a host of conflicting state regulations.

In *In re Rahrer* (1891) the Court managed to uphold the Wilson Act by carving the first of a series of exceptions from the traditional understanding of the federal system.[130] Perhaps reluctant to pick a fight with the other branches of the federal government—the measure had passed both houses of Congress by wide margins—or perhaps sensitive to the lawlessness unfolding in dry states and counties, Chief Justice Fuller now appeared to reject the logic of the Court's earlier importation rulings. In particular, Fuller held that it was within Congress's power to "divest" particular items of their commercial character: "No reason is perceived why, if Congress chooses to provide that certain designated subjects of interstate commerce shall be governed by a rule which divests them of that character at an earlier period of time than would otherwise be the case, it is not within its competency to do so." Fuller's opinion seemed to suggest that the "commercial" nature of commodities was no longer fixed and inherent in the commodities themselves: Congress could now subject "commercial" items to the operation of the states' police powers by enacting legislation that stripped particular commodities of their "commercial character." But this begged the question of whether the Wilson Act did not invite precisely the sort of piecemeal dismantling of the national market that the Court had condemned in its *Bowman* and *Leisy* rulings. How, in other words, could the Wilson Act be squared with the framers' "great object" of "secur[ing] uniformity of commercial regulations" throughout the Union?[131] Here Fuller resorted to an incredible leap of logic, pointing out that the legislation had, in a formal sense, established a single, uniform rule to govern the interstate traffic in liquor:

> In [enacting the Wilson Act] Congress has not attempted to delegate the power to regulate commerce, or to exercise any power reserved to the states, or to grant a power not possessed by the states, or to adopt any state laws. It has taken its own course and made its own regulation, applying to these subjects of interstate commerce one common rule, whose uniformity is not affected by variations in state laws in dealing with such property.[132]

That the Court's ruling in *In re Rahrer* has received scant attention from legal scholars and historians is likely due to the apparently narrow scope of the constitutional question at issue. Indeed, the decision is regularly filed away under the rather obscure category of "dormant" Commerce Clause jurisprudence.[133] But because *Rahrer* blurred the allegedly natural distinction between "commerce" and "police"—or, rather, permitted Congress to blur this distinction—its implications extended far beyond the narrow class of cases involving state-level obstacles to interstate commerce. In sum, Fuller had resolved the "original package" crisis by declaring, in an opinion that cited no precedent to support its key holding, that Congress possessed the authority to move subjects of regulation from the category of "commerce" to the category of "police"—or at least to establish the physical point at which this transformation took place. In the view of one astonished commentator, it seemed that the Fuller Court had "overthrow[n]" the entire doctrine of "exclusive [state and federal] power" with its discovery that Congress possessed the power to subject "established . . . [and] legitimate articles of commerce to state regulation."[134] And in light of this revelation, it was a relatively short step to the idea that subjects of regulation could similarly move in the opposite direction. If Congress could by legislation contract the definition of commerce, in other words, why could it not expand it to reach subjects that had traditionally fallen under the heading of "police"?

The Louisiana Lottery and the Rise of the Federal Police Power

The development of the federal police power, which followed quickly on the heels of *In re Rahrer*, resulted in large part from the states' inability to curb the interstate market in lottery tickets. The Court's 1880 decision in *Stone v. Mississippi*, as we have seen, made it possible for states to abolish their existing lottery grants, notwithstanding the federal Contract Clause. But while *Stone* appeared to seal the fate of the Louisiana Lottery, the Lottery subsequently outmaneuvered its opponents by securing a state constitutional provision authorizing it to conduct drawings for another two decades.[135] As a result, the company's interstate operations continued to flourish, prompting Congress to enact a series of measures designed to prevent the company from selling tickets through the mail.[136] Not surprisingly, lottery operators argued that the new postal measures had invaded privacy, restricted speech, and impinged upon the police powers of the states. The Supreme Court rejected these arguments, however, on the grounds that the postal power was a "plenary" power. As a congressional creation, the postal system was under the sole control of Congress; and the Constitution did not require Congress "to arbitrarily . . .

assist in the dissemination of matters condemned by its judgment, through the governmental agencies which it controls."[137] At the same time, the Court *initially* made plain that the ability to exclude lottery materials from the mail marked the outer extent of congressional authority over the lottery industry. As the Court explained in *Ex Parte Jackson* (1878), Congress did not possess "the power to prevent the transportation in other ways, as merchandise, of matter which it excludes from the mails."[138]

By the early 1890s, however, it was apparent that neither state lottery bans nor federal postal regulations could be counted on to curb the Louisiana Lottery's interstate operations. In 1890, when Congress at last enacted a total ban on the mailing of lottery tickets and advertisements, the Louisiana Lottery simply turned to shipping its wares through private express companies.[139] And in 1892, when the Louisiana legislature at last succeeded in repealing the company's charter, the Lottery quickly convinced the Florida legislature to allow it to base its interstate operations in that state (although the company was required to hold its drawings in Honduras).[140] As the influential jurist Thomas Cooley lamented in the pages of the *Atlantic Monthly*, it appeared that the company might carry on its interstate operations indefinitely, for "so long as a single State permits the setting up of a public lottery . . . the tickets issued in one will be sold in all, notwithstanding any diligence that the public authorities may employ for the purpose of prevention." The problem, as Cooley pointed out, was that the states were *unable* to curb the interstate traffic in lottery tickets, while Congress, in turn, lacked constitutional "jurisdiction to act upon the subject." The only apparent remedy, Cooley concluded, was for Congress to use its enumerated powers to "indirectly" target the Lottery's interstate operations—a move which Cooley supported, despite its obvious tendency to destabilize the federal system:

> It will not be denied that, under a constitutional government, there are serious objections to the powers conferred upon [Congress] being exercised in an indirect way, which keeps the actual purpose out of view. What it has been empowered to do should be done directly; and what it has not been empowered to do, or what it cannot do directly, it ought not, in general to do at all. That which is plainly within the jurisdiction of a member of the federal Union ought not to be drawn into the jurisdiction of the Union itself by any indirect means. *The indirect method, though employed in such a manner as to be, when considered by itself, a benefit to the people, will constitute a precedent which may possibly be troublesome hereafter.*[141]

The point bears emphasis: in 1892, the nation's leading legal commentator—a thinker who in his academic treatises regularly implored the nation's judges to guard "against the encroachment of federal upon state power"—took to the pages of a widely read periodical to urge enactment of federal morals legislation about which he himself seems to have harbored serious doubts.[142] The "demoralizing" effects of the Louisiana Lottery upon the nation—from wasted livelihoods, to political corruption, to "murders, robberies, and suicides"—were so severe, Cooley reasoned, as to justify a momentary departure from the traditional principles of American federalism. That such a precedent might invite further "encroachments" of federal power upon the states was a problem that would have to be dealt with in the future, after the Louisiana Lottery had met its end.

Cooley's preferred "indirect" method of targeting the Louisiana Lottery was for Congress to use its taxing power to drain the company's coffers. But in 1895, following a two-year period of intense lobbying by religious groups and the press, federal lawmakers settled on the commerce power as the most convenient vehicle for ending the Louisiana Lottery's interstate operations.[143] The resulting legislation, which made it a federal offense for any person or express company to transport lottery tickets or other lottery-related materials in interstate commerce, is usually cited as the first clear exercise of the federal police power. To be sure, previous federal laws had arguably advanced "police" purposes (as when the Animal Industry Act of 1884 banned the shipment of diseased cattle in interstate commerce), but the anti-lottery act of 1895 marked the first occasion in which Congress had used its commerce power to pursue an objective that was plainly noncommercial in nature.[144] Stated otherwise, although some previous commercial regulations had touched upon traditional police functions, such as protecting public health, the "police" dimension of these regulations was easily characterized as ancillary to a valid "commercial" objective.[145] In the case of the anti-lottery act, in contrast, there was no avoiding the fact that Congress was acting for the *sole* purpose of promoting a "police" objective—namely, the eradication of an immoral industry.

Remarkably, despite its potentially transformative impact on the federal system, the anti-lottery act of 1895 encountered relatively little resistance in Congress. Although the measure was for a time held up in committee, it ultimately passed both houses of Congress without a recorded vote.[146] That the measure encountered so little opposition can only be explained by the fact that opposition to lotteries was, by this point, so universal as to transcend the usual divisions of party and section. By 1895, thirty-eight of the forty-four states had enacted constitutional lottery bans, including virtually all of the Southern states. And following Louisiana's revocation of the Louisiana Lottery Company's charter in 1892, there remained not a single state that authorized lottery drawings within its borders. (Florida merely permitted the Louisiana Lottery Company to print tickets and disseminate them to other states.) Hatred of the Louisiana Lottery was as intense in the South as elsewhere, and leading Southern Baptists, Methodists, and Presbyterians—who typically spurned calls for federal morals regulation—now joined together with their Northern counterparts to press for the enactment of federal anti-lottery legislation. And indeed, a number of prominent Southern Democrats, including Speaker Charlie F. Crisp of Georgia, played key roles in shepherding the 1895 anti-lottery bill through Congress.[147]

Given the absence of debate in Congress, it fell to the nation's lottery operators to point out that the 1895 lottery law had all but obliterated the traditional distinction between "police" and "commerce." More specifically, attorneys for the lottery industry advanced two seemingly unassailable propositions. First, lotteries and lottery tickets—unlike liquor and livestock—had never been regarded as "commercial" items, and for this reason they could not be reached under the commerce power. To allow Congress to transform a traditional "police" subject into a "commercial commodity" would be to allow "Congress [to] determine for itself the extent and limit of its own powers and enlarge them at will." Second, even if lottery tickets *were* regarded as commercial items (based on the fact that they were bought and sold across state lines), it was clear that the purpose of the anti-lottery law had not been to facilitate the efficient movement of goods in interstate commerce but rather to regulate public morality. In other words, even if one adopted the view that any tangible item transported across state lines could be classed as "commerce," then it was all the more necessary to insist that congressional regulations bear some reasonable relation to a valid "commercial" purpose. Otherwise, the era of strictly enumerated federal powers would be at end, since a blanket power to prohibit the movement of goods or people across state lines would allow Congress to override the police regulations of the states—or even to destroy interstate commerce itself.[148]

That the Court was greatly troubled by these arguments is clear from the fact that the case was argued three times (with the Court's members reportedly dividing 4–4 on the first two arguments).[149] In the end, however, the Court upheld the measure in the landmark case of *Champion v. Ames* (1903). Writing on behalf of four dissenters, Chief Justice Fuller echoed the constitutional arguments of the lottery operators, noting that lottery tickets, like insurance contracts, had never been regarded as "commercial" items. Moreover, although it was true that the Court had previously upheld commercial regulations that *indirectly* promoted public health or morals, it had always insisted that such regulations be directed at subjects that were "themselves injurious to the transaction of interstate commerce . . . and . . . essentially commercial in their nature."[150] Unlike diseased cattle, lottery tickets did not disrupt the flow of goods in interstate commerce (unless, Fuller wrote in jest, it could be said that "these pieces of paper . . . can communicate bad principles by contact.") And indeed, the title of the 1895 law openly acknowledged that Congress had had no other purpose than "the suppression of lotteries."[151] To Fuller, it seemed that the lottery law had erased "all the differences between that which is, and that which is not, an article of commerce. . . . It is a long step in the direction of wiping out all traces of state lines, and the creation of a centralized Government."[152]

But where the four dissenters insisted that the "scope of the commerce clause . . . [could] not be enlarged because of present views of the public interest," Justice Harlan's majority opinion dwelt at length on the fact that lotteries had "become offensive to the entire people of the Nation."[153] To be sure, Harlan did not base his opinion on appeals to mores or expediency alone. Rather, he advanced the entirely plausible argument that lottery tickets, which were bought and sold across state lines, ought to be regarded as "commercial" items; and if even if it were true that the lottery law amounted to a surreptitious exercise of a federal police power, Harlan reasoned that the Court could not inquire into Congress's motives. But in response to Fuller's broader charge—that upholding the lottery law would pave the way for an inexorable expansion of federal authority—Harlan embraced the frankly pragmatic logic of Thomas Cooley's *Atlantic Monthly* essay. The American people, at least in Harlan's mind, were unified in their hatred of the lottery industry. But while the states had done everything in their power to eradicate the business, state-level efforts had plainly failed. To invalidate the federal lottery law would therefore be to authorize lottery companies to carry on their operations indefinitely, and in blatant defiance of the public will, as expressed in both state and federal legislation. Not surprisingly, this was an outcome that Harlan, like Cooley, was unprepared to accept:

> In legislating upon the subject of the traffic in lottery tickets, as carried on through interstate commerce, Congress only supplemented the action of those States—perhaps all of them—which, for the protection of the public morals, prohibit the drawing of lotteries, as well as the sale or circulation of lottery tickets, within their respective limits. It said, in effect, that it would not permit the declared policy of the States, which sought to protect their people against the mischiefs of the lottery business, to be overthrown or disregarded by the agency of interstate commerce. *We should hesitate long before adjudging that an evil of such appalling character, carried on through interstate commerce, cannot be met and crushed by the only power competent to that end.*[154]

Harlan's *Champion* opinion thus introduced into American constitutional law the idea that the federal commerce power could be used to address social "evils" in cases where the states' police powers had proved inadequate to the task. Indeed, Harlan's opinion clearly suggested that there were no longer any *substantive* limits to the reach of the commerce power; if Congress could use the newly expanded commerce power to "indirectly" target a traditional subject of state regulation like lotteries, it followed that the same power could be used to indirectly target other social ills. Numerous progressive commentators therefore praised the ruling, believing that the decision had paved the way for aggressive federal regulation of trusts and even child labor.[155] As a commentator in the *Michigan Law Review* explained, *Champion* had opened the door for Congress to block the interstate movement of "any property which [it] considers detrimental to the interests of the whole people."[156] A few conservative commentators echoed Fuller's dissent, warning that the Court had unwisely "stretched" the boundaries of the commerce power on the theory that "the end will be deemed to justify the means."[157]

Both supporters and opponents of the ruling read Harlan's opinion as holding that the commerce power extended to the regulation of anything that moved in interstate commerce, regardless of the impact on the states' police powers. It therefore came as no surprise to legal commentators when, in the period immediately following the *Champion* decision, the Court permitted Congress to use the commerce power as a proxy for a federal police power in a range of cases involving threats to public morality.[158] In 1910, for example, Congress responded to popular outrage at the "white slave" traffic—a shadowy (and possibly fictional) network of prostitution rings that preyed on immigrant women and innocent country girls—by enacting the Mann Act.[159] The measure made it a federal crime for any person to transport a woman or girl across state lines for purposes of prostitution or "immorality." Like the 1895 lottery act, the Mann Act plainly used the commerce power to target a traditionally "local" evil; and yet the Court not only upheld the measure (unanimously) but also ruled that the federal prohibition against sexual "immorality" should be construed liberally so as to apply to adultery and fornication as well as prostitution.[160] A few years later, the Court proved similarly accommodating of Congress' increasingly aggressive attacks on the interstate liquor traffic. In 1917, it upheld the Webb-Kenyon Act, which authorized the states to prohibit entirely the importation and sale of out-of-state liquor (thus closing a court-created loophole in the Wilson Act).[161] Although President Taft had vetoed the Webb-Kenyon Act on the grounds that the law unconstitutionally delegated Congress' commerce power to the states, Justice White's majority opinion in *Clark Distilling Co. v. Western Maryland Railway Co.* simply declared, without further explanation, that liquor was an "exceptional" subject and could therefore justify the use of "exceptional . . . power."[162] Two years later, the Court went further, permitting Congress to directly penalize the interstate shipment of liquor even in cases where no violation of state law was alleged, thus removing any doubt that the commerce power had become the preferred vehicle for the enactment of federal police regulations.[163]

As in cases involving the contract and due process clauses, however, the Court soon realized that the seemingly narrow doctrinal exception established in *Champion* might well undermine the entire federal system if doctrinal firewalls were not established. Thus, in the *Employers' Liability Cases* (1908) and *Adair v. U.S.* (1908), the justices began to set limits to the "indirect" purposes for which Congress' enumerated powers could be employed.[164] The commerce power, the Court now declared, was not a suitable vehicle for the indirect regulation of labor relations and working conditions: it could not reach workers who did not physically move across state lines in the course of their duties (even in cases where the employer was plainly engaged in interstate operations); nor, under any circumstances, could Congress use the commerce power to set limits to the terms of employment contracts (for example, by barring employers from conditioning employment upon a worker's agreement not to join a union). But if these decisions hinted at a retreat from *Champion*, the most glaring doctrinal departure came in the child labor case of *Hammer v. Dagenhart* (1918).[165] In *Hammer*, a five-member majority of the

Court invalidated the Owen-Keating Act, which banned child-made goods from interstate commerce, on the grounds that the law represented a surreptitious attempt to regulate "production" and had thus impinged upon the states' police powers. In a last-ditch effort to establish limits to Congress' newly discovered police powers, the majority developed the novel doctrine that the commerce power could not be used to bar the interstate transportation of "harmless" items – items that were not in themselves dangerous or immoral, and thus posed no immediate danger to residents of the destination state. In this way, the *Hammer* majority effectively distinguished the Owen-Keating Act from the federal lottery, liquor, and prostitution measures that had inspired it.[166] But, as Oliver Wendell Holmes and three other dissenting justices were quick to point out, the Court's efforts to rein in the commerce power came at a steep cost in terms of doctrinal clarity. For the Court had, in the years since 1903, repeatedly suggested that so long as a purported "commercial" regulation targeted tangible entities that moved across states lines, its constitutionality would be assumed. The Court's previous rulings upholding federal morals laws had thus opened a door that the Court, if it wished to preserve any semblance of intellectual consistency, could no longer close.[167]

The *Hammer* ruling and its corrosive impact on the traditional federal system will be examined at length in the next chapter. For now, the important point to note is that the Court had in *Hammer* wandered into precisely the same sort of doctrinal morass that already plagued its Contract Clause and economic due process jurisprudence. After sanctioning a series of unprecedented departures from the traditional understanding of the federal system, the justices were attempting to reestablish a workable boundary between state and federal authority. But as in the Contract Clause and due process cases, efforts to reinforce the crumbling foundations of the traditional order were open to entirely plausible charges of arbitrariness. Indeed, following the Court's admission that the boundaries of the federal system were neither fixed and unchanging, nor rooted in the natural attributes of particular subjects of regulation, any attempt to establish new boundaries merely highlighted the oddity of a federal commerce power that could reach liquor, lotteries, and prostitution, but whose application to the field of industrial regulation was sharply limited.

{5}

Reexamining the Collapse of the Old Order

> Intoxicating liquor has mellowed the stiffness of constitutional law. . . .
> Any notion that in that hot Philadelphia summer of 1787 the Fathers
> froze forever a rigid framework of government is wide of the mark.
> —Thomas Reed Powell, *Address to the North Carolina Bar Association* (1935)[1]

In the early decades of the twentieth century, a series of Supreme Court rulings invalidating broadly popular progressive reforms—from wage and hours laws to child labor restrictions—provoked a sustained assault on the doctrinal underpinnings of the traditional constitutional order. The critics of the old order were a professionally diverse group: their ranks included law professors (Roscoe Pound, Felix Frankfurter), political scientists (Edward Corwin, Thomas Reed Powell), economists (Robert Lee Hale, John R. Commons), philosophers (Morris Cohen, John Dewey), and Supreme Court justices (Oliver Wendell Holmes, Louis Brandeis). Regardless of professional background, however, these critics of the old order shared at least three core convictions. First, they agreed that the Supreme Court's federalism and due process rulings were incoherent, self-contradictory, and horribly out of touch with modern social and economic conditions. Second, they deemed it unlikely that such flawed decisions could have issued from misguided but otherwise well-intentioned justices; rather, it appeared that the justices were actively manipulating the concepts and categories of classical legal thought in order to achieve results that benefited employers and corporations at the expense the broader public. Finally, the critics agreed on the need to abandon the rigid categorical distinctions that lay at the heart of the Court's federalism and economic due process jurisprudence. Indeed, present circumstances seemed to demand a radically new approach to constitutional interpretation, an approach that would permit constitutional meaning to evolve in tandem with changing social and economic conditions—in short, a "living Constitution."

The progressive critique of the early-twentieth-century Court and its juris-prudence has, of course, generated an enormous literature.[2] Largely absent from the scholarly discussion, however, is any consideration of the critical role that moral reform played in the progressive assault the old order. This oversight is unfortunate. As this chapter will demonstrate, major progressive thinkers relied extensively on the liquor and lottery precedents to make the point that legal concepts and categories were inherently indeterminate and that traditional constitutional principles merely served to mask the judiciary's subjective preference for laissez-faire economic policies. Indeed, both the cri-tique of "mechanical" jurisprudence and the drive for a dynamic approach to constitutional interpretation drew inspiration—as well as specific legal argu-ments—from the Court's prior accommodation of liquor and lottery reform. Again and again—in academic articles, popular polemics, and arguments be-fore the Supreme Court—progressives cited these rulings to show that it was indeed possible to adjust constitutional doctrine to accommodate evolving popular mores. If the public's evolving attitude towards liquor and lotteries had been sufficient to justify a rethinking of economic rights and federalism constraints, the argument went, then what else but the subjective policy pref-erences of the justices themselves could explain the Court's stubborn resis-tance to other, broadly popular forms of "social" legislation?

One aim of this chapter, then, is simply to correct an oversight in the dominant narrative of early-twentieth-century constitutional development. But there is a more important reason why this neglected aspect of the pro-gressive critique deserves attention: namely, because it helps to explain why early-twentieth-century Americans found the progressives' sometimes out-landish arguments regarding the indeterminacy of constitutional doctrine and the subjective nature of judging to be inherently *plausible*. The progressive legal theorists of the early twentieth century have, after all, come in for rough treatment at the hands of scholars in recent years. Revisionist historians have demonstrated that the jurisprudence of the early-twentieth-century Court was far more coherent than its critics were willing to admit,[3] and legal scholars have raised entirely credible doubts about whether the Court's rulings were, in fact, characterized by a rigidly "formalistic" style of reasoning, as its critics claimed.[4] But to conclude that the progressive critics of the old order were, to some extent at least, arguing with a straw man is to raise anew the question of why so many Americans found the progressives' vastly exaggerated account of judicial dissembling to be entirely credible. This chapter will argue that the widely noted tension between the Court's liquor and lottery rulings, on the one hand, and its rulings on industrial and economic regulation, on the other, points the way to an answer. My claim is not that the two lines of decisions were irreconcilable at the level of doctrine; rather, it is that any doctrinal distinction capable of reconciling them was bound to strike most Americans as little better than sophistry. Progressive commentators were well aware of this fact, and they exploited it to their advantage. The liquor and lottery cases served, in effect, as the flexible and pragmatic backdrop against which the Court's rigid opposition to progressive economic regulation could plausibly be described as hypocritical.

As this brief overview suggests, the dominant thread of the narrative shifts in this chapter from evangelical reformers and cases involving liquor and lottery regulation to the progressive commentators who used the liquor and lottery precedents to advance a broader agenda of constitutional reform. To be clear, this is not to suggest that the progressive jurists of the 1920s and 1930s who pressed the case for a "living" Constitution were, in any literal sense, the intellectual heirs of the nineteenth-century evangelicals. The links between evangelicalism and progressivism are complex, and a full examination of this relationship is beyond the scope of this study.[5] Suffice it to note here that while the progressive thinkers examined below owed a certain intellectual debt to the nineteenth-century evangelicals, most were far from sympathetic to the evangelical policy agenda; indeed, many seem to have agreed with Walter Lippmann in viewing liquor prohibition, in particular, as a doomed experiment that rested on an ill-considered view of human nature.[6] And yet, even the most secular of twentieth-century progressives agreed with the nineteenth-century evangelicals on one critical point: the primary aim of the constitutional enterprise was *not* to protect established property rights or ancient jurisdictional boundaries, but rather to provide for the wellbeing of the present generation of Americans. This shared conviction explains why even thinkers who privately ridiculed the evangelical campaign against vice were happy to use the liquor and lottery precedents as a rhetorical lever to attack the doctrinal underpinnings of the old order.

Moral Storms and Apologetic Phrases: Justice Holmes's Critique of the Traditional Order

Scholarly accounts of the traditional order's collapse often begin with the academic writings and judicial opinions of Oliver Wendell Holmes, Jr.—and with good reason. Almost from the moment of his appointment to the Supreme

Court in 1902, Holmes used his new platform to attack the traditional approach to both economic rights and state–federal relations. In cases involving the due process and Contract Clauses, Holmes ridiculed the notion that there existed an inviolable sphere of economic liberty, whether defined in terms of natural law or legal custom. And in cases involving clashes between state and federal authority, Holmes was equally dismissive of the notion that there existed an inviolable sphere of state sovereignty—"created by some invisible radiation from the general terms of the Tenth Amendment"—that could not be reached under Congress's commerce power.[7]

Holmes's critique of *Lochner*-era constitutionalism was rooted in a broader legal philosophy, the key features of which were a rejection of formalist or categorical modes of legal reasoning and a belief that judges should rarely, if ever, defy the clearly expressed will of legislators or the general public.[8] These defining features of Holmes's legal philosophy were interconnected. Because Holmes believed that the act of judging often amounted to a largely subjective choice between competing social policies—rather than "an inevitable unfolding of common law principles"—it was only logical for the judge to defer "especially arbitrary policy choices to some other body, such as a legislature or jury, that arguably reflected community sentiment."[9] Perhaps the best example of Holmes's judicial philosophy in action is his famous 1905 dissenting opinion in *Lochner v. New York.* Here, in response to the majority's declaration that a New York law limiting the workday of bakery employees to ten hours had interfered with the "liberty of contract," Holmes objected that "general propositions do not decide concrete cases." Although the majority opinion turned on the question of whether the New York bakeshop law constituted a valid "police" measure, Holmes insisted that this formulation of the problem only served to mask the majority's subjective dislike of labor regulation. Given that "reasonable men" might well disagree as to whether the bakeshop law was necessary to protect public health, Holmes thought it best to read the due process clause narrowly and leave matters of economic policymaking to legislative bodies. Moreover, judicial obstruction of popular policies was ultimately pointless, Holmes argued, since in the end "[e]very opinion tends to become a law."[10]

The basic features of Holmes's critique of classical legal thought are, of course, well known. And yet, scholars have largely overlooked the critical role that the liquor and lottery precedents played in Holmes's attack on the old order. Consider Holmes's majority opinion in *Otis v. Parker,* his first as a member of the Court.[11] The case involved a Fourteenth Amendment challenge to a California law that prohibited "all contracts for sales of shares of corporate stock on margin."[12] Although the challenged law was apparently intended to restrain wildcat speculation in mining stocks, opponents argued that the measure had unconstitutionally restrained the "liberty of contract." To this Holmes replied that, although it was true that the Fourteenth Amendment barred purely "arbitrary" state interference with "private business or transactions," such "general propositions do not carry us far." Turning to the facts of the case, Holmes agreed that California had abolished an important and arguably useful form of business transaction, and the argument that this amounted to an "arbitrary" interference with "the liberty of adult persons in making contracts" was certainly not unreasonable.[13] But neither was it unreasonable to argue that contracts for the sale of stock on margin threatened the public welfare by encouraging unbridled speculation.[14] There were plausible arguments on both sides, in other words, and in such a case, categorical modes of reasoning alone could never produce a decision. The proper course for judges in such cases was *not* to void legislation simply because it appeared "excessive, unsuited to its ostensible end, or based upon conceptions of morality with which they disagree." Rather the Court should allow "[c]onsiderable latitude . . . for differences of view as well as for possible peculiar [local] conditions which it can know but imperfectly," otherwise the Constitution, "instead of embodying only relatively fundamental rules of right . . . would become the partisan of a particular set of ethical or economical opinions."[15]

Having articulated a clear, if subtle, case for a narrow reading of the due process clause, Holmes concluded his first majority opinion with a broader plea for judicial deference:

> If the state thinks that an admitted evil cannot be prevented except by prohibiting a calling or transaction not in itself necessarily objectionable, the courts cannot interfere, unless . . . they can see that "it is a clear, unmistakable infringement of rights secured by the fundamental law." No court would declare a usury law unconstitutional, even if every member of it believed that Jeremy Bentham had said the last word on that subject. . . . The Sunday laws, no doubt, would be sustained by a bench of judges, even if one of them thought it superstitious to make any day holy. *Or, to take cases where opinion has moved in the opposite direction, wagers may be declared illegal without the aid of a statute, or lotteries forbidden by express enactment, although at an earlier day they were thought pardonable at least. The case would not be decided differently if lotteries had been lawful when the Fourteenth Amendment became law, as indeed they were in some civilized states.*[16]

The passage sounds a series of themes that would be repeated two years later in the *Lochner* dissent. Yet, for present purposes, the most interesting aspect of the passage is the critical role played by the example of the recent abolition of lotteries. In a little more than a month, the Court would hand down its landmark *Champion v. Ames* ruling upholding the federal anti-lottery law of 1895.[17] For Holmes, the remarkable shift in the public perception of the lottery industry, coupled with the courts' recent accommodation of anti-lottery legislation, belied any suggestion that there existed a fixed and immutable sphere of economic liberty. The ancient examples of Sunday laws and usury laws, which Holmes would repeat in several of his best-known dissents, were also useful in this regard, since they demonstrated that the liberty to enter into contracts had long been circumscribed in Anglo-American law. But the lottery example was the lynchpin of the argument. It demonstrated that public opinion had at times moved "in the opposite direction"—that is, towards prohibiting economic activities that were traditionally protected by law—and that the judiciary had, in this instance at least, modified constitutional doctrine to reflect the public's evolving sense of morality. Indeed, when public opinion had turned against the lottery industry, neither the Contract Clause nor the Fourteenth Amendment had long succeeded in blocking the anti-lottery crusade. The lottery example thus suggested that where a "deep-seated conviction" regarding the immorality of a particular "calling or transaction" existed, the public would ultimately have its way; and, provided that the case for regulation was at least "reasonable," the proper course of action for the judiciary was to defer to the considered judgment of the people.

Two years later, when Holmes found himself in the *Lochner* minority, he reworked his *Otis* opinion into a biting dissent. If a state could regulate the stock market in the name of protecting public morals, Holmes saw no reason why it could not similarly regulate the hours of employment in the name of public health. The only truly novel feature of the *Lochner* dissent was the charge that the majority's expansive reading of the due process clause represented an attempt to write the "laissez faire" philosophy of "Mr. Herbert Spencer's Social Statics" into the Fourteenth Amendment.[18] This barb aside, Holmes merely repeated the argument that the Constitution was "made for people of fundamentally differing views," and that the Court ought not to substitute its own judgment for that of the public in any case where a "reasonable man" might deem the law in question necessary to protect public health or morals.[19] Once again, the example of anti-lottery laws demonstrated the essential fluidity of legal categories: "It is settled by various decisions of this court that state constitutions and state laws may regulate life in many ways which we as legislators might think as injudicious or if you like as tyrannical as this, and which equally interfere with the liberty to contract. Sunday laws and usury laws are ancient examples. *A more modern one is the prohibition of lotteries.*"[20]

The *Lochner* dissent, with its oft-quoted charges of class bias, made Holmes a hero to progressive critics of the Court.[21] Yet it is Holmes's 1927 dissent in *Tyson and Brother v. Banton* that careful students of constitutional development have often described as laying the groundwork for the Court's ultimate rejection of economic due process.[22] The case involved a due process challenge to a New York law that prohibited theater ticket brokers from reselling tickets at a price greater than 50 cents above face value. Significantly, the statute explicitly referred to the theater industry as a "business affected with a public interest"—a conscious attempt to link the regulation to the line of cases in which the Court had upheld laws regulating the prices charged by grain storage facilities, railroads, and a narrow class of industries deemed particularly essential to the public welfare.[23] Writing for a bare majority of five, however, Justice Sutherland denounced the New York measure as an unconstitutional interference with the property rights of ticket brokers. The "right . . . to fix a price at which . . . property shall be sold," Sutherland concluded, was "an inherent attribute of the property itself . . . and as such within the protection of the due process . . . clauses."[24] Although Sutherland acknowledged that the Court had permitted rate regulation in previous cases involving businesses "affected with a public interest," he rudely rebuffed New York's attempt to shoehorn the ticket-selling business into this category. In Sutherland's mind, the fact that theaters had never before been subject to this sort of regulation was essentially dispositive: "While theaters have existed for centuries . . . it does not appear that any attempt hitherto has been made to fix their charges by law. This . . . fact . . . persuasively suggests that by general legislative acquiescence theatres, historically, have been regarded as falling outside the classes of things which should be thus controlled."[25]

A better set-up for a Holmesian assault on the rigid dichotomies of the Court's economic due process jurisprudence is difficult to imagine. Sutherland had turned to history to demonstrate that the ticket-selling business did not belong in the category of businesses "affected with a public interest." In response, Holmes lambasted Sutherland and the majority for deliberately ignoring the Court's liquor and lottery decisions, which plainly demonstrated the fluidity of the distinction between public and private economic concerns. If the historical novelty of the anti-scalping measure was an argument against its constitutionality, then surely the same could be said of prohibitory liquor laws and lottery bans. And yet, after a brief period of resistance, the judiciary had now endorsed the constitutionality of both prohibition and anti-lottery measures. On what basis, then, could the Court justify its decision to defy public opinion on the question of ticket scalping?

> The truth seems to be that . . . the legislature may forbid or restrict any business when it has a sufficient force of public opinion behind it. Lotteries were thought useful adjuncts of the state a century or so ago; now they are believed to be immoral and they have been stopped. Wine has been thought good for man from the time of the Apostles until recent years. But when public opinion changed it did not need the Eighteenth Amendment, notwithstanding the Fourteenth, to enable a state to say that the business should end. What has happened to lotteries and wine might happen to theaters in some moral storm of the future, not because theaters were devoted to a public use, but because people had come to think that way.[26]

At first glance, the passage may seem merely to reiterate themes already seen in Holmes's *Lochner* dissent. Yet it is important to note that the *Lochner* dissent was, at bottom, merely a plea for setting the bar of "reasonableness" as low as possible in cases involving due process review of police regulations; at no point, that is, did Holmes's earlier opinion advocate a wholesale abandonment of the jurisprudential underpinnings of economic due process. In *Tyson*, in contrast, the aged Holmes was advancing the more radical view that the very concept of a "police" regulation—and the associated category of business "affected with a public interest"—was simply an empty vessel for whatever regulatory policies happened to enjoy majority support at a particular moment in history. To be sure, he had previously made plain his belief that courts should not—and ultimately could not—block regulatory experiments that enjoyed broad public support; but now he went further, arguing that judges should simply abandon the entire complex of "apologetic phrases" that had previously supported—and marked the limits of—state power in cases involving economic regulation:

> [W]hen legislatures are held to be authorized to do anything considerably affecting public welfare, it is covered by apologetic phrases like the police power, or the statement that the business concerned has been dedicated to a public use. The former expression is convenient, to be sure, to conciliate

the mind to something that needs explanation. . . . I do not believe in such apologies. I think the proper course is to recognize that a state legislature can do whatever it sees fit to do unless it is restrained by some express prohibition in the Constitution. . . . [T]he notion that a business is clothed with a public interest and has been devoted to a public use is little more than a fiction intended to beautify what is disagreeable to the sufferers.[27]

In other words, there was simply no way to draw an immovable barrier between public power and private right; all attempts to do so, whether rooted in history or natural law, had failed. Regardless of whether Holmes was correct to view legal categories such as "police" and "affected with a public interest" as *inherently* devoid of substantive content, his frequent dissents in economic due process cases raised entirely credible doubts about the present Court's ability—or willingness—to apply these categories in an intellectually consistent manner. As one contemporary commentator explained, Holmes's *Tyson* dissent had laid bare "the utter baselessness of the distinction between industries affected with a public interest and those not so affected." Holmes had correctly surmised that the entire doctrinal edifice of economic due process rested "on a house of cards," and his opinion was "a well directed blow destined to cause a realignment of decisions on the basis of sound . . . constitutional interpretation."[28]

The morals precedents were equally central to Holmes's devastating critique of the Court's federalism jurisprudence. Indeed, the collapse of the traditional conception of the federal system can be traced, in no small part, to Holmes's characteristically biting dissent in the child labor case of *Hammer v. Dagenhart*.[29] In *Hammer*, as we as we saw in chapter 4, the Court was asked to determine whether Congress could indirectly regulate child labor by banning the shipment of child-made goods in interstate commerce. Writing for a bare majority, Justice William Day held that the Owen-Keating Act was a surreptitious attempt to regulate the conditions of "production"—a traditional state function—and therefore beyond the scope of the commerce power. Holmes, writing for four dissenters, penned a point-by-point rebuttal of Day's conception of the federal system. One by one, Holmes skewered the various arguments that opponents of the child labor law had used to distinguish the Owen-Keating Act from the post-*Champion* line of precedents upholding the use of the commerce power to reach traditional "police" subjects ranging from lotteries to impure food and drugs. The theory that Congress's Article I power to "regulate" commerce did not entail the power to "prohibit" commerce,

Holmes noted, had been jettisoned in *Champion v. Ames*. The theory that the Court should review the "purpose" of congressional acts—in order to prevent enumerated powers from being used to interfere with the "domestic policy" of the states—had been similarly rejected in decisions upholding the federal oleomargarine tax and a federal ban on the distribution of immoral films.[30] Moreover, Holmes observed that the Court's decisions upholding federal liquor laws and the Mann Act had acknowledged that commercial regulations might "have the character of police regulations"—i.e., be indistinguishable from them.[31]

Yet these doctrinal objections merely served as prelude to the soaring rhetoric of the opinion's concluding section, in which Holmes advanced a pair of broader—and more radical—claims. First, he cited the Court's accommodation of liquor prohibition to suggest that the term "interstate commerce" was no less susceptible to judicial manipulation than "police" or "affected with a public interest." How else, Holmes asked, could one explain the discrepancy between the Court's pre-Eighteenth Amendment liquor decisions—which had appeased an "emotionally aroused" public by endorsing congressional regulation of the liquor traffic—and its subsequent rejection of federal child labor legislation in *Hammer?*[32] Both the liquor and child labor laws had interfered with traditionally "local" questions; moreover, both had done so through the indirect method of denying the offensive businesses access to interstate markets. That federal liquor laws had survived constitutional scrutiny under the Commerce Clause while the child labor law had not suggested that the constitutional category of "commerce" was simply a fig leaf for whatever social policies commanded the support of five members of the Court: "But I had thought that the propriety of the exercise of a power admitted to exist in some cases was for the consideration of Congress alone and that this Court always had disavowed the right to intrude its judgment upon questions of policy or morals. *It is not for this Court to pronounce when prohibition is necessary to regulation if it ever may be necessary—to say that it is permissible as against strong drink but not as against the product of ruined lives.*"[33]

Having highlighted the jarring contrast between the Court's treatment of liquor prohibition and child labor, Holmes then concluded the opinion by spelling out his own expansive understanding of the commerce power. The only plausible reading of the Commerce Clause—at least in light of recent rulings—was one that viewed Congress's power over the interstate movement of goods and people as plenary and in no way constrained by the traditional police powers of the states. The fact that a "commercial" regulation interfered with—or blatantly contradicted—the domestic policies of certain states was no argument against its constitutionality, since Congress was duty-bound to advance the general welfare through all means at its disposal. Holmes sealed the argument by pointing out that this understanding of the federal system was hardly novel; it was, rather, the precise theory put forward by Justice Harlan in the course of sustaining the 1895 Lottery Act:

> If, as has been the case within the memory of men still living, a State should take a different view of the propriety of sustaining a lottery from that which generally prevails, I cannot believe that the fact would require a different decision from that reached in *Champion v. Ames*. Yet, in that case, it would be said with quite as much force as in this that Congress was attempting to intermeddle with the State's domestic affairs. The national welfare, as understood by Congress, may require a different attitude within its sphere from that of some self-seeking State. It seems to me entirely constitutional for Congress to enforce its understanding by all the means at its disposal.[34]

As should be clear from this brief overview, the broader impact of Holmes's assault on the traditional order was surely magnified by the memory of the Court's frankly pragmatic accommodation moral reform. And in at least one case, *Knickerbocker Ice Co. v. Stewart*, Holmes frankly acknowledged the polemical motivation behind his frequent references to liquor and lottery prohibition. *Knickerbocker Ice* involved the question of whether Congress could authorize the states to establish their own rules for workmen's compensation in admiralty cases.[35] A majority of the Court answered in the negative, on the grounds that the framers' decision to vest the federal judiciary with admiralty jurisdiction had been intended to ensure that a single, uniform system of rules would govern admiralty cases. Congress, in short, could not delegate to the states a power that the framers had vested in the national government. In dissent, Holmes pointed out that the decision seemed to contradict the Court's prior rulings on the subject of liquor regulation, many of which appeared to endorse the delegation of Congress's commerce power to the states. The only possible explanation for the discrepancy, Holmes suggested, was that "special constitutional principles exist against strong drink." But this seemed unlikely, since "[t]he framers of the Constitution, so far as I know approved [of] them."[36]

Holmes clearly believed he had landed a solid blow; indeed he specifically mentioned the remark in letters to both Harold Laski and Felix Frankfurter.[37] Also mentioned in the letters to Laski and Frankfurter was the fact that

Holmes had received at least one piece of hate mail attacking the *Knickerbocker Ice* dissent. The anonymous correspondent had said nothing about the arcane subject of admiralty jurisdiction, however, but had instead focused his or her ire on Holmes's remark about the framers' affinity for liquor. As Holmes informed Laski, the letter "refer[red] me copiously to the Old Testament and [said] that A. Lincoln would have read his Bible and asked God about it before he gave it to the public—but A.L. was a great man and he guesses that men like me don't read our Bibles."[38] That a single critical remark about liquor prohibition in an otherwise unremarkable opinion on admiralty jurisdiction could provoke such a reaction serves, in a way, as evidence in favor of Holmes's larger critique of *Lochner*-era constitutionalism. The reason why "general principles" could no longer govern in due process or Commerce Clause cases was because the people and their representatives had long since abandoned them in their quest for a morally purified republic. As John Dewey would soon write in *The Public and Its Problems,* few prohibition-era Americans ever stopped to consider "the relationship between their professed general principle[s] and their special position on the liquor question." At a time when a nation founded on the ideals of federalism and limited government had endorsed national prohibition, one could only conclude that constitutional principles "persist[ed] as emotional cries rather than as reasoned ideas."[39]

The Morals Precedents and the Erosion of Economic Rights

By the time Holmes retired from the Court in 1932, his once-unconventional understanding of the constitutional enterprise had gained widespread acceptance within the legal academy. Over the course of the following decade, the Supreme Court itself would embrace Holmes's contention that the traditional conceptions of economic rights and federalism were broken beyond repair. The question of precisely when and why the Court abandoned the traditional understandings of economic rights and state–federal relations is, of course, the subject of intense scholarly debate.[40] My aim in what follows is not to resolve these controversies, but rather to address the critical but often-neglected question of how Holmes's once-radical views began to acquire legitimacy in the eyes of legal commentators and the wider public. How, in other words, did Holmes's vision move from the periphery to the mainstream of American constitutional discourse?

On one level, of course, the answer to this question is obvious: Holmes's views were disseminated in hundreds of academic articles and popular works authored by progressive academics in the 1920s and early 1930s.[41] Thus, early public law scholars, including Roscoe Pound, Felix Frankfurter, Edward Corwin, and Thomas Reed Powell, drew on Holmes's opinions to make the case that traditional rules of constitutional adjudication were indeterminate; that that the *Lochner*-era Court had read into the constitutional text its own idiosyncratic economic philosophy; and that the Constitution should be understood as a "living" document whose meaning evolved in tandem with societal norms and changing economic conditions. Viewed on another level, however, the critical question is not how such views were transmitted to a wider public, but rather, what made them *credible?* And it is here, I believe, that the Supreme Court's turn-of-the-century accommodation of moral reform played a critical—and previously neglected—role. For, like Holmes, the major academic critics of the *Lochner*-era Court regularly bolstered their arguments for "constitutional laxity" by stressing the fact that the Court had already bent the traditional rules of constitutional adjudication in cases involving liquor and lotteries.[42] The morals precedents thus brought the abstract arguments of the sociological jurists and Legal Realists down to earth. They provided progressive critics of the Court with a powerful rhetorical tool that could be used to chip away at the foundations of the old order, since even Americans who cared nothing for the finer points of constitutional law or legal philosophy could perceive the tension between the Court's accommodation of moral reform and its stubborn resistance to industrial and economic regulation.

The Academic Critique of Lochner-Era Economic Rights

The progressive assault on the traditional understanding of economic rights can be traced through three relatively distinct phases, each of which relied heavily on the example of liquor and lottery precedents to press the case for constitutional change. The first phase, which began around 1910, focused on what G. Edward White has termed the issue of "constitutional adaptivity."[43] The critical question was whether the interpretation of the constitutional text should be governed by the original understanding of the framers, or whether constitutional meaning should be understood to evolve in tandem with changing economic and social conditions. Traditionally, American jurists had understood constitutional interpretation as a relatively straightforward task in which judges functioned as passive mouthpieces for the will of the sovereign "people," as expressed in a "timeless" and unchanging constitutional text.[44] Beginning shortly after the turn of the century, however, a number of prominent scholars began to challenge this understanding of the interpretive enterprise. The traditional approach to constitutional interpretation, they argued, rested on at least two flawed premises. First, it tended to conflate specific textual provisions with the vast body of judicially created *doctrine* that had grown up around those provisions. The growth of judicially created rules, which were necessary to fill out the often open-ended language of the constitutional text, was, of course, inevitable, but such rules were not permanent and unalterable in the same sense as the text itself. Judicially crafted doctrine, the argument went, could—and should—be modified to reflect altered social and economic conditions. Second, the traditional understanding of the interpretative enterprise rested on a flawed understanding of the judicial function. Judges, as Holmes had made clear in various dissents, could not act as passive mouthpieces for the sovereign will of the people, for the simple reason that "general principles" could rarely decide concrete cases. Legal texts and doctrines were often indeterminate, and the task of judging was therefore inherently subjective. So long as the American public remained blind to this fact, the Constitution's judicial interpreters would enjoy perfect immunity to read their own policy preferences into the text—all while claiming to be the passive agents of the people themselves.[45]

One of the first scholars to challenge the traditional understanding of the interpretative enterprise was Roscoe Pound. Although the phrase "living Constitution" did not come into widespread usage until the 1920s, Pound's 1909 article "Liberty of Contract" articulated all of the key components in the progressive case for a dynamic approach to constitutional interpretation. In particular, Pound argued that it was

> contrary to [the framers'] principles to assume that they intended to dictate philosophical or juristic beliefs and opinions to those who were to come after them. What they did intend was the *practical* securing of each individual against arbitrary and capricious governmental acts. They intended to protect the people against their rulers, not against themselves. They laid down principles, not rules, and rules can only be illustrations of those principles so long as facts and opinions remain what they were when the rules were announced.[46]

In other words, it was critical to distinguish between constitutional principles and the judicially created rules through which principles were applied to specific situations; the former were permanent, while the latter had to be adjusted to changing social and economic circumstances, lest the entire constitutional edifice collapse. To illustrate the point, Pound noted that even though jurists had long asserted that the Constitution protected the "natural" right to possess and enjoy property, the content of this right had changed radically over time. For example, political thinkers from Aristotle to Grotius had insisted that the institution of slavery possessed "a natural basis"; but once public opinion began to turn against the institution, slavery was reconceptualized as antithetical to natural law. Liquor prohibition provided an even more striking example of the same phenomenon. As recently as the 1850s, Pound observed, many jurists had viewed the right to sell or possess liquor as a natural right that could not be destroyed by "simple legislative declaration." "Since that time," however, "people [had] changed their minds." Indeed, in the short span of three decades, the judiciary had reversed course and permitted lawmakers to transform liquor into a "nuisance per se."[47] To Pound, this transformation perfectly illustrated the futility of the *Lochner*-era Court's crusade against industrial regulation. Although the legal accommodation of social change was clearly inevitable, the Court continued to decide employment cases by "rigorous logical deduction from predetermined conceptions in disregard of and often in the teeth of the actual facts."[48]

The legal philosopher Morris Cohen, another early and prominent advocate of the "living" Constitution, frequently cited the abolition of lotteries to make essentially the same point. In an influential 1915 article entitled "Legal Theories and Social Science," for example, Cohen lamented that the "prevailing theory" of constitutional interpretation had "erected a Chinese wall around the . . . legal intellect" so as to shield judges from social and economic change.[49] The most important brick in this wall was what Cohen labeled the "phonograph theory of the judicial function." On this view, judges "had no share in the making of constitutional law" but were merely the passive "mouthpiece[s] of a pre-existing definite will of the people" as expressed in the constitutional text.[50] The absurdity of this theory, according to Cohen, stemmed from the fact that modern "constitutional issues . . . are often of a kind that could not possibly have been present in the minds" of "the people" who had ratified the Constitution—a fact that was nowhere clearer than in the incoherent muddle of Commerce Clause rulings that had followed in the wake of *Champion v. Ames:* "It is absurd to maintain that when 'the people' in 1789 adopted the Federal Constitution with its Commerce Clause, they actually intended to give Congress the authority to *prohibit lotteries* (an honorable and established institution in those days), but not to regulate insurance . . . or to prohibit [railroads] from discharging their men for joining trade unions."[51] The lottery example was central to Cohen's argument because it demonstrated not only that the "phonograph theory" offered a flawed depiction of the interpretive process, but also that the Court had effectively admitted as much in upholding the federal anti-lottery law.[52] The Court had accommodated social change in some areas but not others, with the result that the "phonograph theory" had lost credibility as an interpretive methodology. The only sensible response to this state of affairs, according to Cohen, was an unapologetic embrace of the living Constitution: Americans "ought to live not as pall bearers of a dead past but as the creators of a more glorious future."[53]

The second phase of the progressive assault on *Lochner*-era economic rights exploited the tension between the Court's deferential treatment of morals laws and its rigid opposition to industrial regulation to argue for a controlled expansion of the police power. In particular, the Court's progressive critics demanded to know why the state's allegedly plenary power to protect public health, safety, and morals was so often subject to judicial limitation in cases involving the regulation of employment relations and working conditions. In a 1917 *Yale Law Journal* article entitled "Social Insurance and Constitutional Limitations," for example, Edward Corwin observed that the nation's courts appeared to alternate between two distinct constitutional philosophies in cases involving the police power. When confronted with constitutional challenges to workmen's compensation laws, minimum-wage legislation, and other "social insurance projects," the Court adhered to a philosophy of constitutional "rigorism"—a philosophy which adamantly refused to adjust traditional concepts and categories to meet the "needs of modern complex society."[54] But in cases involving the regulation of liquor, the nation's courts, after a period of resistance, had adopted a philosophy of constitutional "laxism" that frankly subordinated private rights to the wellbeing of the community:

> Thus, shortly before the Civil War, the New York Court of Appeals, in the famous *Wynehamer* case, set aside an anti-liquor law on the ground that, as to existing stocks of liquor, it constituted an act not of regulation but of *destruction,* and so of *taking* without compensation. Thirty years later, in *Mugler v. Kansas,* the United States Supreme Court sustained precisely the same kind of law as within the police power, to which, it said, all property

is at all times held subject. In other words, the state may, in the exercise
of its police power, absolutely outlaw what was good property when it was
acquired. But even as to property remaining under the protection of the law
it may, by the same power, limit the owner's use and control thereof for the
public benefit.[55]

The liquor example illustrated that the boundary between a permissible police regulation and an unconstitutional taking of private property was "by no
means a stationary one" and raised the question "whether its present place-
ment is necessarily so definite, after all."[56] Given that the judiciary had plainly
adopted a philosophy of "laxism" in morals cases, Corwin demanded to know
"why . . . the maxim against confiscation should [not] meet with the like fate,
if confronted with a well-considered Minimum Wage [law] or other Social
Insurance scheme?"[57]

Ray Brown of the University of Wisconsin juxtaposed the Court's liquor
and labor rulings to make a similar point in a pair of *Harvard Law Review*
articles published in the mid-1920s. Specifically, Brown noted that in its "later
liquor cases"—i.e., those decided after *Mugler v. Kansas* but before the adoption of the Eighteenth Amendment—the Court had fully endorsed the theory
that "property, contract, and liberty are social and not personal concepts." For
Brown, the courts' accommodation of prohibition marked the "overthrow of
[the] individualistic concepts on which much of our common law is based"
and announced the advent of a new constitutional era in which "ordinary legal
dogmata" would "cease to be of assistance in the deciding of cases." Instead of
attempting to force concrete cases into outmoded and purely abstract categories, courts confronted with due process challenges would henceforth focus
on a series of "practical" considerations: "Is there, in fact, a danger to the
health or safety of the members of the state in the existing situation? Will the
method adopted by the state guard against it? Is the burden on the individual
too heavy to justify the claimed benefit?" Striking a Holmesian note, Brown
declared that the answer to such questions could not "be forecast by the pro-
nouncement of general rules" but would depend "on a clear insight into the
facts of the specific case, and a keen intuition as to what is generally regarded
as just, and what will in the end work toward the welfare of all."[58] Brown
warned, however, that while this more enlightened approach to constitutional
adjudication had clearly prevailed in cases involving liquor regulation, it had
not yet taken hold in the realm of labor regulation. When viewed in light of
the judiciary's deferential treatment of liquor laws, the Court's hostile reaction

to minimum-wage laws—most recently in the case of *Adkins v. Children's Hospital*—stood out in sharp relief.[59] Given that the liquor decisions had so clearly endorsed "the state's claim of dominance over the individual," Brown could only conclude that decisions invalidating minimum-wage legislation reflected "an instinctive dread of price fixing" which had "obscured in the Court's mind the health aspects of the legislation."[60] The simple need for logical consistency suggested that the Court would soon be compelled to extend to labor regulations the same deferential treatment it had already extended to liquor.[61]

The third phase of the progressive assault on *Lochner*-era economic rights used the example of liquor prohibition to mount a somewhat more radical challenge to the jurisprudential underpinnings of the due process and Contract Clauses. In this phase, the prohibition cases were useful not because they could be used to push for an expansion of the police power, but rather because they could be used to show that the major concepts and categories used to enforce traditional property protections were essentially *meaningless*. Thus, the economist and law professor Robert Lee Hale argued in a series of influential articles—published shortly before Holmes's *Tyson and Brother v. Banton* dissent—that the public/private distinction on which so much of the Court's economic due process jurisprudence depended was essentially arbitrary.[62] Where American law had traditionally permitted rate regulation only in a narrow class of cases involving businesses "affected with a public interest," Hale made the case that "there is not a single advantage possessed by a business affected with a public use which cannot be matched in the case of some unregulated concern."[63] Indeed, the very idea of a "private" economic concern was a misnomer, according to Hale, since all property rights were in the end defined and enforced by the state; the market was not "an abstract meeting of the minds or convergence of wills" but "an interlocking system of power relations" backed by official coercion.[64] Nowhere was this fact more clearly illustrated, Hale reasoned, than in cases where "[a] change in the law . . . prohibits the manufacture of [a] type of product" which had previously enjoyed the full protection of law.[65] That previously legitimate businesses, such as breweries, had in the past been shuttered without warning—and without compensation—suggested that there existed no stable or natural baseline against which the confiscatory effects of regulation could be measured. Hale thus concluded that the concepts and categories which underpinned economic due process analysis were clearly in flux—and always had been.[66]

Significantly, such views were not confined to the radical circles of the Legal Realists. Even relatively conservative scholars were by the late 1920s citing liquor prohibition to make the case that the traditional conception of economic due process had broken down. Writing in the *Atlantic Monthly* in 1927, for example, Charles Warren put forward a somewhat simplified version of Hale's basic thesis. Citing an unnamed case in which a man had "lawfully purchase[d] liquor valued at four hundred dollars," only to have his liquor seized and destroyed when the state legislature "later [made] the possession of liquor illegal," Warren endorsed the view that the terms "due process," "confiscation," and "police power" were essentially "meaningless."[67] When ancient forms of property could be abolished at the whim of state legislatures, it was clear that such terms had "no fixed and unalterable meaning, no absolute meaning which is unaffected by times or circumstances and unrelated to social and economic conditions." In reality, Warren informed his readers, the border between public power and private right was not determined by abstract formulas, but rather by the subjective policy judgments of the courts. The police power, then, was simply "the right of the State to cause discomfort, injury, loss, or ruin to a part of the community in the interest of a greater part—up to the point where the court says that the State has gone too far."[68] Significantly, Warren bolstered this claim with an approving citation to Holmes's *Tyson* dissent, handed down earlier the same year. The entire conceptual apparatus of due process analysis, as Holmes had shown in *Tyson*, was simply a complex of "meaningless" phrases designed to "conciliate the mind to something that needs explanation."[69]

Other scholars writing in the same period employed a similar logic to challenge the conceptual foundations of the Court's Contract Clause jurisprudence. As we have seen, the incoherence of the Court's Contract Clause rulings was a popular topic of discussion among legal scholars as early as the 1890s. With the emergence of sociological jurisprudence and Legal Realism, however, the general tenor of academic writing on the Contract Clause underwent a decisive shift. Instead of expressing bemusement at the Court's convoluted and arguably contradictory Contract Clause rulings, scholars now cited the same rulings to argue that the Contract Clause was devoid of substantive content. In 1921, for example, a writer in the *Michigan Law Review* set out to explain how a clause that had once protected a virtually inviolable sphere of economic liberty had been narrowed to the point where contractual rights were "almost subservient to that vast state power, the Police Power." Citing *Stone v. Mississippi* as a critical turning point, the writer concluded that the history of the Contract Clause evinced the essential fluidity of constitutional rights. Although modern Contract Clause cases were "not materially different" from the cases that arose under the Marshall Court, it was clear that judicial "interpretation" of the Contract Clause "had changed." In light of this fact, one could only conclude that "the Supreme Court is, in the final analysis, a law-making body."[70] An early 1933 *Harvard Law Review* article offered a similarly succinct summary of the trajectory of Contract Clause doctrine in the post-Civil War period: "The decline of the clause *began* in cases in which the obligations of corporate charters were urged against the validity of *lottery and liquor prohibition legislation.* Such legislation was held a proper exercise of the police power in 1878. By 1905 it seems to have been apparent that private persons' contracts were given no special protection by the Contract Clause . . . and that such contracts were subject to modification by legislatures in the exercise of their police powers." The post-*Stone* Contract Clause decisions thus illustrated the Court's "creative power," its ability to ensure that significant social and economic developments "find their place in the constitutional system."[71]

From here, it was a short step to the conclusion that the views of the Marshall Court—as well as the original understanding of the framers—had become irrelevant to the task of interpreting and applying the Contract Clause. Thus, when the onset of the Great Depression led many states to experiment with mortgage moratoria—precisely the type of "debtor relief" legislation that the Constitution's framers had understood the clause to bar—the general consensus among legal commentators was that the Court would have to sustain these laws, lest it contradict its past assertions regarding the plenary nature of the police power. A second writer in the *Harvard Law Review* concluded in 1933 that "the legal armory" was "plentifully furnished with precedents for or against the constitutionality" of "moratory legislation." Indeed, the once-robust Contract Clause had become so riddled with exceptions that virtually any plausible "police" rationale was now sufficient to warrant the abolition of contractual rights. In moratoria cases, "the choice to be made among conflicting . . . principles" would depend not upon any analysis of original intent or precedent but rather "upon the sensitiveness of the courts to the dangers threatening the general economic structure."[72] A writer in the *University of Pennsylvania Law Review* reached a similar conclusion. In its rulings on lottery grants, the writer noted approvingly, the Waite Court had refused to sacrifice "social advancement" to the "the claims of vested rights," thus opening the door to a pragmatic reading of the Contract Clause.[73] The increasingly incoherent rulings that followed in the wake of *Stone v. Mississippi,* in turn, had foreclosed any possibility of articulating a "consistent theory of the relation between contract and the police power." Now that the nation was facing an unprecedented economic crisis, the time was right for the Court to acknowledge that all contractual rights were ultimately subordinate to "the power to make regulations for the general welfare, in all its manifestations."[74]

By the early 1930s, a significant swath of the legal community had reached the conclusion that the conceptual underpinnings of the due process and Contract Clauses were damaged beyond repair. To be sure, a good deal of the skepticism regarding the traditional conception of economic rights was probably motivated by policy considerations and unspoken assumptions regarding the proper relationship between the state and the economy. Indeed, for those who wished the Court to uphold the unprecedented regulatory innovations of the New Deal period, it was essential to cast doubt on the Court's prior rulings in cases involving industrial and economic regulation. The important point to note, however, is that proponents of an expanded regulatory state had by the early 1930s developed an entirely credible case for jettisoning the traditional framework. Given that the Court had already discarded traditional property protections in the liquor and lottery cases, progressive academics and members of the Realist movement argued that there could be no principled justification for reviving these doctrines at a moment when the national economy was on the brink of collapse.

The Transformative Decisions: Blaisdell and Nebbia

Scholarly opinion, as we have seen, is sharply divided on the question of exactly when the New Deal-era "constitutional revolution" was completed. For present purposes, however, it is not necessary to map every twist and turn of the Court's response to the New Deal. Rather, it suffices merely to examine the two 1934 decisions—*Home Building and Loan Association v. Blaisdell* and *Nebbia v. New York*—in which the progressive understanding of the police power first won the support of a majority of the Court. The critical point to note in both decisions is the majority's frank rejection of the categorical approach which had previously governed in due process and Contract Clause cases (at least in theory). Although the *Blaisdell* and *Nebbia* decisions did not mark the end of all judicial opposition to economic regulation—the Court struck down a number of innovative state and federal regulations in 1935 and 1936—they nonetheless signaled the Court's acceptance of the basic features of the progressive critique. From this point forward, it was clear that the burden of proof in cases involving the police power had shifted from the state to the private economic actors who sought protection under the due process and Contract Clauses.

The *Blaisdell* litigation began when the Minnesota legislature, in an effort to arrest an epidemic of farm foreclosures, enacted a moratorium law that extended the time available for mortgagors to redeem their mortgages. Not surprisingly, banks and other lenders immediately challenged the law on Contract Clause grounds. A bare majority of the Court rejected this argument, however, in a landmark opinion authored by Chief Justice Charles Evans Hughes. Hughes began his opinion by emphasizing the extraordinary nature of the economic crisis then gripping the nation. Although the Chief Justice denied that an "emergency" could "create power," he nonetheless found enough play in the joints of the Constitution to permit extraordinary regulatory measures in cases where the text was not so "specific . . . as not to admit of construction."[75] Thus, while the existence of an "emergency" would furnish no grounds for permitting a state to "coin money" (in violation of Article I, Section 8), the Contract Clause was a relatively vague provision that required judicial "construction . . . to fill in [its] details."[76] To illustrate the fact that the Contract Clause could "not . . . be read with exactness like a mathematical formula," Hughes offered a lengthy summary of the myriad decisions in which the Court had made clear that the clause did not bar *all* interferences with contractual rights. Not surprisingly, the liquor and lottery cases featured prominently in this review of precedent. The lottery at issue in *Stone v. Mississippi,* Hughes observed, had been "a valid enterprise when established under express state authority," and yet the Court had held that "the legislature in the public interest could put a stop to it." And in the years since the *Stone* decision, a "similar rule [had] been applied to the control by the states of the sale of intoxicating liquors."[77] In this line of decisions subordinating contractual rights to the police power, Hughes saw indisputable evidence that the Contract Clause was now "qualified" by "the measure of control which the State retains . . . to safeguard the vital interests of its people."[78]

In the end, however, Hughes was forced to face the fact that *Blaisdell* differed from most previous cases in which the Court had upheld the destruction of contractual rights, in the sense that the Minnesota law involved *precisely* the type of debtor relief that the clause had been designed to bar. For this reason, there could be no couching the decision as a mere gloss on the original intent of the framers. Rather, the majority was forced to confront squarely the fact that a decision upholding the law would be, in effect, an endorsement of the "living Constitution" theory of constitutional interpretation. Hughes frankly admitted as much in the opinion's most famous passage. The critical consideration in interpreting the Contract Clause, Hughes wrote, was not the original intent of the framers, but rather "the essential content and spirit" of the text. The framers had intended the Constitution to endure for generations, and there was every reason to believe that they expected the text's vaguely worded provisions to assume new meanings "in the conditions of the later day."

> It is no answer to say that this public need was not apprehended a century ago, or to insist that what the provision of the Constitution meant to the vision of that day it must mean to the vision of our time. If by the statement that what the Constitution meant at the time of its adoption it means today, it is intended to say that the great clauses of the Constitution must be confined to the interpretation which the framers, with the conditions and outlook of their time, would have placed upon them, the statement carries its own refutation. It was to guard against such a narrow conception that Chief Justice Marshall uttered the memorable warning—"We must never forget that it is *a constitution* we are expounding . . . a constitution intended to endure for ages to come, and consequently, to be adapted to the various *crises* of human affairs."[79]

Hughes's assertion that the meaning of constitutional provisions should reflect "the vision of our time" is rightly viewed as marking a new era in constitutional interpretation.[80] It should therefore come as no surprise that the opinion has generated an enormous amount of scholarly commentary, much of which faults Hughes for apparently reading his own policy preferences into the text. Indeed, critics of the New Deal Court regularly describe the *Blaisdell* decision as the first step in a constitutional coup. Knowing full well that its preferred regulatory schemes were incompatible with the Constitution, the argument goes, the *Blaisdell* majority simply expunged those provisions, like the Contract Clause, which it deemed incompatible with the regulatory demands of a modern industrial economy.[81]

But while critics of the New Deal Court are correct to identify *Blaisdell* as a transformative decision, they have generally misunderstood the nature of the interpretive dilemma that confronted Hughes and the *Blaisdell* majority. Far from inventing an interpretive methodology in order to achieve a preferred policy outcome, Hughes was actually attempting to provide a new theoretical foundation for a clause that had long ago been severed from its original purposes. This was the point of Hughes's lengthy review of precedent, most of which focused on the post-*Stone* line of cases in which the Court had carved out a series of ever-wider police-power exceptions. Again and again, Hughes noted, the Court had held that the Contract Clause would not be permitted to trump "vital public interests"—even in cases, like the abolition of lottery grants, where the framers would have been unlikely to view the interests in question as "vital."[82] The only conceivable way of making sense of these decisions was to adopt a dynamic understanding of the constitutional enterprise in which the protection afforded contractual rights was constantly recalibrated to reflect the evolving moral sense of the community.[83] As Hughes put the point, it was "manifest from this review of our decisions that there has been a growing appreciation of public needs and of the necessity of finding ground for a rational compromise between individual rights and public welfare."[84] Given that the Court had already subordinated private rights to alleged public needs in dozens—if not hundreds—of post-Civil War rulings, there could be no principled basis for invalidating mortgage moratoria at a time when the entire "economic structure" appeared on the verge of collapse.[85] Thus, when Hughes declared that the Contract Clause should be understood in light of the "vision of our time," his point was less hermeneutical than factual. No intellectually honest reading of the Court's post-*Stone* Contract Clause decisions could deny that contractual rights were *already* subject to "a reservation of state power" to "protect the vital interests of the community."[86]

Nebbia v. New York, the decision typically cited as marking the demise of economic due process, similarly takes on new meaning when seen as the culmination of a decades-long process of doctrinal decay.[87] Handed down a mere two months after *Blaisdell, Nebbia* involved a due process challenge to a New York law that imposed price regulations on the dairy industry. In 1932, milk prices in New York had fallen below the cost of production, at which point the state legislature had created a control board with the power to fix prices so as to protect the state's dairy farmers. Shortly thereafter, Leo Nebbia, the operator of a Rochester grocery store, was convicted of selling milk at a price below that established by the control board. Traditionally, as we have seen, the Court had limited the state's power to fix prices to a relatively narrow category of businesses "affected with a public interest." The New York milk regulation scheme, like the ticket-scalping measure challenged in *Tyson and Brother v. Banton,* thus tested the limits of the states' police powers by imposing price regulations on an industry that was not traditionally classed in the "public" category.

But where the *Tyson* majority had stubbornly refused to blur the distinction between "public" and "private" economic concerns, the *Nebbia* majority all but endorsed Holmes's contention that these categories were essentially subjective.[88] Writing for the majority (composed of the same five justices as the *Blaisdell* majority), Justice Owen Roberts openly acknowledged that the dairy industry had never been regarded as a "public utility."[89] And yet Roberts insisted that this fact was irrelevant to the question of the New York law's constitutionality, since a frank review of precedent revealed that there existed no "closed class or category of businesses affected with a public interest."[90] Decisions such as *Otis v. Parker* and *Mugler v. Kansas* had established that the "Constitution does not guarantee the unrestricted privilege to engage in a business or to conduct it as one pleases." Even ancient professions could be "prohibited" or subjected to onerous "conditions" when necessary to protect the public welfare.[91] In the end, the notion of a "public" economic concern was simply "another way of saying that if one embarks in a business which public interest demands shall be regulated, he must know that regulation will ensue."[92] Roberts thus laid to rest the notion of an inviolable sphere of economic liberty, using language that, as Barry Cushman has written, was "more reminiscent of Holmes's *Tyson and Brother v. Banton* dissent than of any previous majority decision."[93] From this point forward, the states would be "free to adopt whatever economic policy may reasonably be deemed to promote public welfare, and to enforce that policy by legislation adapted to its purpose." So long as economic regulations were not "arbitrary" or "discriminatory," the courts would be "without authority to . . . override" them.[94]

Not surprisingly, critics of the New Deal revolution argue that the *Nebbia* Court's decision to jettison the public/private distinction had less to do with concern for the integrity of constitutional doctrine than with the majority's obvious preference for centralized economic planning.[95] The problem with this narrative, however, is that it shifts attention away from the critical question of how the concepts and categories associated with economic due process analysis became so discredited as to permit the *Nebbia* majority to simply discard them as unworkable. Stated otherwise, the characterization of *Nebbia* as sheer interpretive chicanery neglects the fact that much of the legal community was, by the early 1930s, genuinely convinced that the Fuller and White Courts had so mangled the jurisprudence of economic due process as to make a constitutional revolution all but inevitable. By this point, it was widely accepted that Holmes's *Tyson* dissent had effectively unmasked the "fictional conceptualism" and "legal apologetics" that undergirded the edifice of economic due process.[96] Again and again, scholars cited Holmes's discussion of liquor and lottery prohibition to make the point that the boundary between public and private economic concerns rested on nothing but the "fashionable conventions" of the moment.[97] Attempts to cast Justice Roberts in the role of villain are therefore misguided. If anything, Roberts's opinion merely acknowledged publicly what careful observers of the Court had known for years: that the *Lochner*-era economic due process framework had suffered an irreparable loss of legitimacy.[98]

"Sweet Morals and Bad Economics": Reexamining the Collapse of Dual Federalism

The traditional federal system met its demise in a series of Supreme Court rulings handed down in the period between 1937 and 1942. That the Court would endorse the constitutionality of the New Deal—and the reconfiguration of the federal system it entailed—was by no means foreordained, however. As late as the 1935–6 term, the Court used the basic formula articulated in *Hammer v. Dagenhart* to weaken or invalidate a number of key New Deal measures, including the Railroad Retirement Act, the National Industrial Recovery Act (NIRA), the Agricultural Adjustment Act (AAA), and the Guffey Coal Act.[99] Beginning in early 1937, however, the Court reversed course and adopted a more expansive understanding of the federal commerce power. Thus, in *NLRB v. Jones & Laughlin Steel* (1937), a bare majority of the Court upheld Congress's use of the commerce power to bar employers from discriminating against workers who attempted to join unions.[100] Two years later, in *Mulford v. Smith* (1939), the Court went further and upheld a revised version of the AAA, thus permitting Congress to regulate agricultural production under the commerce power. Finally, in *U.S. v. Darby* (1941), the Court upheld the Fair Labor Standards Act, which used the commerce power to establish a national minimum wage and to prohibit certain forms of child labor. The *Darby* ruling, which explicitly overturned *Hammer*, sounded the death knell of the traditional federal system; indeed, the *Darby* Court went so far as to endorse the Holmesian view that the Tenth Amendment was "but a truism" and not an independent check on Congress's enumerated powers.[101] The key conceptual move in the post-1937 decisions was the discovery that the constitutional category of "commerce" was no more susceptible to fixed definition than the categories that had previously undergirded economic due process.[102] Where the pre-1937 Court had struggled mightily to construct firewalls around the commerce power—insisting, for example, that it did not extend to the regulation of "production" or to activities that only "indirectly" affected interstate commerce—the New Deal Court ultimately concluded that all efforts to contain the commerce power through the "mechanical application of legal formulas" had failed.[103] In order to explain the collapse of the traditional federal system, then, one must first explain how the legal community—and ultimately the Court—came to believe that the traditional rules of American federalism "could no longer be faithfully and uncontroversially applied."[104]

From Hammer to the New Deal: The Academic Critique

Situated in the broader stream of constitutional development, the pivotal post-1937 Commerce Clause rulings can be seen as the final episode in an interpretive crisis that began with the turn-of-the century morals rulings and which escalated significantly following the Court's bitterly divided ruling in *Hammer v. Dagenhart*. In order to appreciate *Hammer*'s corrosive effect on the legitimacy of the Court's Commerce Clause jurisprudence, one need only glance at the academic reaction to the decision. In particular, it is important to note the near unanimity with which commentators endorsed Holmes's contention that the distinction between child labor, on the one hand, and the social "evils" of liquor, lotteries, and prostitution, on the other, rested on nothing more than the policy preferences of the Court's conservative majority. As a commentator in the *California Law Review* explained in late 1918, the *Hammer* ruling was blatantly at odds with a long line of decisions in which the Court had permitted Congress to regulate "lottery tickets and other articles innocuous in themselves" on the grounds that citizens of "the more morally-minded states" were entitled to protection against "the evil practices of less advanced communities." *Hammer* thus threatened the stability of the entire federal system, since it seemed to suggest that decisions upholding the federal regulation of liquor, lotteries, and prostitution had been "decided wrongly, [based] on no constitutional principle at all, but simply in response to a popular emotion."[105] A second commentator, writing in the *Harvard Law Review*, saw the *Hammer* opinion as confirmation that the distinction between "harmful" and "harmless" commodities was "largely a matter of opinion." Liquor had once been considered a "legitimate" commodity and lotteries had long been viewed as a "proper method of endowing schools and churches." But then the "judgment of the community" had "change[d]," and the Court had responded by permitting Congress to address these "evils" under the auspices of the commerce power. The majority's refusal to adopt the same deferential attitude in the case of the child labor law could only be described as arbitrary, since "gambling, fraud, poisoning, and drunkenness" had also been viewed as "exclusively subject to state control" prior to the early twentieth century.[106] Harvard's Thomas Reed Powell, a future adviser to the Roosevelt White House, echoed the charge in the *Southern Law Quarterly*. Contrasting the Court's efforts to keep "intoxicants from inebriants" with its refusal to protect "the young from the perils of the mine and mill," Powell could only conclude that the boundary between state and federal power was not determined by "the logic or the language of the Constitution." Rather, on the question of the extent of the commerce power, it was clear that the justices "think as for some reason they like to think."[107] The editors of the *New Republic* reiterated the point. Given that the Court had in so many of its "prior decisions" declared that "legislative motive or policy" had no bearing on the constitutionality of commercial regulations, one could only conclude that the child labor decision—the Court's worst effort "since the Dred Scott case"—had been driven by "intellectual bias" and a "fear of future social legislation."[108]

No scholar did more to popularize this skeptical view of the Court's Commerce Clause jurisprudence than Princeton's Edward Corwin. Arguably "the most important [legal] commentator" of the first half of the twentieth century, Corwin authored dozens of articles and several books describing a titanic clash between two theories of the American federal system.[109] The first theory, which Corwin labeled "cooperative federalism," viewed the state and federal spheres as overlapping and complementary. On this view, which Corwin saw reflected in the Court's rulings upholding federal liquor, lottery, and prostitution laws (as well as Holmes's *Hammer* dissent), there were no *substantive* limits to Congress's enumerated powers; rather, the enumerated powers could be used in "the service of" any "of the major objects of civilized society."[110] Opposed to this cooperative theory was the theory of "dual federalism," which

Corwin saw reflected in the Court's decisions invalidating federal child labor laws and other forms of industrial regulation. Under the theory of dual federalism, the state and federal spheres were mutually exclusive and the preexisting or "reserved" powers of the states were understood to constitute an independent check on Congress's enumerated powers.[111] A proponent of an activist federal government—and, like Powell, an adviser to the Roosevelt administration—Corwin viewed the "cooperative" theory of the federal system as the "historically authentic" view. Dual federalism, on the other hand, he dismissed as a mere "judicial gloss" on the constitutional text.[112] What was worse, the theory of dual federalism, according to Corwin, had the unfortunate and illogical effect of creating a "twilight zone" in the constitutional system—an area of commercial activity that could not be reached by either the states or the federal government. Thus, in the case of child labor, neither the states nor the federal government possessed the authority to bar the importation of child-made goods: any state that tried to do so would be impermissibly interfering with the federal commerce power; but, for Congress to do so would be to violate the state-controlled sphere of "production."[113]

What was novel in Corwin's analysis, however, was not his exegesis of these competing theories of federalism, but rather his insistence that the justices alternated between the two theories in an effort to reach desired outcomes. As a practical matter, the fact that there existed two competing theories of the federal system, both amply supported by precedent, meant that the Court enjoyed "the sovereign prerogative of choice" when it came to determining the scope of the commerce power: "In short, the existence of certain standardized, but conflicting views of the Constitution both confers upon the judges perfect freedom of decision where the issue before them is one that can be stated in the terms of such views, and at the same time sets up a defense against any attack based on conventional notions of judicial function, which is extremely difficult to break down."[114] Or as Corwin put the point at the height of the Court's confrontation with the New Deal, the theory of dual federalism was "one of a pair of horses which the Court has . . . saddled and bridled, depending on the direction it wishes to ride."[115]

One need not accept Corwin's conclusions regarding the indeterminacy of legal doctrine to grasp the power of his critique as a description of the state of Commerce Clause jurisprudence in the 1920s and early 1930s. Even if Corwin was wrong to characterize dual federalism as a mere "gloss" on the constitutional text, he was almost certainly correct in arguing that the Fuller and White Courts had developed two distinct readings of the Commerce Clause—one stemming primarily from morals cases, the other primarily from cases involving economic regulations—that were becoming increasingly difficult to reconcile.[116] He was right, moreover, to point out that the Court had explicitly denied the potential existence of "twilight zones" in the constitutional system when it had permitted the federal government to aid the states in ridding themselves of liquor, lotteries, and the "white slave" traffic; indeed, decisions such as *Champion v. Ames* and *Hoke v. U.S.* were bottomed on the premise that, where the states had proved unable or unwilling to defeat a great social evil, the Constitution did not bar the federal government—"the only power competent to that end"—from doing so.[117] That the Court was unwilling to adopt the same pragmatic reading of the Commerce Clause in cases involving labor and industrial regulation—thus creating precisely the sort of twilight zone it had refused to accept in the morals cases—suggested pure opportunism. In the words of Thomas Reed Powell, Corwin's analysis of the Court's post-1900 Commerce Clause rulings demonstrated that "[t]he holy name of states' rights is easily forgotten when employers wish their laborers sober and unctuously invoked when they wish their laborers young. The name is a name to conjure with only when convenient."[118]

By the time of the Supreme Court's confrontation with the New Deal, Corwin's skeptical take on the Court's Commerce Clause jurisprudence was thoroughly ingrained in the progressive legal consciousness. Indeed, supporters of the New Deal consistently characterized their struggle against the Court as a clash between two readings of the Commerce Clause, one stemming from the straightforward nationalism of the post-*Champion* morals rulings (a reading the New Dealers traced to John Marshall's *Gibbons v. Ogden* opinion), the other springing from the tortured logic of *Hammer*. Given that the Court had repeatedly refused to impose substantive limits on Congress's enumerated powers in the post-*Champion* line of decisions, the argument went, there could be no principled basis for preventing Congress from using the commerce power to regulate employment relations, coal production, or agricultural outputs. Thus, Theodore Cousens, an academic supporter of the New Deal, declared in 1934 that the Court tended to "tolerate the regulation of interstate matters when it liked (as in cases involving morality . . . such as the Lottery case and the Mann Act cases)," while "refus[ing] to tolerate it when it did not like (as in cases involving social [i.e., industrial] interests primarily)." As a result, the commerce power was now virtually "unlimited in the moral field" but strictly circumscribed in the area of industrial regulation. This state of affairs would not likely endure, however, due to the patently arbitrary nature of the distinction between moral and economic subjects of regulation. In short, "[p]rostitution and lotteries" were "evil things, but no less evil is a system of commerce which drags down wage scales and work standards all over the Union to feed the callous greed of a few backward states."[119] In a similar vein, John Dickinson, who was soon to be named Assistant Attorney General and charged with defending the AAA and other New Deal measures before the Court, declared in early 1935 that only "one outstanding case" raised any "doubt[s]" as to the plenary nature of the federal commerce power. *Hammer v. Dagenhart* was a thin reed on which to base opposition to the New Deal, however, since the Court had previously upheld such indirect uses of the commerce power as "the prohibition of lottery tickets, impure food, and prize fight films," and Dickinson could perceive no basis for distinguishing "economic subjects" from "moral and sanitary subjects."[120] Also writing in 1935, Morris Cohen used an essay in *The Nation* to argue for the constitutionality of the NIRA—and also to repeat his familiar claim that the image of a passive judiciary giving life to the eternal principles of the framers was a "childish fiction." As evidence of the inevitable evolution of constitutional meaning, Cohen cited the "judge-made" determination that Congress's commerce power could reach liquor, but not other traditional "police" subjects such as insurance contracts and child labor—a determination that, "whether justified or not by [its] practical consequences," was not based on "anything written in the Constitution."[121]

To be sure, not all commentators accepted the New Dealers' contention that the dual federalism line of rulings represented a modern-day gloss on the constitutional text. Many, in fact, viewed the Court's conservative block as the heirs of the framers while dismissing Corwin and the New Dealers as dangerous radicals.[122] Nor should one ignore the fact that plausible arguments *did* exist for distinguishing the landmark regulatory experiments of the New Deal period from earlier measures that had used the commerce power to indirectly reach activities that were traditionally classified as "police" matters. (In many of the critical New Deal cases, for example, Congress and the Roosevelt administration were claiming authority not only to reach all items that *moved* in interstate commerce, but also to regulate intrastate activities that substantially *affected* interstate commerce.) And yet, by the mid-1930s many Americans were finding it difficult to take seriously those who advanced subtle doctrinal distinctions to challenge the constitutionality of the New Deal. Simply put, the undeniable existence of an expansive, Court-sanctioned federal regulatory apparatus dedicated to the control of *morality*—perhaps the most quintessential of traditional state functions—provided powerful support for the New Dealers' contention that the choice between "cooperative" and "dual" federalism was essentially arbitrary. As a pair of contributors explained in the "police power" entry of the 1934 *Encyclopedia of the Social Sciences,* Congress had "grafted on" to its enumerated powers a "federal police power," the very idea of which would have been "an anomaly to Marshall, Taney, Bradley, and Field." Citing federal regulation of lotteries, obscene matter, narcotic drugs, and oleomargarine, the authors concluded that the federal government was now possessed "of a power which was once but another name for 'the residual sovereignty' of the states."[123] Anyone who at this point still doubted that Congress had, in fact, appropriated the states' traditional role of regulating morality could consult Charles and William Beard's massive reference tome, *The American Leviathan* (1931), an overview of the federal bureaucracy which contained no less than thirteen pages on federal regulation of liquor, lotteries, prostitution, obscenity, and other threats to "public morals."[124]

But criticism of the Court's mercurial federalism jurisprudence was not limited to academic circles. In 1937, on the eve of the Court's dramatic reinterpretation of the Commerce Clause, *Time* magazine published a satirical essay in which a fictional Supreme Court justice attempted to explain the definition of "interstate commerce" to a confused public.[125] The author of the essay, a law professor named Thomas Cowan, began by admitting that many Americans were likely perplexed by the Court's decision to uphold the 1932 Federal Kidnapping Act as a valid "commercial" regulation while simultaneously invalidating the NIRA, the AAA, and the Guffey Coal Act for exceeding the scope of the commerce power.[126] To the layperson, it no doubt appeared that the latter statutes had far more to do with commerce than did the federal kidnapping statute. But this was only because the public held the mistaken belief that "commerce has to do with trade, business, commercial enterprise, adventure involving profit or loss." In reality, kidnappers were more appropriate targets for commercial regulation than industrialists, since "precedent was abundant" that the commerce power was primarily a device for reaching moral deviants, such as prostitutes and car thieves. Paradoxically, the types of activities included in the popular definition of "commerce" were virtually the only activities that Congress could *not* reach with its commerce power: "For example, it would never do to presume that the United States

Steel Corporation is engaged in interstate commerce. Similarly, we could not presume that dealers in live poultry"—the industry at heart of the NIRA decision—"are engaged in interstate commerce. In fact, we cannot conceive how this could even be proved. If Congress, by statute should presume that the products of the bituminous coal industry"—the target of the Guffey Coal Act—"move in interstate commerce, we should have no hesitation in setting the act aside." Of course, Cowan's essay played fast and loose with the facts of the cases it discussed, and also with the doctrinal underpinnings of the Court's decisions. But on a polemical level, it was highly effective. As *Time*'s legal editor observed in comments appended to the essay, Cowan had effectively demonstrated "just how loose has been the courts' usage of this constitutional phrase, 'commerce . . . among the several States.'" Cowan had shown that the Court was often "willing to expand the meaning of 'interstate commerce' when a law involves 'morals,' but [had] narrowly circumscribed Congress' power where business and industry were concerned."[127]

By the mid-1930s, then, there existed a widespread perception that the Court's Commerce Clause jurisprudence had come to reflect, in the words of a pair of commentators in the *Virginia Law Review*, "a peculiar blend of sweet morals and bad economics."[128] From the perspective of constitutional development, this fact is significant because it suggests a new way of viewing the Court's encounter with the New Deal. In particular, it suggests that one reason why the Court ultimately failed to prevent a reconfiguration of the federal system was because the doctrinal tools necessary to accomplish this task had already been thoroughly discredited. Viewed in this light, the Court's post-1937 shift to an expansive conception of the federal commerce power was less a response to naked political pressure than a frank admission that the turn-of-the-century morals rulings had in fact undermined the philosophical foundations of the traditional federal system.

The Transformative Commerce Clause Decisions

The extent to which the New Deal Court was haunted by the post-*Champion* line of morals precedents becomes evident when we turn to the cases themselves. A review of the government's briefs in the major Commerce Clause cases decided between 1935 and 1942 reveals that Roosevelt administration lawyers kept the morals precedents constantly before the eyes of the justices. In fact, beginning with the 1936 cases of *U.S. v. Butler* (challenging the constitutionality of the AAA) and *Carter v. Carter Coal* (challenging the constitutionality of the Guffey Coal Act), the administration recruited Professors Corwin and Powell to assist in making the case for an expansive conception of Congress's enumerated powers.[129] Not surprisingly, Corwin and Powell steered the administration towards what they regarded as the weak link in the doctrinal edifice of dual federalism, namely, the dozen or so cases in which the Court had upheld the use of the commerce power to achieve such obviously non-commercial purposes as combating drunkenness, gambling, prostitution, and auto theft.

Thus, the bulk of the government's 300-page brief in *Carter Coal* was dedicated to rebutting the claim that the commerce power could not be used to regulate labor relations in the coal industry, since mining belonged within the inherently "local" or state-controlled sphere of "production." The flaw in this theory, according to the brief, was that it rested on "a complete confusion between a governmental *power* on the one hand, and the *subject matter . . . or objective* for which the power may be exercised, on the other."[130] In light of *Champion v. Ames*, the administration argued, it was clear that nothing in the Constitution confined the use of the commerce power to the promotion of "commercial" objectives. Nor, in light of that ruling, could one claim that the states' police powers constituted an independent check on the commerce power: "Congress has no general power to protect . . . morals . . . and, more specifically, no power to give such protection by the suppression of lotteries. On the other hand, each state, within its own limits, may employ its police power to suppress lotteries. Nevertheless, this Court has held that the commerce power may be used with the objective of suppressing lotteries so far as that objective may be obtained by regulations of commerce, and the regulations are not invalid because the suppression of lotteries is their objective."[131] If an inviolable sphere of inherently "local" activities existed, in other words, one would expect to find lotteries within that sphere. That the Court had plainly denied the existence of any such sphere in upholding the federal lottery law—as well as subsequent "commercial" regulations aimed at prostitution and auto theft—suggested that neither Congress's "objective" in passing the Guffey Coal Act, nor the extent of the Act's interference with state regulations of "production," should bear on the latter measure's constitutionality. Rather, the sole question at issue in *Carter Coal* was whether labor strife in the coal industry bore a "real and substantial relation" to interstate commerce—a question that the administration brief argued was easily answered in the affirmative, given the industry's integral role in the national economy.[132]

These arguments failed to convince the Court in *Carter Coal*, as a bare majority—composed of the conservative "Four Horsemen" (Justices Butler, McReynolds, Van Devanter, and Sutherland) and Justice Roberts—found that the Guffey Coal Act was directed at purely "local controversies and evils" and thus beyond the scope of the commerce power.[133] And yet *Carter Coal*, as it turned out, would be the last time that the Court would invalidate a New Deal measure as exceeding the scope of the commerce power. That the justices were aware of the problematic tension between the competing *Champion* and *Hammer* lines of precedent became clear the following year in the critical but little-remembered case of *Kentucky Whip & Collar v. Illinois Central Railroad*, decided in January 1937.[134] *Kentucky Whip* involved a Commerce Clause challenge to the Ashurst-Sumners Act, a recently enacted federal law barring the interstate transportation of convict-made goods where such transportation was undertaken for the purpose of violating state law. (Many states had banned the sale of imported convict-made goods, which were believed to depress prices and wages, and the federal law was intended to aid the states in making these bans effective.) The measure was a carbon copy of the federal bans on interstate transportation of liquor which Congress had enacted prior to the adoption of the Eighteenth Amendment and which the Court had upheld in *Clark Distilling Co. v. Western Maryland Railroad Co.* and *U.S. v. Hill*. Like the earlier liquor laws, the prison labor law reflected the theory that Congress could use its commerce power to prevent miscreants from using the "instrumentalities of commerce" to undermine the police regulations of the states. But the Ashurst-Sumners Act also bore a strong resemblance to the Owen-Keating child labor law, in that it penalized the interstate shipment of commodities that were in themselves harmless—and arguably with the aim of affecting *production* processes in the states (the chief difference being that the prison labor statute imposed penalties only in cases where the importation of convict-made goods would violate state law).

Kentucky Whip thus provided a perfect opportunity for the administration to urge a narrow reading of *Hammer*. What distinguished the new prison labor law from the invalidated child labor statute, according to the government's brief, was that the latter measure had been sloppily drafted: instead of professing to target an evil involving the "instrumentalities of commerce"—such as depressed wages resulting from child labor—its authors had focused on the purely "local" evil of child labor itself. The authors of the prison labor law, in contrast, had followed the lead of congressional anti-liquor crusaders in emphasizing the extraterritorial consequences (namely, depressed prices and wages) of prison labor.[135] In essence, the brief urged the Court to set aside the distinction between "harmful" and "harmless" commodities—a distinction most commentators viewed as central to the *Hammer* holding—and to focus instead on whether interstate transportation of the commodities in question contributed to a particular "harm" or "evil" in the state of destination.[136] This way of reading *Hammer* was not entirely implausible; the majority opinion had in fact suggested that one reason why Congress could prohibit the interstate transportation of lottery tickets and women was because these "traffics" in items that were in themselves harmless nonetheless contributed to "the accomplishment of harmful results."[137] But the argument raised serious questions about the sorts of "harmful results" that could justify federal regulation under the commerce power. If this category now included depressed prices and wages resulting from substandard labor conditions, then there would seem to be little room left in the constitutional system for an exclusively state-controlled sphere of "production."[138]

In the end, the parallel to federal liquor regulation was too perfect even for the Four Horsemen to ignore, and the result was a unanimous decision upholding the Ashurst-Sumners Act.[139] The price of this unanimity was a rather narrow opinion, written by Chief Justice Hughes, that stopped short of explicitly overturning *Hammer*. But in the process of upholding the prison labor law, Hughes so weakened *Hammer* as to virtually expunge it from the Commerce Clause canon. Acknowledging that liquor and stolen automobiles, like convict-made goods, were "useful and harmless" in themselves, Hughes denied that the question of whether a particular commodity was inherently "harmful" had any bearing on Congress's power to prohibit its interstate transportation. Congress's power to prohibit transportation, Hughes insisted, did not depend on the harmful nature of the commodities themselves, but rather on the question of whether their transportation contributed to a harmful "result."[140] In the case at bar, it was clear that permitting "the sale of convict-made goods in competition with the products of free labor" contributed to the "evil" of depressing wages for "free laborers."[141] Congress was therefore free to prohibit the interstate transportation of such articles, either with the aim of "preventing the frustration of valid state laws," or simply because of a desire to further "the fundamental interests of free labor."[142] Hughes's decision to follow the administration's lead and transfer the "harmful" label from the commodities themselves to their effects—and to include the purely economic harm of depressed wages within this category—suggested that the disjunction between the two strands of Commerce Clause jurisprudence could not long endure. Summarizing the decision, *Time* and other major media outlets concluded that the Court had "apparently given Congress carte blanche" to forbid the interstate movement of goods produced under substandard labor conditions, thus "rais[ing] hopes in all those who want to revive [the] NRA."[143]

Any doubts about whether the Court had, in fact, begun to distance itself from the *Hammer* majority's conception of the federal system were put to rest four months later in *NLRB v. Jones & Laughlin Steel*, when a bare majority of the Court upheld the Wagner Act's use of the commerce power to impose collective bargaining requirements on employers throughout the nation.[144] Again writing for the majority, Hughes went so far as to endorse the administration's argument that even "productive" activities could be reached under the commerce power whenever such activities bore a "close and substantial relation" to interstate commerce, so that "their control is essential or appropriate to protect . . . commerce from burdens and obstructions."[145] But while *Jones & Laughlin* is rightly remembered as a landmark decision, the fact that it was handed down shortly after President Roosevelt's threat to "pack" the Court with sympathetic justices—thus suggesting a politically motivated "switch in time"—has perhaps led scholars to exaggerate its significance. In reality, *Jones & Laughlin* left a great deal of uncertainly in its wake, in part because Hughes's opinion repeatedly emphasized the massive *size* of the steel company to make the point that the company's labor relations had an inherent—or "direct"—impact on interstate commerce.[146] The decision thus left in place the test of "direct" versus "indirect" effects as a limit on the commerce power; and for this reason, it stopped short of the wholesale federalism revolution advocated by Corwin, Powell, and other administration allies.[147]

In order to set the "second" New Deal on a secure footing, the administration needed the Court to expand its definition of "interstate commerce" to include even activities that were not directly related to the movement or transportation of goods in national markets. Put differently, the New Dealers needed the Court to acknowledge that under modern economic conditions there could be no fixed set of activities that were inherently intrastate in nature, since even small-scale productive activities, when viewed in the aggregate, exerted a significant impact on national markets. An opportunity to press this argument yet again arose in *Mulford v. Smith* (1939), when tobacco farmers in Georgia and Florida challenged the constitutionality of the

Agricultural Adjustment Act (AAA) of 1938.[148] The original AAA of 1933, which reduced agricultural production by imposing acreage restrictions on the nation's farmers (who were then compensated through a tax on processors), had been invalidated in *U.S. v. Butler* (1936).[149] The revised AAA was also directed at the problem of overproduction, but the tax on processors was dropped and the supply of agricultural commodities was regulated indirectly through marketing quotas rather than acreage restrictions. Despite these changes, the tobacco growers maintained, reasonably enough, that the true aim of the legislation was to control the amount of grain and tobacco produced by the nation's farmers; and any attempt to achieve this objective, they argued, even through the indirect method of marketing quotas, amounted to an impermissible interference with the states' reserved powers.

The administration responded to these objections by first denying that the revised AAA had in fact imposed any restrictions on agricultural production. In particular, the brief pointed out that the revised AAA, unlike its predecessor, imposed no restrictions whatsoever on the amount of tobacco a farmer could plant or harvest; instead, it aimed to stabilize the tobacco market by imposing limits on how much tobacco a given producer could *sell*. Later in the brief, however, the administration lawyers abandoned this line of argument in favor of the broader—and by now familiar—claim that the idea of an inherently state-controlled sphere of "production" was ultimately untenable.[150] "Even if it were true that . . . marketing quotas necessarily affected production," the brief argued, "it would not follow that the revised AAA had exceeded the scope of the commerce power." The Court's endorsement of federal "liquor laws, and the Lottery, White Slave, and Kidnapping Acts" made clear that "collateral" interference with the states' police powers did "not determine the constitutionality of legislation."[151] Given that the Court had refused to draw the line at federal morals laws, it was difficult to perceive any principled basis for erecting an immovable barrier around "production." And indeed, drawing the line at precisely this point produced a rather absurd sort of "commerce" power—one that could reach prostitutes and lottery promoters but not large-scale economic problems such as agricultural overproduction:

> That stabilization of the flow of commodities in interstate commerce and of the prices at which such goods are marketed for the benefit of producers and consumers, is an appropriate purpose under the commerce clause cannot be gainsaid. . . . The prevention of these economic effects upon commerce and upon those engaged in commerce is *much more closely related to the*

underlying objectives of the commerce clause than protection of the public morals against lotteries, or prostitution, or [automobile] theft, or kidnapping, or the protection of the public health against diseased livestock, or adulterated foods and drugs. . . . *The original purpose of the commerce clause was primarily economic,* and the objectives of the most important commerce legislation enacted by Congress, like those of this Act, [have been] to improve the economic well-being of the nation.[152]

Even if one conceded that the scope of the commerce power was governed by the original intent of the framers, that is, the AAA's marketing quotas were surely more closely related to the goal of protecting national markets than were the federal lottery or prostitution laws.[153] This was not to suggest that the morals cases were wrongly decided: they had targeted items and people that moved across state lines in the course of corrupting public morality, and a strong case could be made that interstate movement was fair game for regulation under the commerce power, regardless of Congress's ultimate purposes. But to hold that the commerce power could reach gambling but not agricultural overproduction—on the grounds that productive activities were by definition excluded from interstate commerce—was, to say the least, a difficult position to defend. A more plausible way of defining the extent of the commerce power, the brief suggested, was to focus on the regulated activity's aggregate effect on the national economy; and given the integrated nature of the twentieth-century economy—with its "comingling of interstate and intrastate operations"—there could be little doubt that intrastate sales of agricultural commodities exerted a significant impact on national markets.[154] In closing, the brief dealt with *Hammer* by observing that, in light of *Kentucky Whip,* it appeared the Court had finally "abandoned the principles which governed the unfortunate decision of a bare majority . . . in *Hammer* . . . and that that case may no longer be regarded as an authority."[155]

By the time *Mulford* reached the Court in the spring of 1939, two of the Four Horsemen (Sutherland and Van Devanter) had retired and been replaced by Roosevelt appointees, meaning there was little doubt that the Court would ultimately uphold the revised AAA. In the end, the justices divided 7–2 in favor of the measure's constitutionality, with Justice Roberts writing for the majority. But while Roberts's opinion offered perhaps the broadest reading of the commerce power to date—declaring that any regulation that prevented "the flow of commerce from working harm to the people of the nation . . . is within the competence of Congress"—the majority again stopped short of explicitly overturning *Hammer*.[156] Perhaps the most revealing feature of the decision, then, was not the majority opinion but rather the almost perfunctory nature of the dissent. Writing for himself and Justice McReynolds, Justice Butler complained that the government's case for an expansive commerce power was based "merely" on *Champion, Hoke,* and the dozen or so additional cases in which the Court had upheld the use of the commerce power to regulate health and morals.[157] But these decisions, according to Butler, were narrow rulings that were based entirely on the peculiar "nature and character" of the subjects regulated. As such, they gave "no support to the view that Congress has power generally to prohibit or limit, as it may choose, transportation in interstate commerce of corn, cotton, rice, tobacco, or wheat."[158] Tellingly, Butler did not offer so much as a hint of what the philosophical foundation for this distinction might be.[159] That the dissenters declined to offer any theoretical justification whatsoever for allowing Congress to impinge upon the local sphere of "morals" while simultaneously barring it from the local sphere of "production" suggested that even the remaining Horsemen were aware that the conceptual foundations of dual federalism were crumbling.

The ultimate collapse of the traditional federal system came two years later in *U.S. v. Darby* (1941).[160] *Darby* involved a Commerce Clause challenge to the Fair Labor Standards Act (FLSA) of 1938, which invoked the commerce power to establish a national minimum wage, require overtime pay in certain industries, and prohibit most forms of child labor. The new labor regulations, which applied only to workers who were engaged in "production for interstate commerce," were enforced in part through a ban on the interstate shipment of goods manufactured under substandard labor conditions. The *Darby* litigation began when a Georgia lumber company challenged the Act's wage and hours provisions on the grounds that the FLSA was not a bona fide commercial regulation but yet another covert attempt to invade the state-controlled sphere of "manufacturing" or "production." Naturally enough, the company's written brief relied heavily on *Hammer,* a ruling that counsel declared to be "directly in point." But while the brief dutifully recited the central holding of *Hammer*—that Congress's "quasi police power" was only applicable in cases where there was something "harmful" in the "goods themselves, or in an incidental activity"—its authors seemed almost embarrassed to be building their case on so flimsy a foundation. *Hammer,* they acknowledged, had "been severely criticized," in part because the majority opinion was "burdened with a brilliant dissenting opinion" by Justice Holmes. Moreover, Holmes and other critics of the decision were correct to note that the holding had not been mandated by the "express" text of the Constitution, at least not by "any solitary constitutional provision." Rather, it seemed to have "aris[en] by implication" from a "combination of provisions" that pointed to a narrow reading of the commerce power. Remarkably, in a brief that relied almost exclusively on the *Hammer* precedent, the best that could be said of the decision was that the majority had not been afraid to "blaze" a novel "line of demarcation" in order to prevent a "national domination" of the states' police powers.[161]

In response, the government again cited the post-*Champion* line of Commerce Clause decisions to make the point that the Court had repeatedly endorsed the use of the commerce power "to accomplish objectives the promotion of which is not expressly conferred on Congress by the Constitution and which were appropriate objections of state legislation." Thus, the Court had sanctioned the use of the commerce power to "suppress lotteries," "promote health," "promote morality," and "to prevent theft of property or persons." "In each of these cases the statutes were sustained because, irrespective of their various objectives, it was interstate commerce that was regulated."[162] From this, it followed that even "productive" activities could be reached under the commerce power, so long as a plausible link to interstate commerce could be identified. In the case of the Fair Labor Standards Act, Congress had acted with the aims of "regulat[ing] interstate competition, . . . avoid[ing] the spread of harmful conditions [i.e., substandard labor conditions] by reason of the channels of interstate commerce, and to prevent labor disputes." These aims were "commercial in the strictest sense," and could be advanced by federal legislation regardless of any collateral impact on the states' police powers.[163] There remained, of course, the problem of *Hammer*. But in light of recent decisions it appeared that the *Hammer* majority's "narrow reading" of *Champion* and its progeny was no longer good law.[164]

Writing for a unanimous Court—the last of the Four Horsemen had by this point left the bench—Justice Stone not only endorsed the constitutionality of the FLSA but also took the opportunity to characterize the entire theory of dual federalism as a modern-day gloss on the constitutional text. Prior to the early twentieth century, he declared, it was accepted that "[w]hatever their motive and purpose, regulations of commerce which [did] not infringe upon some constitutional prohibition [were] within the power conferred on Congress by the commerce clause."[165] Then came *Hammer*, an anomalous decision that—as "Mr. Justice Holmes" had pointed out in "now classic dissent"—was based on a "novel" doctrine that was "unsupported by any provision of the Constitution."[166] *Hammer* had "not been followed," however, with the result that "such vitality, as a precedent, as it [once] had has long since been exhausted." The child labor decision, Stone declared, "should be and now is overruled."[167] Having thus purged *Hammer* from the constitutional canon, the way was open for Stone to expunge the doctrine of dual federalism as well, which he did in the opinion's most famous passage:

> The [Tenth] amendment states but a truism that all is retained which has not been surrendered. There is nothing in the history of its adoption to suggest that it was more than declaratory of the relationship between the national and state governments as it had been established by the Constitution before the amendment or that its purpose was other than to allay fears that the new national government might seek to exercise powers not granted, and that the states might not be able to exercise fully their reserved powers. From the beginning and for many years the amendment has been construed as not depriving the national government of authority to resort to all means for the exercise of a granted power which are appropriate and plainly adapted to the permitted end.[168]

With this declaration, the reconstituted Court of the early 1940s announced the arrival of a new epoch in the history of American federalism. Henceforth, the Court would no longer inquire into whether the "motive . . . or . . . effect" of a given regulation was "to control . . . production" or otherwise interfere with the "police powers" of the states.[169] Nor would the scope of the commerce power be limited to the regulation of activities that hindered the *movement* of goods in interstate commerce. Rather, it now appeared that the commerce power could reach any activity that, when viewed in the aggregate, could be said to exert a substantial effect on national markets—a test broad enough to encompass even the most quintessential of "productive" activities.[170]

Not surprisingly, Justice Stone's *Darby* opinion, with its expansive conception of federal authority, has long functioned as a lightning rod for controversy. To supporters of the New Deal, including Corwin, *Darby* was an inspired decision that purged American constitutional law once and for all of the "laissez faire" ideals that the judicial supporters of "Big Business" had grafted onto the constitutional text. The effect of *Darby* was merely to take constitutional law "straight back to . . . Marshall's opinions," with their "latitudinarian construction" of the necessary and proper clause and "uncompromising application" of the supremacy clause.[171] Modern-day critics of the New Deal Court, in contrast, view *Darby* as a "cavalier" ruling that gave "back-of-the-hand treatment" to the Founding-era ideal of "enumerated powers."[172] What is easily overlooked in this battle of competing "originalisms" is that *Darby* was merely the final decision in a half-century-long process of doctrinal decay. To be sure, modern-day critics of *Darby* are on solid ground when they challenge Stone's characterization of dual federalism as a "novel" doctrine. But even if we accept that the *Hammer* Court's characterization of the federal system was broadly consistent with the ideals of the framers—and a strong case can be made that it was—this does not mean that Stone was wrong to describe *Hammer* as an anomalous decision *at the time it was decided.* For by 1918 the Court had already endorsed federal regulation of a range of activities that had long been considered the exclusive province of the states. As a result, when the *Darby* Court dismissed the doctrines announced in *Hammer* as having "long since ceased to have force," it was able to support this claim with numerous Commerce Clause decisions handed down *before* the child labor case.[173] To criticize the Hughes Court for abandoning the ideals of the framers, then, is to ignore the fact that it was the Fuller and White Courts who first opened the door to federal regulation of traditional "police" subjects. Had the early-twentieth-century Court not opened this door, Holmes could not have penned his "now classic" *Hammer* dissent, and the *Darby* Court could not have so easily expunged the theory of dual federalism from the constitutional canon.

This is not to suggest that the demise of the traditional federal system resulted solely from the early-twentieth-century Court's accommodation of federal morals legislation. Certainly, the federal system was by this point buffeted by a host of economic pressures, most of which pushed in the direction of centralization; and the added pressure of the greatest economic crisis in American history was bound to produce significant doctrinal adjustments, with or without the precedent of federal morals regulation. Moreover, it should be noted that federal morals laws were far from the only precedents available to support a more expansive conception of federal regulatory authority. As Howard Gillman has reminded us, constitutional reformers rarely confess to a lack of precedential support for their endeavors. In the case of the New Deal, the Roosevelt administration and its allies "used every idea at their disposal to make their case"—from decisions upholding wartime emergency measures, to the turn-of-the-century Court's "stream of commerce" decisions endorsing the federal regulation of meatpackers and stockyards.[174]

Notwithstanding these caveats, however, the evidence examined in this chapter suggests that the morals precedents deserve a far more prominent role in the story of the New Deal revolution than they have traditionally received. It is no accident that virtually every argument for an expansive conception of the commerce power advanced during the New Deal period began by quoting from Justice Harlan's opinion in *Champion v. Ames*. Supporters of an expanded regulatory state knew that the tension between the competing visions of the federal system articulated in *Champion* and *Hammer* resonated on a level that other, perhaps more technically on point precedents, did not. If the federal *commerce* power could reach liquor, lotteries, prostitution, and adultery, then common sense suggested that the same power should be capable of reaching nationally significant economic ills, from labor relations to agricultural overproduction.

Indeed, one need only revisit Justice Fuller's dissenting opinion in *Champion* or Thomas Cooley's early 1890s warning about the likely consequences of "indirect" federal lottery regulation to recall that the New Dealers were merely exploiting a doctrinal disjunction that had troubled legal commentators for a generation. Writing some four decades before *Darby*, both men predicted with uncanny accuracy the subsequent course of the Court's federalism jurisprudence. In its haste to rid the nation of the lottery evil, Fuller complained, the Court had "enlarged" the "scope of the commerce clause" to accommodate "present views of the public interest." But having once embraced the idea that the nation's "fundamental law is flexible," there could be no returning to an era of strictly enumerated powers. The Court would constantly be met with demands "to ease the shoe where it pinches," until nothing but the empty shell of the framers' constitutional vision remained.[175]

Conclusion

The Evangelical Origins of the Modern Constitutional Order

> It is amusing to see in the law how in a century what was thought
> natural and wholesome may become anathema—like rum and the
> lottery—but they generally are argued about as if the
> present view was an eternal truth.
>
> —Oliver Wendell Holmes, Jr., to Harold Laski (February 1, 1925)[1]

To a remarkable extent, American constitutional theory is even today dominated by questions surrounding the legitimacy of the New Deal-era constitutional revolution. Indeed, the basic terms of the debate have remained more
or less stagnant since the 1930s. On one side, critics of the modern order
echo the complaints of the New Deal Court's Four Horsemen, lamenting the
collapse of economic rights, the uncontrolled expansion of federal power, and
the judiciary's disregard for the original intent of the framers. In this telling,
the story of the constitutional revolution is a story of national corruption. In
thrall to the possibilities of modern science and bureaucratic administration,
or perhaps merely panicked at the prospect of economic collapse, Americans
abandoned the ideals of the framers in favor of a "living" Constitution that
would permit state and federal governments to respond to novel social and
economic ills without regard for traditional constitutional limitations.[2] On
the other side, defenders of the modern order offer variations on the themes
of Holmes, Pound, and Corwin. From this perspective, the collapse of the
traditional order was both popularly sanctioned and probably inevitable. The
constitutional revolution thus reflects the "magic of the dialogic system of
determining constitutional meaning." Voters and elected officials expressed
their displeasure with the courts' reading of the constitutional text, and the
judiciary eventually came "into line with the considered views of the American public."[3] Opposition to the interpretive shifts of the 1930s, on this view,

can only be explained by a misguided and hidebound attachment to the technicalities of the Article V amendment process.[4]

Although the present study cannot settle the question of whether the constitutional changes of the 1930s should be regarded as legitimate, it does call into question a number of critical assumptions that inform the contemporary debate. The first concerns the intellectual provenance of the "living" Constitution. Writing more than seventy years ago, Morton White traced the origins of the idea of a flexible or "organic" fundamental law to American pragmatist philosophers who, in turn, drew inspiration from Darwin and Hegel. Focusing on Holmes, in particular, White concluded that the jurisprudential revolution of the 1920s and 1930s was merely one front in a broader "revolt against formalism" in which economists, historians, and political scientists simultaneously purged their disciplines of the rigid, a priori concepts and categories that had traditionally guided scholarly inquiry. The framers' conception of the constitutional order, White argued, was swept away by the same intellectual tidal wave that buried (for the time being) the political economy of Adam Smith and the political philosophy of John Locke.[5]

The evidence presented above, while not inconsistent with White's account, provides some crucial missing context—and in so doing calls into question some of the more extravagant normative conclusions that scholars have drawn from his interpretive framework. In particular, critics of the modern order have long described the interpretive revolution of the 1930s as a constitutional coup engineered by a small cabal of progressive intellectuals. Thus, we are told that the impetus behind the early twentieth-century "movement to abandon the Founders' Constitution" came not from the broader public or even elected officials, but from "the scholarly community." Swept up in "the scientific enthusiasms of the day," scholars including Woodrow Wilson and Edward Corwin led the charge to replace the framers' "Newtonian conception of constitutional law and politics" with a "Darwinian" or "evolutionary approach" to constitutional meaning.[6] Having thus freed themselves from the "binding force of language" the way was open for progressive jurists to "rewrite" the Constitution—that is, to turn the "literal provisions" of the text "into their contrarieties" for the sake of accommodating a vastly expanded regulatory state.[7] Pressing the point further, Richard Epstein writes that early-twentieth-century progressives "saw in constitutional interpretation the opportunity to rewrite a Constitution that showed at every turn the influence of John Locke and James Madison into a different Constitution, which reflected the wisdom of the leading intellectual reformers of their own time." Only by ex-punging property protections and federalism constraints from the text could progressive jurists ensure that "their vision of the managed economy [would] take precedence in all areas of life."[8]

The narrative of the progressive "rewriting" of the Constitution is, to say the least, greatly complicated by the evidence examined in this study. There is, of course, no denying that progressive intellectuals shaped their constitutional theories with an eye towards the emergent regulatory state.[9] But the idea of the living Constitution was neither invented for the purpose of furthering the progressive economic agenda, nor foisted on the nation by academics searching for a new arena in which to apply the insights of pragmatist philosophers. Rather, it emerged at a very early point in the nation's history, when Revival-era evangelicals found their moral agenda blocked by the rigid property protections and jurisdictional boundaries of the founding-era constitutional order. Writing decades before Darwin and Hegel were fully integrated into the American intellectual milieu, evangelical thinkers from Charles Finney to Justin Edwards argued that the rights and duties of citizenship should be understood to evolve with the moral progress of the community. And while some moral reformers advocated using constitutional amendments to effect the destruction of "immoral" forms of property, far more expressed confidence that the language of the state and federal constitutions was capacious enough to permit a dynamic understanding of constitutional guarantees.[10]

Moreover, although it is certainly true that the progressives and New Dealers were well versed in intellectual trends ranging from pragmatist philosophy to evolutionary biology, the evidence presented in this study helps to explain *why* these approaches were intuitively appealing. As Justice Holmes observed in a 1925 letter to Harold Laski, one of the most important lessons of "a century" spent in the law was that things "thought natural and wholesome may become anathema." The remark reminds us that, at the age of eighty-three, Holmes was old enough to remember a time when few Americans had regarded either "rum" or "the lottery" as moral abominations. More to the point, he could remember when liquor and lottery grants had been regarded as constitutionally protected forms of *property*. He could no doubt recall that lottery operators had once been insulated from state regulation by the federal Contract Clause; that federal courts had once endorsed Fourteenth Amendment challenges to state prohibition laws; and that federal regulations of morality had once been viewed as incompatible with the basic structure of the federal system. One by one, however, the constitutional obstacles blocking the path to moral regeneration had fallen; at each point where contemporary mores had clashed with entrenched constitutional commitments, contemporary mores had triumphed. Not only, then, did the idea of an organic fundamental law comport with the world that progressive thinkers hoped to bring into being; it also helped to explain the world they had known—a world in which the "eternal truths" of one generation had, in fact, become the "darkness and ignorance" of the next.[11] Only when this crucial context is omitted from the story can one plausibly describe the early proponents of the living Constitution as radical innovators, or dismiss the idea of an organic fundamental law as the product of a fleeting intellectual fad.

The question of intellectual provenance represents only one facet of the larger debate concerning the legitimacy of the New Deal revolution, however. For other critics of the New Deal Court, the problem has less to do with doctrinal innovation per se than with the relative merits of the pre- and post-New Deal frameworks. Recent years have, after all, witnessed an explosion of revisionist historical studies that have gone some way towards restoring the *Lochner*-era Court's formerly tarnished reputation. Following this trend in the historical literature, it was perhaps inevitable that constitutional theorists of a libertarian or conservative bent would undertake to rehabilitate the jurisprudence of the pre-New Deal Court. And indeed, a number of theorists have recently argued for a revival of *Lochner*-era federalism principles and economic rights.[12] If only Americans were made aware of the "lost Constitution" that the progressives discarded, the argument goes, we could begin planning our return to a time when constitutional meaning was fixed and unchanging[13]; when our natural liberties were secure[14]; when the size and scope of the federal government was kept within meaningful bounds[15]; and when contentious moral questions were resolved by democratic majorities, and not by unelected judges.[16]

Although the story of evangelical reform cannot settle the question of whether Americans should welcome or resist a revival of nineteenth-century constitutional principles, it does call into question the assumption that these principles provided the basis for a smoothly functioning regime. Stated differently, it is only when *moral* subjects are excluded from the analysis that the nineteenth century becomes a libertarian golden age, a time when courts merely protected property rights and interstate markets from excessive regulation while leaving the social order to evolve according to its own lights.

Certainly, the framers envisioned such an arrangement, as I have argued above. But they failed to account for the possibility of radical social change on the order of the post-Revival shift in mores—that is, social change that could not be confined to the private sphere or the lower levels of government, and which therefore blurred the crucial categorical distinctions that undergirded much of the traditional constitutional order. This history suggests that, for constitutional theorists concerned with the legitimacy of the modern order, there can be no ignoring the inevitably intercurrent relationship between constitution and society. For those who seek to revive the "lost Constitution," it is not enough simply to advance normative arguments on behalf of an expansive conception of economic liberty or a narrow conception of Congress's enumerated powers. Rather, such scholars must grapple with the more basic question of how the allegedly superior constitutional principles of the *Lochner* era became, as a result of social change, so discredited as to permit the New Deal Court to discard them as unworkable.

At the same time, the evangelical encounter with the constitutional system offers important lessons for the modern order's defenders. Recall that, for most defenders of the New Deal Court, the critical question is whether the constitutional changes of the 1930s reflected the will of "we the people." Such theorists, in other words, typically concede that the revolution was not merely a restoration of founding-era constitutional principles, as its contemporary defenders sometimes claimed, but rather a fundamental reinterpretation of inherited constitutional commitments.[17] But this was no top-down constitutional coup. Rather, the revolution reflected the considered judgment of the American people, who had determined that existing constitutional doctrine was ill suited to modern economic conditions and that state and federal policy makers required greater flexibility to respond to the economic catastrophe of the Great Depression. Perhaps not surprisingly, Roosevelt's landslide 1936 reelection victory features prominently in such accounts. The public's unequivocal expression of support for the President, coming in the midst of the administration's widely publicized confrontation with the Court, becomes in this telling a vote for a reconstructed constitutional framework.[18]

But if one accepts that the doctrinal shifts of the New Deal period were natural outgrowths of the nineteenth-century revolution in mores, it is no longer clear why efforts to establish the popular bona fides of the constitutional revolution must involve an obsessive focus on the minutia of the Roosevelt administration's confrontation with the Hughes Court. Indeed, the story of evangelical reform demonstrates that significant constitutional change need not occur in a single "constitutional moment" or burst of public engagement in order to lay claim to popular legitimacy.[19] Such change may just as easily occur gradually, over the course of several decades, and even, I would argue, without a clear sense of how particular doctrinal or policy changes will alter the underlying structure of the constitutional system.[20] Certainly, no one would claim that the doctrinal shifts described above were popularly "ratified" in the sense that that term has been applied to the critical rulings of the New Deal Court; there was no national plebiscite in which a majority of Americans voted to discard the Marshall Court's interpretation of the Contract Clause or the traditional distinction between the police and commerce powers. And yet these departures from the constitutional principles of the founding generation were clearly necessary to bring the constitutional order into alignment with the broadly shared moral convictions of post-Revival society. Whenever Americans mobilized on behalf of the goal of eradicating newly immoral forms of property—a goal that could only be achieved by discarding settled property rights and traditional jurisdictional boundaries—they were voting, in effect, for a novel conception of the constitutional enterprise.

Notes

Acknowledgments

Index

Notes

Introduction

1. In the Pew Research Center's 2011 political typology survey, for example, 90 percent of respondents in the "staunch conservative" category reported that religion was a "very important part" of their lives. Eighty-eight percent of these same respondents endorsed the view that the Constitution should be interpreted as "originally written" and not in light of what it has come to mean in "current times." Among individuals in the most secular category of respondents—"solid liberals"—only 15 percent expressed support for an "originalist" approach to constitutional interpretation. *Beyond Red vs. Blue: Political Typology* (Washington: Pew Research Center for the People and the Press, 2011). The quotation is from presidential candidate Newt Gingrich's 2011 address to the Values Voter Summit. "Gingrich Values Voter Summit Transcript." http://thepage.time.com/2011/10/08/gingrich-values-voter-summit-transcript. (10/25/2011)

2. See, generally, Henry Mayer, *All on Fire: William Lloyd Garrison and the Abolition of Slavery* (New York: Norton, 1998), Ch. 15. Garrison's famous declaration was based on a passage from the book of Isaiah: "And your covenant with death shall be disannulled, and your agreement with hell shall not stand; when the overflowing scourge shall pass through, then ye shall be trodden down by it" Isaiah 28:18 (King James Version). On the public reaction to Garrison's demonstration, see Michael Kammen, *A Machine That Would Go of Itself: The Constitution in American Culture* (New York: Alfred A. Knopf, 1986), 98.

3. Henry W. Blair, *The Temperance Movement* (W.E. Smythe, 1887), 388, 389.

4. By *mores,* I mean simply the fundamental and broadly shared moral values of a particular society, the violation of which is likely to be perceived as a threat to stability. The Oxford English Dictionary, on which I rely here, defines mores as "[t]he shared habits, manners, and customs of a community or social group; spec[ifically] the normative conventions and attitudes embodying the fundamental moral values of a particular

society, the contravention or rejection of which by individuals or subgroups is liable to be perceived as a threat to stability."

5. Roger Finke and Rodney Stark, *The Churching of America, 1776–2005: Winners and Losers in Our Religious Economy*, 2d Ed. (New Brunswick, NJ: Rutgers University Press, 2005), 23. The term "evangelical" is notoriously difficult to define. Nonetheless, Mark Noll and other leading historians of evangelicalism agree that the label entails at least the following four characteristics: (1) emphasis on an individual conversion experience; (2) emphasis on the Bible as the ultimate source of spiritual truth; (3) a crucicentric approach to salvation, or belief that sinful humans are reconciled to God through Christ's death on the cross; and (4) a commitment to activism on the part of all believers, particularly with respect to spreading the gospel message to non-believers. See Mark A. Noll, *The Rise of Evangelicalism: The Age of Edwards, Whitefield, and the Wesleys* (Downers Grove, IL: InterVarsity Press), 19; David W. Bebbington, *Evangelicalism in Modern Britain: A History from the 1730s to the 1980s* (London: Unwin Hyman, 1989), 1–17.

6. On the emergence of the "national sin" concept, see Michael P. Young, *Bearing Witness against Sin: The Evangelical Birth of the Modern Social Movement* (Chicago: University of Chicago Press, 2006). Young has persuasively argued that the emergence of reform movements focused on specific "national sins"—such as slavery and intemperance—was in part a response to the sense of alienation which accompanied the unprecedented economic and political changes of the early nineteenth century. The "reform cosmology," he writes, "envisioned the individual as morally implicated in national expansion and taught that she could not ignore large-scale problems *because* they held the keys to her spiritual fate." Ibid., 198. Emphasis in the original.

7. Karen Orren and Stephen Skowronek, *The Search for American Political Development* (New York: Cambridge University Press, 2004), 113.

8. Ibid., 22–3.

9. As Morton Horwitz has written, the view of judging as a "science" in which judges impartially interpreted the fixed categories articulated in legal texts was central to the framers' constitutional vision: "It was hoped that [law] could provide a non-political cushion or buffer between state and society. Unless law could be rendered non-political, how could it avoid becoming simply an instrument of democratic politics?" Horwitz, *The Transformation of American Law, 1870–1960* (New York: Oxford University Press, 1992), 9–10. Also see Jennifer Nedelsky, *Private Property and the Limits of American Constitutionalism: The Madisonian Framework and its Legacy* (Chicago: University of Chicago Press, 1990); Christopher Tomlins, *Law, Labor, and Ideology in the Early American Republic* (New York: Cambridge University Press, 1993), 19–100.

10. *Federalist* 39, in Alexander Hamilton, James Madison, and John Jay, *The Federalist Papers*, ed. Garry Wills (New York: Bantam, 1982), 194.

11. Quoted in Fran Grace, *Carry A. Nation: Retelling the Life* (Bloomington: Indiana University Press, 2001), 152.

12. Major studies of the period that provide only a cursory discussion of morals regulation include Horwitz, *The Transformation of American Law, 1870–1960*, 28; Howard

Gillman, *The Constitution Besieged: The Rise and Demise of Lochner Era Police Powers Jurisprudence* (Durham, NC: Duke University Press, 1993), 72–3; James W. Ely, *The Chief Justiceship of Melville W. Fuller, 1888–1910* (Columbia: University of South Carolina Press, 1995), 151. A noteworthy exception to this general rule is Owen Fiss's study of the Fuller Court, which devotes the better part of a chapter to analyzing the prohibition movement's impact on American federalism. Owen M. Fiss, *Troubled Beginnings of the Modern State, 1888–1910* (New York: Macmillan, 1993), 257–92.

13. Steven K. Green, *The Second Disestablishment: Church and State in Nineteenth-Century America* (New York: Oxford University Press, 2010); David Sehat, *The Myth of American Religious Freedom* (New York: Oxford University Press, 2011).

14. Sehat's study is somewhat broader than Green's and does include some discussion of the relationship between Protestantism and property rights in the late-nineteenth and early-twentieth centuries. In particular, Sehat argues that evangelicals in this period "aligned themselves with owners in the ongoing industrial conflict" and helped to legitimate "economic libertarianism under the protective canopy of moral norms." Although there is certainly a grain of truth in this characterization of the relationship between evangelicalism and constitutionalism—most evangelicals outside of the Social Gospel movement were indeed skeptical of organized labor and of "socialism in all its forms"—it leaves unexplored the myriad ways in which specific *policies* enacted at the evangelicals' behest worked to erode the foundations of the traditional constitutional system. In other words, even as many leading evangelicals professed support for strong property protections and federalism constraints, they were simultaneously pressing for morals laws that flaunted these constitutional principles, and thus worked to undermine their legitimacy. *The Myth of American Religious Freedom,* 189–90.

15. A few legal scholars and political scientists have recently begun to explore the impact of national liquor prohibition on American constitutional development—and with promising results. For the most part, however, these scholars continue to downplay the constitutional impact of morals regulation in the period prior to the adoption of the Eighteenth Amendment. See, for example, Kenneth M. Murchison, *Federal Criminal Law Doctrines: The Forgotten Influence of National Prohibition* (Durham, NC: Duke University Press, 1994); Ken I. Kersch, *Constructing Civil Liberties: Discontinuities in the Development of American Constitutional Law* (New York: Cambridge University Press, 2004), 72–89; Robert C. Post, "Federalism, Positive Law, and the Emergence of the American Administrative State: Prohibition in the Taft Court Era," *William & Mary Law Review* 48 (2006): 1–173.

16. Theodore J. Lowi, *The End of the Republican Era* (Norman: University of Oklahoma Press, 1995), 30.

17. William J. Novak, *The People's Welfare: Law and Regulation in Nineteenth-Century America* (Chapel Hill: University of North Carolina Press, 1996), 149–70, 187, 9, 149. Although Novak acknowledges that Americans who ran afoul of liquor and other morals laws occasionally invoked the rights provisions of the state and federal constitutions, he insists that such appeals consistently fell on deaf ears. Thus, despite occasional signs of "dissent, discontent, and dispute," a single "distinctive understanding of public powers

and rights was consistently victorious in nineteenth-century courtrooms, assembly halls, and council chambers." Ibid., 17.

18. Herbert Hovenkamp, "Law and Morals in Classical Legal Thought," *Iowa Law Review* 82 (1997): 1427–65.

19. James W. Ely, *The Chief Justiceship of Melville W. Fuller, 1888–1910* (Columbia: University of South Carolina Press), 151.

20. Lawrence Friedman, *A History of American Law* (New York: Simon and Schuster, 1973), 312. Also see Michael Les Benedict, "Victorian Moralism and Civil Liberty in the Nineteenth-Century United States," in *The Constitution, Law, and American Life*, ed. Donald G. Nieman (Athens: University of Georgia Press, 1992), 108; and John J. Dinan, *Keeping the People's Liberties: Legislators, Citizens, and Judges as Guardians of Rights* (Lawrence: University Press of Kansas, 1998), 13, 16. Benedict notes that constitutional challenges to morals laws, while not unheard of, usually fell on deaf ears. Because judges believed that Victorian moral standards embodied universal truths about humanity, they therefore placed "placed scant value on people's right to challenge orthodoxies." Dinan argues that prohibition measures and other innovative morals laws encountered little opposition in state and federal courts, notwithstanding the fact that they obviously interfered with property rights. The fact that judges generally upheld prohibition laws, he argues, provides clear evidence of "a dominant norm" which held that legislatures should be left free to use their police powers to "respond to changing conditions," and not constrained by overly rigid interpretations of constitutional rights provisions.

21. See, for example, Richard A. Epstein, *How Progressives Rewrote the Constitution* (Washington, DC: Cato Institute, 2006); Randy E. Barnett, *Restoring the Lost Constitution: The Presumption of Liberty* (Princeton, NJ: Princeton University Press, 2004), 108–9; Hadley Arkes, *The Return of George Sutherland: Restoring a Jurisprudence of Natural Rights* (Princeton, NJ: Princeton University Press, 1994); Gary L. McDowell, "The Corrosive Constitutionalism of Edward S. Corwin," *Law and Social Inquiry* 14 (1989): 603–14.

22. Bruce Ackerman, *We the People: Foundations* (Cambridge, MA: Belknap Press, 1991); *We the People: Transformations* (Cambridge: MA, Belknap Press, 1998); Barry Friedman, *The Will of the People: How Public Opinion Has Influenced the Supreme Court and Shaped the Meaning of the Constitution* (New York: Farrar, Straus, and Giroux, 2009).

23. See, in particular, Ackerman, *We the People: Transformations*, 306–16.

24. Some of the major works in the revisionist vein include Fiss, *Troubled Beginnings of the Modern State;* Horwitz, *The Transformation of American Law;* Gillman, *The Constitution Besieged;* Barry Cushman, *Rethinking the New Deal Court: The Structure of a Constitutional Revolution* (New York: Oxford University Press, 1998); G. Edward White, *The Constitution and the New Deal* (Cambridge, MA; Harvard University Press, 2000); Julie Novkov, *Constituting Workers, Protecting Women: Gender, Law, and Labor in the Progressive Era and New Deal Years* (Ann Arbor: University of Michigan Press, 2001); Richard D. Friedman, "Switching Time and Other Thought Experiments: The Hughes Court and Constitutional Transformation," *University of Pennsylvania Law Review* 142 (1994): 1891–1984. For overviews of the revisionist literature, see Gary D. Rowe, "*Lochner* Revisionism Revisited," *Law and Social Inquiry* 24 (1999): 221–52; and

Laura Kalman, "The Constitution, the Supreme Court, and the New Deal," *American Historical Review* 110 (2005): 1052–80.

25. Or to cite a slightly different example, Ken Kersch has recently documented the extent to which modern civil rights and civil liberties jurisprudence was shaped by a series of seemingly unrelated Progressive-era policy debates concerning labor organization, prohibition enforcement, and compulsory public education. *Constructing Civil Liberties: Discontinuities in the Development of American Constitutional Law* (New York: Cambridge University Press, 2004).

26. Cushman, *Rethinking the New Deal Court,* 141–76.

27. On the antislavery movement's confrontation with the judiciary, see Robert M. Cover, *Justice Accused: Antislavery and the Judicial Process* (New Haven, CT: Yale University Press, 1975); Paul Finkelman, *An Imperfect Union: Slavery, Federalism, and Comity* (Chapel Hill: University of North Carolina Press, 1981).

28. William M. Wiecek, *Sources of Antislavery Constitutionalism in America, 1760–1848* (Ithaca, NY: Cornell University Press, 1977); William E. Nelson, "The Impact of the Antislavery Movement upon Styles of Judicial Reasoning in Nineteenth-Century America," *Harvard Law Review* 87 (1974): 513–66; Gerald N. Magliocca, *Andrew Jackson and the Constitution: The Rise and Fall of Generational Regimes* (Lawrence: University Press of Kansas, 2007).

29. On the antislavery movement's impact on American constitutionalism, see Michael Vorenberg, *Final Freedom: The Civil War, the Abolition of Slavery, and the Thirteenth Amendment* (New York: Cambridge University Press, 2001); "Bringing the Constitution Back In: Amendment, Innovation, and Popular Democracy during the Civil War Era," in *The Democratic Experiment,* ed. Meg Jacobs, William J. Novak, and Julian E. Zelizer (Princeton, NJ: Princeton University Press, 2003), 120–45; J. David Greenstone, *The Lincoln Persuasion: Remaking American Liberalism* (Princeton, NJ: Princeton University Press, 1993); Mark A. Graber, *Dred Scott and the Problem of Constitutional Evil* (New York: Cambridge University Press, 2006); Mark E. Brandon, *Free in the World: American Slavery and Constitutional Failure* (Princeton, NJ: Princeton University Press, 1988); Garry Wills, *Lincoln at Gettysburg: The Words that Remade America* (New York: Simon and Schuster, 1992).

30. The question of which branch bears primary responsibility for the failure of Reconstruction is, of course, hotly contested. For an important recent contribution the debate, see Pamela Brandwein, *Rethinking the Judicial Settlement of Reconstruction* (New York: Cambridge University Press, 2011).

31. See, for example, Michael Les Benedict, "Preserving Federalism: Reconstruction and the Waite Court," *Supreme Court Review* (1978): 39–79.

32. This is a major point of emphasis in the revisionist literature. More specifically, revisionist scholars tend to emphasize the continuities in antebellum and postwar jurisprudence and also to describe the New Deal as more significant turning point in American constitutional development than the Civil War. See, for example, Gillman, *The Constitution Besieged;* "The Struggle Over Marshall and the Politics of Constitutional History," *Political Research Quarterly* 47 (1994): 877–86; Barbara Young Welke, *Law*

and the Borders of Belonging in the Long Nineteenth Century United States (New York: Cambridge University Press, 2010).

33. Richard M. Valelly, *The Two Reconstructions: The Struggle for Black Enfranchisement* (Chicago: University of Chicago Press, 2004); Kevin J. McMahon, *Reconsidering Roosevelt on Race: How the Presidency Paved the Road to Brown* (Chicago: University of Chicago Press, 2004).

34. Vorenberg, "Bringing the Constitution Back In."

35. Hamm, *Shaping the Eighteenth Amendment,* 243–4. Hamm notes that the Supreme Court's 1917 decision in *Clark Distilling Co. v. Western Maryland Railway Co.*—upholding a federal law banning importation of liquor into dry states—forced prohibition supporters to develop a new rationale for their proposed amendment. In the end, many drew a parallel to the abolition of slavery, declaring that the Constitution would remain a "covenant with death" until formally amended to prohibit the liquor traffic. 242 U.S. 311.

36. Speaking at the Values Voter Summit in the fall of 2011, for example, presidential candidate Newt Gingrich traced the decline of traditional values to the New Deal period, when the nation's elite law schools had endorsed an "anti-American . . . judicial model" which viewed the Constitution as "old and antiquated." Freed from the need to concern themselves with the original intent of the framers, judges trained in this environment had embarked on a campaign to "radically [change] our society" through decisions that banned school prayer, barred states from regulating abortion and—eventually—legalized same-sex marriage. "Gingrich Values Voter Summit Transcript." http://thepage.time.com/2011/10/08/gingrich-values-voter-summit-transcript. (10/25/2011)

37. Epstein, *How Progressives Rewrote the Constitution,* 3, 135.

38. James R. Stoner, *Common-Law Liberty: Rethinking American Constitutionalism* (Lawrence: University of Kansas Press, 2003), 166.

39. Bradley C.S. Watson, *Living Constitution, Dying Faith: Progressives and the New Science of Jurisprudence* (Wilmington, DE: ISI Books, 2009), 55.

40. Christopher Wolfe, *The Rise of Modern Judicial Review: From Constitutional Interpretation to Judge-Made Law* (Lanham, MD: Rowman and Littlefield, 1994), 208.

41. Paul O. Carrese, *The Cloaking of Power: Montesquieu, Blackstone, and the Rise of Judicial Activism* (Chicago: University of Chicago Press, 2003), 232–3.

1. The Evangelical Challenge to American Constitutionalism

1. See, for example, Martin Diamond, "Ethics and Politics: The American Way," in Robert Horwitz, ed. *The Moral Foundations of the American Republic* (Charlottesville: University Press of Virginia, 1986), 75–108; Robert H. Horwitz, "John Locke and the Preservation of Liberty: A Perennial Problem of Civic Education," in ibid., 136–64; Stephen L. Elkin, *Reconstructing the Commercial Republic: Constitutional Design after Madison* (Chicago: University of Chicago Press, 2006).

2. *Federalist 10; Federalist 12; Federalist 70,* in Alexander Hamilton, James Madison, and John Jay, *The Federalist Papers,* ed. Garry Wills (New York: Bantam, 1982), 43, 55, 358. As Gordon Wood has written, the Federalists broke with tradition by resting "their

government . . . on the assumption that most people were self-interested and absorbed in their private affairs." *The Radicalism of the American Revolution* (New York: Knopf, 1992), 264.

3. Thus, Oliver Ellsworth, in the midst of the ratification debate, drew attention to the fact that the new Constitution barred the federal government from regulating religion, while at the same time giving the states free rein to "punish gross immoralities and impieties," such as "drunkenness, profane swearing, blasphemy, and professed atheism." "A Landholder, No. 7," in *The Debate on the Constitution: Federalist and Antifederalist Speeches, Articles, and Letters During the Struggle over Ratification,* ed. Bernard Bailyn (New York: Library of America, 1981), 1:521–25, 524.

4. Benjamin Barber, "The Compromised Republic: Public Purposelessness in America," in *The Moral Foundations of the American Republic,* ed. Robert H. Horwitz (Charlottesville: University Press of Virginia, 1986), 47–8. William Sullivan echoes the basic point: "The novelty of the conception of politics embodied in the Federalist Constitution was its assertion that the end of government was not the achievement of a particular moral quality of civic life but, rather, the guarantee of individual security" and the promotion of "a commercially competitive civil society." William M. Sullivan, *Reconstructing Public Philosophy* (Berkeley: University of California Press, 1982), 12. Also see Diamond, "Ethics and Politics"; Barry Shain, *The Myth of American Individualism: The Protestant Origins of American Political Thought* (Princeton, NJ: Princeton University Press, 1994), 143–9.

5. Diamond, "Ethics and Politics," 92. This is not to deny the existence of serious internal tensions within the Federalist worldview. As would become apparent in the early nineteenth century, rapid economic development worked to undermine other aspects of the Federalist philosophy, including its hierarchical conception of the social order. See Wood, *The Radicalism of the American Revolution,* 325–47.

6. Sheldon S. Wolin, *The Presence of the Past: Essays on the State and the Constitution* (Baltimore, MD: John Hopkins University Press, 1989), 86–7.

7. On the affinities between the Marshall Court's jurisprudence and the political philosophy of the Federalists, see, for example, Jennifer Nedelsky, *Private Property and the Limits of American Constitutionalism: The Madisonian Framework and its Legacy* (Chicago: University of Chicago Press, 1990), 189.

8. Broadly speaking, the early Court's constitutional achievement rested on four sets of decisions handed down in the period between 1803 and 1824. First, in a line of cases that included *Fletcher v. Peck* (1810), *New Jersey v. Wilson* (1812), *Sturges v. Crowninshield* (1819), and *Dartmouth College v. Woodward* (1819), Marshall and his colleagues employed a broad reading of the Constitution's Contract Clause to shield rights arising out of both public and private contracts from state legislative interference. Second, in *McCulloch v. Maryland* (1819), the Court ruled that Congress's implied powers were broad enough to authorize the incorporation of a National Bank and, second, that the exercise of this federal power preempted the states' powers of taxation. Third, in a line of Commerce Clause decisions that included *Gibbons v. Ogden* (1824), the Court worked to create a single national market unencumbered by excessive state regulation. In

keeping with the *Federalist*'s prediction that ratification of the Constitution would open "the veins of commerce" and promote "intercourse" between the states, *Gibbons* and its progeny ensured that attempts to interfere with the interstate movement of goods and people would be met with a presumption of unconstitutionality—even in the absence of a clear conflict with federal legislation. Finally, the Court in *Marbury v. Madison* (1803) declared itself the final arbiter in questions of constitutional interpretation, thus validating the conception of judicial review first articulated by Hamilton in *Federalist* 78.

9. To be sure, they recognized that there would be disagreement about how vaguely worded constitutional provisions should be applied to particular cases. But once the meanings of textual provisions had been "liquidated and ascertained by a series of particular discussions and adjudications," as Madison wrote in *Federalist* 37 (in Wills, ed., *The Federalist Papers*, 181) it was assumed that their meanings would solidify, thus providing a stable framework for constitutional adjudication. Or as Hamilton put the point, the "variety of controversies which grow out of the folly and wickedness of mankind" would inevitably cause the volumes of judicial rulings to "swell to a considerable bulk," so that both judges and politicians would in time be "bound down by strict rules and precedents." *Federalist* 78, in ibid., 399.

10. "By a limited constitution," Hamilton wrote, "I understand one which contains certain specified exceptions to the legislative authority. . . . Limitations of this kind can be preserved in no other way than through the medium of the courts of justice; whose duty it must be to declare all acts contrary to the manifest tenor of the constitution void. Without this, all the reservations of particular rights or privileges would amount to nothing." *Federalist* 78, in *The Federalist*, 413–414.

11. David Flaherty, "Law and the Enforcement of Morals in Early America," in *Perspectives in American History, Vol. 5: Law in American History*, ed. Donald Fleming and Bernard Bailyn (Cambridge, MA: Harvard University Press, 1971), 208, 211. Also see Shain, *Myth of American Individualism*, 209–11; William J. Novak, *The People's Welfare: Law and Regulation in Nineteenth-Century America* (Chapel Hill: University of North Carolina Press, 1996), Ch. 5.

12. Quoted in Flaherty, "Law and the Enforcement of Morals," 211.

13. David Hackett Fischer has argued that colonial-era mores differed significantly from region to region. It is important to note, however, that the widespread reception of English common law—as well as simple legislative diffusion, or the tendency copy the statutes of neighboring colonies—tended to mitigate such differences. Thus, while the criminal codes of the New England colonies occasionally called for harsher penalties than those of the Southern and Mid-Atlantic states, the list of moral and religious offenses was roughly the same. In the Mid-Atlantic colony of Delaware, for example, the statute books contained criminal prohibitions against adultery, fornication, gambling, stage plays, blasphemy, profane swearing, Sabbath-breaking, public drunkenness, cock-fighting, and horse-racing. *Laws of the State of Delaware* (New Castle, DE: Samuel and John Adams, 1797), 1:105–9, 120, 173–4; 2:866, 1209–10, 1304–7. Further south, the colony of Virginia enforced criminal prohibitions against gambling, Sabbath-breaking, profane swearing, public drunkenness, adultery, fornication, and "buggery." *A*

Collection of All Such Acts of the General Assembly . . . (Richmond, VA: Samuel Pleasants, 1803), 1:174–9, 275–6. On regional variation in moral and religious matters, see David Hackett Fischer, *Albion's Seed: Four British Folkways in America* (New York: Oxford University Press, 1989).

14. Flaherty, "Law and the Enforcement of Morals"; William E. Nelson, *Americanization of the Common Law: The Impact of Legal Change on Massachusetts Society, 1760–1830* (Cambridge, MA: Harvard University Press, 1975) 36–41; Hendrik Hartog, "The Public Law of a County Court: Judicial Government in Eighteenth Century Massachusetts," *The American Journal of Legal History* 20 (1976): 282–329; Kermit L. Hall, *The Magic Mirror: Law in American Society* (New York: Oxford University Press, 1989), 32–3.

15. See, for example, Wood, *The Radicalism of the American* Revolution, 59.

16. In his influential pamphlet "Thoughts on Government," for example, John Adams was forced to admit that "the very mention of sumptuary laws" (which Adams supported) was likely to "excite a smile." John Adams, "Thoughts on Government," in *American Political Writing During the Founding Era, 1760–1805,* ed. Charles S. Hyneman (Indianapolis, IN: Liberty Fund, 1983) 1: 407.

17. See, for example, Thomas L. Pangle, *The Spirit of Modern Republicanism: The Moral Vision of the American Founders and the Philosophy of Locke* (Chicago: University of Chicago Press, 1988), 73–111.

18. Hiram Caton, *The Politics of Progress: The Origins and Development of the Commercial Republic* (Gainesville: University of Florida Press, 1988), 378–9.

19. Pangle, *Spirit of Modern Republicanism,* 92. Benjamin Franklin, who made a literary career out of simultaneously promoting the Calvinist virtues and mocking those who were overly zealous in enforcing them, provides a particularly striking illustration of the general trend. On this aspect of Franklin's thought, see Caton, *The Politics of Progress,* 374–81.

20. Quoted in Flaherty, "Law and Morals in Early America," 248.

21. Nelson, *Americanization of the Common Law,* 37–8, 110. Hendrik Hartog confirmed Nelson's basic findings in a second study of local court records. Hartog, "The Public Law of a County Court," 282–329. Also see Hall, *Magic Mirror,* 169; Flaherty, "Law and Morals," 246–9.

22. Hartog, "The Public Law of a County Court," 299–308; Flaherty, "Law and Morals," 246–7; Nelson, *Americanization of the Common Law,* 110–1.

23. Hartog, "The Public Law of a County Court," 288–91.

24. Lawrence M. Friedman, *A History of American Law,* 2nd Ed. (New York: Simon and Schuster, 1985), 294.

25. See, for example, *The Federalist,* Nos. 11 and 14. For a recent discussion of the Founding-era conception of "intercourse," which clearly informed the framing of the Commerce Clause, see Jack M. Balkin, *Living Originalism* (Cambridge, MA: Belknap Press of Harvard University Press, 2011), 140–69.

26. Mark A. Noll reports that the ratio of churches to population declined from 1:598 to 1:807 in the period between 1700 and 1780. *America's God: From Jonathan Edwards to Abraham Lincoln* (New York: Oxford University Press, 2002), 162.

27. Roger Finke and Rodney Stark, *The Churching of America, 1776–2005: Winners and Losers in Our Religious Economy*, 2d Ed. (New Brunswick, NJ: Rutgers University Press, 2005), 23. Noll, *America's God*, 162–3. As a rough measure of religion's relative strength within the broader culture, it is worth noting as well the dramatic decline in the proportion of printed works devoted to religious subjects. Noll reports that, as late as 1740, religious publications made up the majority of all nongovernmental works published in the colonies; by 1760 the percentage of religious publications had plummeted to 38 percent, and by 1775, with the onset of the Revolution, religious publications composed a paltry 16 percent of the nation's printed output.

28. Noll, *America's God*, 162.

29. See, for example, William G. McLoughlin, *New England Dissent, 1630–1833: The Baptists and the Separation of Church and State* (Cambridge, MA: Harvard University Press, 1971), Vol. 2; Johann N. Neem, "The Elusive Common Good: Religion and Society in Massachusetts," *Journal of the Early Republic* 24 (2004): 381–417.

30. See, for example, Sidney E. Ahlstrom, *A Religious History of the American People*, 2d Ed. (New Haven, CT: Yale University Press, 2004), 388–402.

31. *Federalist* 10, in Wills, ed. *The Federalist Papers*, 48. This assumption seems to have been widely shared by members of the Founding generation. Tench Coxe, in the first major defense of the Constitution published in the United States, informed his readers that they need not fear the "danger of ecclesiastical tyranny," since "[a]ll religious funds, honor and powers are [in America] in the gift of numberless, unconnected, disunited, and contending corporations." "An American Citizen I," in *The Documentary History of the Ratification of the Constitution*, ed. Merrill Jensen (Madison: State Historical Society of Wisconsin, 1976–) 2:138–142, 140.

32. See, for example, Philip Greven, *The Protestant Temperament: Patterns of Child-Rearing, Religious Experience, and the Self in Early America* (Chicago: University of Chicago Press, 1977), 358–61.

33. Ruth H. Bloch, "Religion and Ideological Change in the American Revolution," in *Religion and American Politics*, ed. Noll and Harlow, 47–63, 58.

34. Michael P. Young, *Bearing Witness against Sin: The Evangelical Birth of the American Social Movement* (Chicago: University of Chicago Press, 2006), 52–3. For example, Benjamin Rush, the only Founder to demonstrate a serious commitment to the legal enforcement of Puritan virtues, was driven from the Presbyterian fold in 1787, in part because of his radical anti-liquor views. Robert H. Abzug, *Cosmos Crumbling: American Reform and the Religious Imagination* (New York: Oxford University Press, 1994), 25–6.

35. On Quaker and Methodist opposition to liquor, see W.J. Rorabaugh, *The Alcoholic Republic: An American Tradition* (New York: Oxford University Press, 1979), 38; John Samuell Ezell, *Fortune's Merry Wheel: The Lottery in America* (Cambridge, MA: Harvard University Press, 1960), 18–22. Together the two denominations totaled a mere 11 percent of the religious population; and while the Quakers were heavily concentrated in Pennsylvania, Quaker-led campaigns for stricter morals laws were generally unsuccessful even in the Quaker State. For the Quaker and Methodist share of the religious population, see Noll, *America's God*, 162. On the failure of Quaker-led

campaigns to improve public morality in Pennsylvania, see Ezell, *Fortune's Merry Wheel*, 33, 52.

36. Walter W. Spooner, *The Cyclopaedia of Temperance and Prohibition* (New York: Funk and Wagnalls, 1891), 425. As David W. Conroy has shown, the profession of tavern keeper grew in both prestige and political influence during the middle decades of the nineteenth century. *In Public Houses: Drink and the Revolution of Authority in Colonial Massachusetts* (Chapel Hill: University of North Carolina Press, 1995), 194, 197–9, 209–15, 222–6, 323–5.

37. See, for example, David Daggett, "Senate Report on Sunday Mails," in *American State Papers Bearing on Sunday Legislation,* ed. William Addison Blakely (New York: National Religious Liberty Association, 1890), 66; Wayne E. Fuller, *Morality and the Mail in Nineteenth-Century America* (Urbana: University of Illinois Press, 2003), 1.

38. Richard R. John, *Spreading the News: The Postal System from Franklin to Morse* (Cambridge, MA: Harvard University Press, 1995), Ch. 5.

39. John, *Spreading the News,* 170–9.

40. Ibid., 174–5; John G. West, *The Politics of Revelation and Reason: Religion and Civic Life in the New Nation* (Lawrence: University Press of Kansas, 1996), 152–3.

41. John, *Spreading the News,* 185–7; West, *Politics of Revelation and Reason,* 162.

42. *Commonwealth v. Knox,* 6 Mass. 76, 77–8 (1809).

43. Quoted in West, *Politics of Revelation and Reason,* 155. It is now widely believed that Johnson's committee reports on the Sunday Mails controversy were ghostwritten by Obadiah Brown, the minister of Washington's First Baptist Church. See Richard R. John, "Taking Sabbatarianism Seriously: The Postal System, the Sabbath, and the Transformation of American Political Culture," *Journal of the Early Republic* 10 (1990): 559.

44. Quoted in Fuller, *Morality and the Mail,* 25.

45. 17 U.S. 518 (1819).

46. For background on the religious origins of the *Dartmouth College* case, see William Gwyer North, "The Political Background of the Dartmouth College Case," *The New England Quarterly* 18 (1945): 181–203; Mark D. McGarvie, *One Nation under Law: America's Early National Struggles to Separate Church and State* (DeKalb: Northern Illinois University Press, 2005), 165–82.

47. The quotation is from Daniel Webster's argument before the Court on behalf of the original trustees. 17 U.S. 518 at 558.

48. On the decision's significance for religious corporations, see McGarvie, *One Nation under Law,* 165–82.

49. On the Federalist-dominated judiciary's efforts to insulate property questions from the political process, see for example, Nedelsky, *Private Property and the Limits of American Constitutionalism,* 187–99 ; Christopher Tomlins, *Law, Labor, and Ideology in the Early American Republic* (New York: Cambridge University Press, 1993), 19–100.

50. Alexis de Tocqueville, *Democracy in America,* ed. Harvey Mansfield and Delba Winthrop (Chicago: University of Chicago Press, 2000), 278–9.

51. Richard J. Carwardine, *Evangelicals and Politics in Antebellum America* (New Haven, CT: Yale University Press, 1993), 44.

52. See, for example, Noll, *America's God,* 165–6; Eldon Eisenach, *The Next Religious Establishment: National Identity and Political Theology in Post-Protestant America* (Lanham, MD: Rowman and Littlefield, 2000); Robert T. Handy, *A Christian America: Protestant Hopes and Historical Realities,* 2d. Ed. (New York: Oxford University Press, 1984).

53. Roger Finke and Rodney Stark, "How the Upstart Sects Won America: 1776–1850," *Journal for the Scientific Study of Religion* 28 (1989): 30.

54. Nathan O. Hatch, *The Democratization of American Christianity* (New Haven, CT: Yale University Press, 1989), 4.

55. Ibid.; Noll, *America's God,* 174–5.

56. Roger Finke and Rodney Stark, *The Churching of America: Winners and Losers in Our Religious Economy, 1776–2005* (New Brunswick, NJ: Rutgers University Press, 2005), 55–117.

57. Ibid., 73–99; Noll, *America's God,* 179–94. The quotation is from Gordon Wood, "Evangelical America and Early Mormonism," *New York History* 61 (1980): 371.

58. In the period between 1776 and 1850, the Methodists' share of all religious adherents increased from 2.5 percent to 34 percent, while the Baptists' increased from 16.9 percent to 20.5 percent. Meanwhile, in the same period, Congregationalists, Presbyterians, and Anglicans all witnessed dramatic decreases in their relative shares of the religious population (though their absolute numbers remained relatively stable). Finke and Stark, *The Churching of America,* 56.

59. Noll, *America's God,* 166.

60. For the Revival's effect on Congregationalist and Presbyterian theology, see Leo P. Hirrell, *Children of Wrath: New School Calvinism and Antebellum Reform* (Lexington: University Press of Kentucky, 1998); Michael P. Young, *Bearing Witness against Sin: The Evangelical Birth of the American Social Movement* (Chicago: University of Chicago Press, 2006), 117.

61. For summaries of the key theological shifts associated with the Second Great Awakening, see Perry Miller, *The Life of the Mind in America: From the Revolution to the Civil War* (New York: Harcourt, Brace, Jovanovich, 1965), 27–35; William G. McLoughlin, *Revivals, Awakenings, and reform: An Essay on Social Change in America, 1607–1977* (Chicago: University of Chicago Press, 1978), 98–140; Hatch, *The Democratization of American Christianity,* 17–46; E. Brooks Holifield, *Theology in America: Christian Thought from the Age of the Puritans to the Civil War* (New Haven, CT: Yale University Press, 2003), 341–369; Hirrell, *Children of Wrath;* Daniel Walker Howe, *What Hath God Wrought: The Transformation of America, 1815–1848* (New York: Oxford University Press, 2009), 285–327.

62. To be sure, not all nineteenth-century evangelicals went so far as Finney in this regard. Beecher, for example, never explicitly repudiated the doctrine of innate depravity, even as he expressed faith that society could be transformed through human agency. That Beecher's children, including the liberal theologian and minister Henry Ward Beecher, unceremoniously abandoned the doctrine of original sin suggests the two beliefs were not entirely compatible. On Henry Ward Beecher's rejection of original sin, see Debby Applegate, *The Most Famous Man in America* (New York: Doubleday, 2006),

38, 121, 300. On the idea of "moral agency" in American Protestant theology and its impact on civil society, see Peter Dobkin Hall, "The Rise of the Civil Engagement Tradition," in *Taking Faith Seriously*, ed. Mary Jo Bane, Brent Coffin, and Richard Higgins (Cambridge, MA: Harvard University Press, 2005), 21–59.

63. Albert Barnes, *The Way of Salvation.* Quoted in Charles C. Cole, Jr. *The Social Ideas of the Northern Evangelists* (New York: Columbia University Press, 1954), 43.

64. Lyman Beecher, *A Sermon Addressed to the Legislature of Connecticut.* Quoted in Daniel Walker Howe, *The Political Culture of the American Whigs* (Chicago: University of Chicago Press, 1979), 152. To be clear, none of these theological tenets originated with Beecher, Finney, or the other leading lights of the Second Great Awakening; most of them can be traced to earlier sources, including the eighteenth-century Methodism of John Wesley and the "New Light" Calvinism that flourished in the aftermath of the First Great Awakening in the 1740s. Yet it was during the 1820s and 1830s, as the historian Paul E. Johnson has written, that the evangelical doctrines of "free agency, perfectionism, and millennialism" moved from the fringes of American society to the mainstream, ultimately assuming the status of "middle-class orthodoxy." *A Shopkeeper's Millennium: Society and Revivals in Rochester, New York, 1815–1837* (New York: Hill and Wang, 1978), 5.

65. *Federalist* 9, in Wills, ed., *The Federalist Papers,* 38.

66. On the framers' "moderate" faith in humanity, see Henry F. May, *The Enlightenment in America* (New York: Oxford University Press), 97–101. For the belief that sound institutional design could compensate for the moral shortcomings of the citizenry, see, for example, Michael G. Kammen, *A Machine That Would Go of Itself: The Constitution in American Culture* (New York: Michael G. Kammen, 1986), 17–18.

67. On the democratic implications of evangelical theology, see Hatch, *Democratization of American Christianity;* Wood, *Radicalism of the American Revolution,* 329–35.

68. Lyman Beecher, *Six Sermons on the Nature, Occasions, Signs, Evils, and Remedy of Intemperance* (New York: American Tract Society, 1827), 93.

69. On Founding-era attitudes with respect to liquor, see Rorabaugh, *Alcoholic Republic,* 5–92. Ian Tyrrell, *Sobering Up: From Temperance to Prohibition in Antebellum America, 1800–1860* (Westport, CT: Greenwood Press, 1979), 16–32. Virtually the only prominent exception to the rule was Dr. Benjamin Rush, the Pennsylvania physician, moral reformer, and signer of the Declaration of Independence. On Rush's early temperance activism, see Rorabaugh, *Alcoholic Republic,* 39–46; Abzug, *Cosmos Crumbling,* 24–9.

70. Zephaniah Swift, *A System of the Laws of the State of Connecticut* (Windham, CT: John Byrne, 1796), 8, 359.

71. Justin Edwards, "Temperance," *Christian Watchman* 17 (February 19, 1836), 32.

72. Ernest H. Cherrington, *The Evolution of Prohibition in the United States* (Montclair, NJ: Patterson Smith, 1920 [1969]), 91–3; Young, *Bearing Witness Against Sin,* 121–5.

73. Rorabaugh, *Alcoholic Republic,* 207–8; Cherrington, *Evolution of Prohibition,* 98–115.

74. John Samuel Ezell, *Fortune's Merry Wheel: The Lottery in America* (Cambridge, MA: Harvard University Press, 1960), 100–60.

75. *Reports of the Proceedings and Debates of the [New York] Convention of 1821* (Albany: E. and E. Hosford, 1821), 4:578. This basic sentiment was echoed in the preambles of Founding-era lottery laws, many of which expressly endorsed the notion that a modicum of immoral behavior was not inconsistent with the welfare of the wider community. Thus, while the New York legislature, in a statute criminalizing private (or unauthorized) lotteries, emphasized lottery gambling's tendency to promote "idleness and dissipation," the same legislature sanctioned a public lottery to fund the construction of Union College, noting that "seminaries of learning are of immense importance to every country, and tend . . . by the diffusion of science and the promotion of morals, to defend and perpetuate the liberties of a free state." The contradiction here is more apparent than real. If Founding-era Americans accepted that lotteries were conducive to greed and idleness, they nonetheless believed that this unfortunate side effect was more than counterbalanced by the social benefits derived from the construction of new schools and churches. *Laws of the State of New York* (Albany: Weed, Parsons, and Co., 1886), 1:523; *Laws of the State of New York* (Albany: Websters and Skinners, 1815), 3:129. In addition, it is worth noting that Founding-era clergymen were similarly enthusiastic about the lottery as a system of revenue generation. According to the leading historical work on early American lotteries, no less than two hundred religious congregations benefited from lottery grants in the Founding era. Ezell, *Fortune's Merry Wheel*, 55–9, 71–2, 140–3.

76. Ibid., 204–29.

77. Jackson Lears, *Something for Nothing: Luck in America* (New York: Penguin, 2003), 60–1.

78. "On the Subject of Legalized Lotteries," *The Theological Review and General Repository of Religious and Moral Information* 1 (1822): 299. For similar statements from the religious press, see "Immorality of Lotteries," *Christian Watchman* (June 23, 1821), 111; "Lotteries," *Christian Watchman* (Feb. 22, 1823), 43; "Lotteries," *Christian Watchman* (Feb. 3, 1826), 35; "On Lotteries," *Religious Remembrancer* (Feb. 9, 1822), 97.

79. Ezell, *Fortune's Merry Wheel*, 205, 219.

80. Daniel Walker Howe, "Religion and Politics in the Antebellum North," in *Religion and American Politics*, ed. Noll and Harlow, 121–43, 130.

81. See, for example, Young, *Bearing Witness against Sin*, 70–1, 121.

82. Ann-Marie Szymanski, *Pathways to Prohibition: Radicals, Moderates, and Social Movement Outcomes* (Durham, NC: Duke University Press, 2003), 30.

83. Young, *Bearing Witness against Sin*, 73. Also see Noll, *America's God*, 198.

84. Noll, *America's God*, 198.

85. Ibid., 174–5.

86. See, for example, Daniel Walker Howe, *The Political Culture of the American Whigs* (Chicago: University of Chicago Press, 1979), 156–63. It is also worth noting that the 1820s and 1830s witnessed the emergence of a new class of professional reformers—individuals who earned their livings as agents and propagandists of voluntary societies and who therefore had a personal and professional stake in the success

of interdenominational outreach. See, for example, Young, *Bearing Witness against Sin,* 80–4; Donald P. Scott, *From Office to Profession: The New England Ministry, 1750–1850* (Philadelphia: University of Pennsylvania Press, 1978), 76–94.

87. See, for example, Howe, *The Political Culture of the American Whigs,* 164; Thomas R. Pegram, *Battling Demon Rum: The Struggle for a Dry America, 1800–1933* (Chicago: Ivan R. Dee, 1998), 34.

88. Rorabaugh, *Alcoholic Republic,* 61–124; Tyrrell, *Sobering Up,* 26.

89. See, for example, Noll, *America's God,* 185; Noll, *The Civil War as a Theological Crisis* (Chapel Hill: University of North Carolina Press, 2006).

90. See, for example, Eisenach, *The Next Religious Establishment,* 24; Edward J. Blum, *Reforging the White Republic: Race, Religion, and American Nationalism, 1865–1898* (Baton Rouge: Louisiana State University Press, 2005); Gaines M. Foster, *Moral Reconstruction: Christian Lobbyists and the Federal Legislation of Morality, 1865–1920* (Chapel Hill: University of North Carolina Press, 2002).

91. On the WCTU, see Theda Skocpol, *Protecting Soldiers and Mothers: The Political Origins of Social Policy in the United States* (Cambridge, MA: Belknap Press of Harvard University, 1992), 326–7. On the Anti-Saloon League, see Peter H. Odegard, *Pressure Politics: The Story of the Anti-Saloon League* (New York: Columbia University Press, 1928); K. Austin Kerr, *Organized for Prohibition: A New History of the Anti-Saloon League* (New Haven, CT: Yale University Press, 1985).

92. Ezell, *Fortune's Merry Wheel,* 221.

93. Cherrington, *The Evolution of Prohibition,* 98–134.

94. For a list of states enacting statewide prohibition laws in the antebellum period, see Szymanski, *Pathways to Prohibition,* 128.

95. Lyman Beecher, "Six Sermons on Intemperance," 66, 72.

96. For example, Charles Grandison Finney, in his *Lectures on Systematic Theology,* offered the following denunciation of the idea of "inalienable" rights: "What is this [that is, the idea of inalienable rights] but maintaining, that . . . we should love others too much to use the indispensable means to secure their good? Or that we should love the whole too much to execute the law upon those who would destroy all good? Shame on such philosophy! It overlooks the foundation of moral obligation, and of all morality and religion." *Lectures on Systematic Theology* (Oberlin, OH: James M. Fitch, 1846), 442–3.

97. Albert Barnes, *The Throne of Iniquity: Or Sustaining Evil by Law* (New York: National Temperance Society, 1852), 11.

98. Beecher, "Six Sermons on Intemperance," 63.

99. The basic regulatory framework can be traced to a late-seventeenth-century English statute that required the permission of the Crown to conduct a lottery. Blackstone, *Commentaries on the Laws of England,* 4:168, 173–4.

100. For typical examples of post-independence lottery grants, see *The Statutes and Large of Pennsylvania from 1682 to 1801* (Harrisburg, PA: Harrisburg Publishing, 1906), 11:252–62; *The Statutes and Large of Pennsylvania from 1682 to 1801* (Harrisburg, PA: Harrisburg Publishing, 1906), 13:276–82, 532–7; *Private and Special Statutes of the Commonwealth of Massachusetts* (Boston: Wells and Lilly, 1823), 4:42–3, 393–6; *Laws of the*

State of New York (Albany, NY: Charles R. and George Webster, 1802), 2:242–5; *Laws of the State of New York* (Albany, NY: Charles R. and George Webster, 1802), 3:302–7; *Laws of the State of New York* (Albany, NY: Weed, Parsons, 1887), 3:114–5, 594–5; *Laws of the State of New York* (Albany, NY: Weed, Parsons, 1887), 4:469–71.

101. Perhaps not surprisingly, these features of the grant system fostered (or perhaps reflected) a thriving late-eighteenth- and early-nineteenth-century trade in the buying and selling of lottery privileges. See, for example, Hugh G. J. Aitken, "Yates and McIntyre: Lottery Managers," *The Journal of Economic History* 13 (1953): 36–57.

102. That the rights afforded lottery grantees were legally enforceable, even against the legislature itself, is clearly evident in the 1818 Massachusetts case of *Commonwealth v. Dearborn*. The litigation began when state lawmakers discovered that the managers of the Kennebec Bridge Lottery had designed a scheme that would net themselves a $51,000 profit while providing only $2,000 towards the construction of a bridge over the Kennebec River. One might imagine that a state legislature would experience little difficulty in reining in a cabal of obviously corrupt lottery managers. But when the state attorney general challenged the managers' authority in an action of *quo warranto*, he was rudely rebuffed by the state Supreme Court. The problem was that the lottery grant in question vested the grantee—in this case, the Kennebec Bridge Corporation—with plenary authority in the hiring and firing of managers. Based on this fact, the state Supreme Court concluded that even if it were to sanction the managers' removal, "such a judgment would be nugatory, for the corporation might immediately reinstate them." *Commonwealth v. Dearborn*, 15 Mass. 125 (1818). Also see Massachusetts House of Representatives, *Report of the Committee Appointed to Inquire into the . . . Conduct of the Managers of All Lotteries* (Boston, 1818); *Resolves of the General Court of the Commonwealth of Massachusetts* (Boston: Russell and Gardner, 1819), 7:532–3.

103. For summary tables describing the number and types of grants issued in this period, see Ezell, *Fortune's Merry Wheel*, 64, 65, 71, 113–18.

104. Aitken, "Yates and McIntyre: Lottery Managers."

105. On petition drives and other tactics used by religious groups and other lottery opponents, see Ezell, *Fortune's Merry Wheel*, 204–29; Anson Phelps Stokes, *Church and State in the United States* (New York: Harper, 1950), 25–9.

106. George William Gordon, *Lecture before the Boston Young Men's Society* (Boston: Temperance Press, 1835), 29.

107. *Fletcher v. Peck*, 10 U.S. 87 at 137.

108. 10 U.S. 87 at 130.

109. 10 U.S. 87 at 139, 130.

110. Here, for example, is how James Kent summarized the Commerce Clause's implications for public contracts in the aftermath of *Fletcher* and *Dartmouth College:* "When a law [is] in its nature a contract, and absolute rights have vested under that contract, a repeal of the law [can] not divest those rights, nor annihilate or impair the title so acquired. A grant [is] a contract within the meaning of the constitution. The words of the Constitution were construed to comprehend equally executory and executed contracts, for each of them contains obligations binding on the parties. A grant is a contract

executed, and a party is always estopped by his own grant. A party cannot pronounce his own deed invalid, whatever cause may be assigned for its invalidity, and though the party may be the legislature of the state. A grant amounts to an extinguishment of the right of the grantor, and implies a contract not to re-assert that right. A grant from a state is as much protected by the operation of the provision of the Constitution, as a grant from one individual to another, and the state is as much inhibited from impairing its own contracts, or a contract to which it is a party, as it is from impairing the obligation of contracts between two individuals. *Commentaries on American Law*, 1:368; also see Joseph Story, *Commentaries on the Constitution of the United States* (Boston: Hilliard, Gray, 1833), 3:257–8.

111. "Lotteries in New York," *The Religious Intelligencer* 11 (1827): 731.

112. *Laws of the State of New York* (Albany, NY: William Gould, 1825), 6:137–9. The lottery privileges in question were originally conferred in 1814. According to the terms of the original grant, the state was to manage the drawings directly. However, the legislature, at the request of Union College and the other beneficiaries, enacted a new grant in 1822 that transferred management of the drawings to the trustees of the colleges. For the original grant, see *Laws of the State of New York* (Albany, NY: Websters and Skinners, 1815), 3:128–30.

113. Clinton's veto message is reprinted in "The Lottery Law," *Nile's Weekly Register* (April 14, 1827), 122.

114. "Lottery Bill," *The Religious Intelligencer* 11 (1827): 747.

115. *Charles River Bridge v. Warren Bridge*, 36 U.S. 420 (1837).

116. See, for example, Kermit L. Hall, *The Magic Mirror: Law in American History* (New York: Oxford University Press, 1999), 132–3; Friedman, *History of American Law*, 198–9.

117. In a major study of the Contract Clause and its development, Benjamin F. Wright concluded that "with very few exceptions, the contract principles of Marshall were those of Taney, and during his chief justiceship the clause was applied much more frequently and to a wider variety of subject matter. The proportion of cases involving this clause in which statutes were held unconstitutional is almost exactly the same in the two periods." *The Contract Clause of the Constitution* (Cambridge, MA: Harvard University Press, 1938), 63.

118. As the author of an 1827 anti-lottery pamphlet framed the issue, lottery tickets were not analogous to "agricultural products" or "species of manufacture" such as "cloths, pails, and corn brooms." They were, rather, "a species of gambling and immorality." For this reason, arguments "drawn from the constitutional principles which protect" other forms of property were "not applicable to the sale of tickets, and cannot be considered as parallel cases." "Civis," [F.O.J. Smith], *A Dissertation on the Nature and Effects of Lottery Systems* (Portland, ME: : Arthur Shirley, 1827).

119. Justin Edwards, "License Laws, No. 9," *Christian Watchman* (Feb. 12, 1836), 28. For an overview of the origins of nineteenth-century evangelical perfectionism, see James A. Morone, *Hellfire Nation: The Politics of Sin in American History* (New Haven, CT: Yale University Press, 2004), 123–31.

120. The various state-level license systems were virtually identical; indeed, all of the original colonies, with two exceptions, modeled their license laws on the English Licensing Act of 1627. Frederick A. Johnson and Ruth R. Kessler, "The Liquor License System—Its Origin and Constitutional Development," *New York University Law Review* 15 (1937–8): 230. For examples of late-eighteenth century license laws, see *Acts and Laws of the State of Connecticut in America* (Hartford, CT: Hudson and Goodwin, 1796), 408–13; *Laws of the State of Delaware* (New Castle, DE: Samuel and John Adams, 1797), 1:192–195; *Digest of the Laws of the State of Georgia* (Milledgeville, GA: Grantland and Orme, 1822), 487–8, 510–12; *The Laws of Maryland* (Baltimore, MD: Philip H. Nicklin and Co., 1811), 1:393–7; *The Perpetual Laws of the Commonwealth of Massachusetts,* (Boston: I. Thomas and E. T. Andrews, 1801), 1:374–382; *Laws of the State of New Hampshire,* (Bristol, NH: Musgrove Printing, 1916), 4:199–201; *Laws of the State of New Jersey* (Trenton, NJ: Joseph Justice, 1821), 281–7; *Laws of the State of New York* (Albany, NY: Weed, Parsons and Co., 1886), 2:707–12; *Laws of the State of North Carolina,* (Raleigh: J. Gales, 1821), 2:906–7, 945; *Laws of the Commonwealth of Pennsylvania,* (Philadelphia: John Bioren, 1810), 1:73–5; *The Public Laws of the State of Rhode Island* (Providence, RI: Miller and Hutchens, 1822), 295–6; *Acts of the General Assembly of the State of South Carolina* (Columbia, SC: D. and J.J. Faust, 1808), 398–403; *A Collection of All Such Acts of the Commonwealth of Virginia* (Richmond, VA: Samuel Pleasants, 1783), 202–4.

121. Often this goal was made explicit in the title of the licensing statute, as in New Hampshire's "Act for the Inspecting, and Suppressing of Disorders in Licensed Houses." *Laws of the State of New Hampshire,* (Bristol, NH: Musgrove Printing, 1916), 4:199–201. In the words of the preamble to the original English license law, a license system was necessary to suppress the "abuses and disorders" associated with "common ale houses and other places called tippling houses." 5 & 6 Edward VI c. 25. Quoted in Johnson and Kessler, "The Liquor License System," 213. Also see Conroy, *In Public Houses,* 27–8.

122. And indeed, this is how many present-day scholars have interpreted the antebellum license system. William Novak, for example, writes that an antebellum "liquor license brought with it no vested rights, no private properties, and no sanction for licentiousness. Rather, it sealed a public trust between community and 'common calling' that brought serious consequences if violated." *The People's Welfare,* 172.

123. Hartog, "The Public Law of a County Court," 288–91. Hartog bases this conclusion on a study of the records of the Middlesex County (Massachusetts) Court of General Sessions. William Nelson similarly concludes that a retail liquor license was by the late-eighteenth century understood to convey "a right in the nature of a property right." *Americanization of the Common Law,* 52, 122–30.

124. Hartog, "The Public Law of a County Court," 288–91. Additional evidence for the emergence of a property-centered conception of the liquor license is evident in the records of the Plymouth County (Massachusetts) Court of General Sessions, which were made available after the studies of Hartog and Nelson were published. The Plymouth Court routinely allowed licenses to pass between individuals and locations; in addition,

the Court granted lengthy grace periods when existing license holders failed to pay the required fee for renewal. *Plymouth Court Records, 1686–1859,* ed. David Thomas Konig (Wilmington, DE: Michael Glazier, 1979), 4:13 ("Petition of Anthony Eames Hatch"), 4:262 ("Court ordered that the Persons who were licensed at August Term last past . . ."), 4:267 ("Petition of John Basset"). Significantly, the situation seems to have been much the same in other regions of the country. In 1791, for example, the North Carolina legislature, noting that most of the state's tavern keepers were not "renew[ing] their licenses according law," passed an act requiring sheriffs to go door-to-door to collect the annual taxes owed by individuals "accustomed to retailing spirituous liquors," thus effectively endorsing the right of previously licensed retailers to stay in business, provided they paid their taxes. *Laws of the State of North Carolina* (Raleigh, NC: J. Gales, 1821), 1:651.

125. Harrison Gray Otis, "Memorial of Harrison Otis Gray and Others," in *Investigation into the Fifteen Gallon Law of Massachusetts* (Boston: J.H. Buckingham, 1839), 6–7.

126. Ibid., 7.

127. Ibid., 6.

128. On the history of the "class legislation" doctrine, see Howard Gillman, *The Constitution Besieged* (Durham, NC: Duke University Press, 1992).

129. Harrison Gray Otis, "Memorial of Harrison Gray Otis and Others," 6–7.

130. As the pro-license politician Benjamin Franklin Hallett declared in 1839: "The legislature has the same right and *no more,* to tax the employment of a farmer or mechanic, as of an attorney, auctioneer, tavern keeper, or retailer of spirituous liquors; and if there is the same right to tax one as the other, there must be the same right, and no more, to *prohibit* the one as the other. Unless, then, the Legislature has power to decree that no *farmer* shall sell less than fifteen bushels of grain or fifteen pounds of pork to be used for food, . . . it follows . . . that the Legislature has not the power to prohibit the sale of any other species of property for its ordinary uses." "Mr. Hallett's Opening Argument," in *Investigation into the Fifteen Gallon Law of Massachusetts,* 21. Emphasis in the original.

131. Pro-license groups in Massachusetts found support for this position in a bit of dictum from an 1815 opinion of the Supreme Judicial Court authored by Chief Justice Isaac Parker. In *Portland Bank v. Apthorp* (12 Tyng 252), Parker had declared it the "natural right" of any man to pursue the calling "of an auctioneer, of an attorney, of a tavern-keeper, of a retailer of spirituous liquors." Significantly, however, Parker also upheld the right of the state to require licensing fees for these professions and to exercise discretion in ensuring that only men of good character were licensed.

132. Otis, "Memorial of Harrison Gray Otis and Others," 8.

133. Marcus Morton, "Address," *Boston Recorder* (Jan. 31, 1840), 1.

134. Justin Edwards, "Sixth Annual Report of the American Temperance Society," in *Permanent Temperance Documents of the American Temperance Society* (Boston: Seth Bliss, 1835), 271.

135. On the structural limitation of federal power in the pre-New Deal period see, for example, Howard Gillman, "Preferred Freedoms: The Progressive Expansion of

State Power and the Rise of Modern Civil Liberties Jurisprudence," *Political Research Quarterly* 47 (1994): 623–53. Of course, the question of whether, or to what extent, Congress's enumerated powers were believed to be constrained by the "reserved" powers of the states remains a subject of controversy among scholars. For two sharply contrasting views, see Robert Lowry Clinton, "Judicial Review, Nationalism, and the Commerce Clause: Contrasting Antebellum and Postbellum Supreme Court Decision Making," *Political Research Quarterly* 47 (1994): 857–76; Howard Gillman, "The Struggle over Marshall and the Politics of Constitutional History," *Political Research Quarterly* 47 (1994): 877–86.

136. *Federalist* 17; *Federalist* 39, in Wills, ed., *The Federalist Papers*, 80, 194. As Madison famously explained in *Federalist* 39, the new government would be neither fully "national" nor fully "federal," but would combine elements of both systems: "The idea of a national Government involves in it, not only an authority over the individual citizens; but an indefinite supremacy over all persons and things, so far as they are objects of lawful Government. . . . In this relation then the proposed Government cannot be deemed a *national* one; since it jurisdiction extends to certain enumerated objects only, and leaves to the several States a residuary and inviolable sovereignty over all other objects."

137. The use of the term "police power" to describe the inherent regulatory powers of the states was not uncommon in the Founding period. Not until the mid-nineteenth century, however, did the term take on a fixed legal or constitutional definition in American courts (as describing a range of regulatory powers that belong exclusively to the states and which may justify significant interference with private property). On the use of the term in the eighteenth century, see Markus Dirk Dubber, *The Police Power: Patriarchy and the Foundations of American Government* (New York: Cambridge University Press, 2005), 81–119; Tomlins, *Law, Labor, and Ideology*, 35–96. On the evolution of the police power doctrine in the nineteenth century, see Leonard W. Levy, *The Law of the Commonwealth and Chief Justice Shaw* (Cambridge, MA: Harvard University Press, 1957), 229–65; Noga Morag-Levine, *Chasing the Wind: Regulating Air Pollution in the Common Law State* (Princeton, NJ: Princeton University Press, 2003), 63–85.

138. See, for example, White, *The Marshall Court and Cultural Change*, 567–85; Herbert A. Johnson, *The Chief Justiceship of John Marshall: 1801–1835* (Columbia: University of South Carolina Press, 1997), Ch. 4.

139. For an overview of the antebellum judiciary's attempts to devise a formula to distinguish the police and commerce powers, see Stuart Streichler, *Justice Curtis in the Civil War Era: At the Crossroads of American Constitutionalism* (Charlottesville: University of Virginia Press, 2005), Ch. 3.

140. Indeed, as W.J. Rorabaugh and other historians have documented, the early nineteenth-century witnessed the emergence of a thriving interstate market in liquor, as transportation networks improved and the opening of the frontier produced a glut of grain. In fact, the vast majority of the liquor consumed in the eastern seaboard states in the early nineteenth century was produced on the Western frontier. By 1810, "western Pennsylvania, Ohio and Kentucky" alone "produced more than half the nation's grain and fruit spirits." Roarabaugh, *Alcoholic Republic*, 76–92.

141. In 1839, for example, the opponents of the Massachusetts Fifteen Gallon Law argued that the power to regulate foreign and interstate commerce had been "wholly ceded" to the federal government at the time of the Founding. The fact that Congress had imposed duties on imported liquor meant that the federal government had occupied the regulatory field with respect to liquor. Massachusetts' experiment with prohibition, on this view, amounted to "an act of nullification of the laws of Congress, rendering the right of importation useless by destroying the right to sell." Otis, "Memorial of Harrison Gray Otis and Others," 6.

142. *Cooley v. Board of Wardens*, 53 U.S. 299 (1852).

143. See especially *Bowman v. Chicago and Northwestern Railway* (125 U.S. 465 [1888]) and *Leisy v. Hardin* (135 U.S. 100 [1890]). Both cases are discussed in detail in chapter 3.

144. Henry William Blair, *The Temperance Movement* (Boston: W.E. Smythe, 1887), 378.

145. See, for example, Bernard C. Gavit, *The Commerce Clause of the United States Constitution* (Bloomington, IN: Principia Press, 1932), 130–9. In his lengthy *Cohens v. Virginia* opinion, handed down in 1821, John Marshall failed to even consider the possibility that a state ban on the importation of lottery tickets might conflict with the federal Commerce Clause. Rather, Marshall concluded that because Virginia's lottery ban was a "penal law," having for its "sole object the internal government" of the state, it had not impinged upon any "legitimate powers of the Union." 19 U.S. 264 at 443.

146. A similar constitutional dilemma can be seen in the Mormon polygamy controversy of the mid nineteenth century. Even in a case where the "rogue state" had not yet attained statehood, the question of the federal government's power to regulate matters of marriage and divorce—which were generally classed under the states' police powers—was sharply contested. In the end, the Supreme Court upheld the constitutionality of federal anti-polygamy laws, but only under Congress's "power to prescribe criminal laws for the Territories." Had the Utah Territory attained statehood prior to the polygamy controversy, a constitutional amendment would likely have been required to justify federal intervention. See, for example, Sarah Barringer Gordon, *The Mormon Question: Polygamy and Constitutional Conflict in Nineteenth-Century America* (Chapel Hill: University of North Carolina Press, 2002); *Reynolds v. United States*, 98 U.S. 145, 162 (1878).

147. "Lotteries," *Friends' Review* 8 (1855): 394.

148. "The Lottery Humbug," *Saturday Evening Post* (August 18, 1860), 2.

149. Edward Dicey, *Spectator of America*, ed. Herbert Mitgang (Athens: University of Georgia Press, 1989), 181, 198–9.

2. Moral Reform and Constitutional Adjudication, 1830–1854

1. Lyman Beecher, *Six Sermons on the Nature, Occasions, Signs, Evils, and Remedy of Intemperance* (New York: American Tract Society, 1827), 84, 60.

2. Ibid., 87.

3. Ibid., 92–3.

4. Ibid., 91, 63.

5. Ibid., 85.

6. Ibid., 58.

7. *Commonwealth v. Blackington*, 24 Pickering 352 (1837), 355. Shaw repeated the basic point in a second 1837 case, *Commonwealth v. Kimball:* "The power to regulate licensed houses, and to provide for the regulation of the sale of spirituous liquors," he noted, "had long been in active operation, in this state, and no doubt in other states, before the Constitution of the United States was adopted." 24 Pickering 359, 361.

8. On the importance of officers' rights in early American law, see Karen Orren, "Officers' Rights: Toward a Unified Field Theory of American Constitutional Development," *Law and Society Review* 34 (2000): 873–909.

9. As Ruffin put the point, if any magistrate, "fully informed that [he has] a discretion to regulate a branch of the public police, should perversely abuse [his] discretion by obstinately resolving not to exercise it at all, or by exercising it in a way purposely to defeat the legislative intention, or to oppress an individual; such an intentional, and, therefore, corrupt violation of duty and law, must be answered for on indictment." *Attorney General v. Justices of Guillford County,* 27 N.C. 315, 331–2 (1844). Also see *City of Louisville v. Kean,* 57 Ky. 9, 15–16 (1857): "In our opinion, although to some extent the [licensing] power . . . is discretionary, it must be exercised, not as an arbitrary, but as a sound legal discretion. [City officials] have not the right of prohibition, but only the right to decide how many taverns, having the privilege of selling spirituous liquors, are required within the city for the public accommodation and convenience, and whether the applicants have the proper legal qualifications to entitle them to a license. The existence of such taverns is not only sanctioned but deemed necessary by the general law, and the city authorities have no power to prohibit their existence within the city."

10. Ruffin's ruling, it should be noted, was anything but a radical innovation; indeed it followed a venerable line of Anglo-American precedent holding that the power to issue liquor licenses was not to be wielded arbitrarily. As early as 1757, Lord Mansfield held (in a case that was subsequently cited by Ruffin and other early American jurists) that any licensing official who was "partially, maliciously, or corruptly influenced in the exercise of [his] discretion" was "liable to prosecution." *R. v. Young and Pitts,* 1 Burr. 556. This declaration was technically dictum, since there was no evidence of corruption in this particular case. However, eight years later, two local Justices were sent to prison for "corruptly" rejecting the liquor license application of a political opponent. *Rex v. Hann and Price,* 3 Burr. 1716 (1765).

11. 3 Del. 441 (1842).

12. 1842 Del. LEXIS 21, at **9–10.

13. Ibid. at **10–12. It is worth noting that the company was represented by John M. Clayton, a former U.S. Senator and Delaware chief justice, and Robert Frame, a former state attorney general. Clayton, a national leader in the Whig party (and future Secretary of State), would also play an important role in defending the state's liquor retailers against the threat of "local option" legislation while serving as counsel in the case of *Rice v. Foster,* discussed below. See Kyle G. Volk, "The Perils of 'Pure Democracy': Minority

Rights, Liquor Politics, and Popular Sovereignty in Antebellum America," *Journal of the Early Republic* 29 (2009): 668–71.

14. 1842 Del. LEXIS 21, at **10–12.

15. 3 Del. 441 at 452–3.

16. The Court was careful, however, to distinguish its holding from the Supreme Court's recent ruling in the famed *Charles River Bridge* case. That case had turned on the question of whether "a contract and sale of a certain legislative power or privilege to build a bridge was a monopoly, and restrained the legislature from granting a similar power to others." The Delaware lottery case, in contrast, involved the very different question of "whether the legislature could directly add to or vary a contract made under its authority." 3 Del. 441 at 455.

17. Ibid. at 452–3. Of course, one might object—as the state in fact did—that merely imposing new license fees on lottery operators was not the same thing as revoking a contractual right. After all, lottery operators were free to continue holding drawings, so long as they paid the higher licensing fees. And yet the Delaware Court refused to concede even this much. Indeed, the Contract Clause, according to the justices, barred any legislative act that would unilaterally alter the terms of the 1839 agreement. For to allow even the narrow exception at issue in *Phalen and Paine* would be to invite further legislative incursions upon a foundational ideal of American constitutionalism: "The simple question we have to settle . . . is, does [the] addition of $10 on each drawing and variation of the time of payment of the installments of the purchase money . . . interfere with the contract . . . so as to impair the obligation thereof? . . . If the legislature [can] add $10 on each drawing, they might add $1,000; *it is a question of power and not of amount. . . .* [W]hen we turn to the clause in the constitution of the United States, which appears there inserted as a shield and defense against all legislative action by a state impairing the obligation of contracts, we feel authorized to say, not only that the legislature had no right, but they had no power to regulate in the manner attempted . . . the existing contract of 1839." Ibid. at 454. Emphasis added.

18. *State v. Hawthorn,* 9 Mo. 389, 394, 396 (1845).

19. Ibid. at 397.

20. 59 Ky. 589 (1859).

21. Ibid. at 598.

22. See, for example, *Boyd and Jackson v. The State,* 46 Ala. 329 (1871); *Webb v. Commonwealth,* 10 Ky. Op. 10 (1878); *Kellum v. The State,* 66 Ind. 588 (1879); *Louisiana State Lottery Company v. Fitzpatrick,* 15 F. Cas. 970 (Cir. Ct., Louisiana 1879).

23. For the dates of enactment of anti-lottery amendments, see Ann-Marie Szymanski, *Pathways to Prohibition: Radicals, Moderates, and Social Movement Outcomes* (Durham, NC: Duke University Press, 2003), 259; John J. Dinan, *The American State Constitutional Tradition* (Lawrence: University Press of Kansas, 2006), 398–9; John Samuell Ezell, *Fortune's Merry Wheel: The Lottery in America* (Cambridge, MA: Harvard University Press, 1960), Ch. 11.

24. According to Ezell, only Delaware, Kentucky, and Missouri were still saddled with active lottery grants at the time of the Civil War. The lottery industry experienced

a major resurgence during the war years, however, as several states resumed the practice of issuing lottery grants. *Fortune's Merry Wheel,* 228–9.

25. Ernest H. Cherrington, *The Evolution of Prohibition in the United States of America* (Montclair, NJ: Patterson Smith, 1969), 276; John Allen Krout, *The Origins of Prohibition* (New York: Alfred A. Knopf, 1925), 275–83.

26. See, for example, Michael F. Holt, *The Rise and Fall of the American Whig Party* (New York: Oxford University Press, 1999), 689.

27. John Locke, *Two Treatises of Government and A Letter Concerning Toleration,* ed. Ian Shapiro (New Haven: Yale University Press, 2003), 163–4.

28. Thomas M. Cooley, *A Treatise on the Constitutional Limitations Which Rest upon the Legislative Power of the States of the American Union* (Boston: Little, Brown, 1868), 121–2. Also see Joseph Story, *Commentaries on the Law of Agency* (Boston: Little and Brown, 1839), 14–15; James Kent, *Commentaries on American Law,* Vol. 2 (New York; O. Halsted, 1832 [2d Ed.]), 633.

29. Argument of counsel, *Bancroft v. Dumas,* 1849 Vt. LEXIS 57, at **6.

30. Argument of counsel, *Rice v. Foster,* 1846 Del. LEXIS 27, at **5.

31. Ibid.

32. Argument of counsel, *Parker v. Commonwealth,* 1847 Pa. LEXIS 193, at **3.

33. For background on the local option controversy Delaware, see Volk, "The Perils of 'Pure Democracy,'" 641–71.

34. Daniel J. Elazar, "'To Secure the Blessings of Liberty': Liberty and American Federal Democracy," *Publius: The Journal of Federalism* 20 (1990):1–13; Dinan, *The American State Constitutional Tradition,* 223–4.

35. 4 Del. 479 at 486, 499.

36. Ibid. at 484.

37. Ibid. at 487.

38. Ibid. at 487–7.

39. Ibid. at 489.

40. Ibid. at 488.

41. Ibid. at 499.

42. On the origins of the local option controversy in Pennsylvania, see Louis Hartz, *Economic Policy and Democratic Thought: Pennsylvania, 1776–1860* (Cambridge, MA: Harvard University Press, 1948), 209–19.

43. 6 Pa. 507 at 513.

44. Although the local option cases of the 1840s and 1850s often appear to turn on arcane procedural questions, they were, at bottom, about the destruction of settled property rights. Indeed, it is worth noting that previous state-level experiments with local option—for example, laws that empowered local electorates to determine administrative boundaries—encountered little judicial opposition. Only in the late 1840s, when the local option procedure was used to prohibit liquor sales—thereby destroying the livelihoods of liquor retailers—did state courts begin to vigorously apply the *delegata potestas* maxim. For examples of early cases in which the constitutionality of local option was sustained, see, for example, *Wales v. Belcher* (20 Mass. 508 [1827]); *Goddin v. Crump*

(35 Va. 120 [1837]); *People v. Reynolds* (10 Ill. 1 [1848]). Also see the discussion in Ellis Paxson Oberholtzer, *The Referendum in America* (New York: De Capo Press, 1900 [1971]), 318–24. Oberholtzer concludes that the bulk of judicial opinions "adverse" to the local option procedure were "called forth by local option liquor laws. If these opinions were disregarded the American courts would [have been] in virtual unanimity respecting this question." *The Referendum in America*, 323.

45. 6 Pa. 507 at 511–14.

46. Ibid. at 519, 514.

47. For state court decisions upholding local option laws, see *People v. Townsey*, 5 Denio (N.Y.) 70 (1847); *Garner v. The State*, 8 Blackf. (Ind.) 568 (1848); *Bancroft v. Dumas*, 21 Vt. 456 (1849). It should be noted, however, that in only one of these cases *(Bancroft v. Dumas)* was the court directly presented with a state *constitutional* objection to a no-license law. In the others, retailers convicted of selling without a license argued unsuccessfully that the passage of local option laws had had the effect of repealing previously existing penal statutes that imposed fines or jail time for retailing without a license.

48. For other opinions invalidating local option on non-delegation grounds, see *Maize v. State*, 4 Ind. 342 (1853): "Nor is it easy to see how, on principle, a public measure can be submitted, in the abstract, to a popular vote, consistently with the representative system. In effect it is changing the government to what publicists call a pure democracy, such as Athens was. If one enactment may be submitted to such vote, so may another, so might all; and thus would the representative system by wholly subverted. If the people desire to resume directly the law-making power which they have delegated to the general assembly, the have only to change the constitution accordingly"; *State v. Swisher*, 17 Tex. 441 (1856): "Under our constitution, the principle of law-making is, that laws are made by the people, not directly, but by and through their chosen representatives. By the act under consideration, this principle is subverted, and the law is proposed to be made at last by the popular vote of the people, leading inevitably to what was intended to be avoided, confusion and great popular excitement in the enactment of laws"; and *Geebrick v. State*, 5 Iowa 491 (1857): "The legislative power must command. It must not leave to the people, the choice to obey, or not to obey its requirements. It is not a law enacted according to the requirements of the constitution, if there is left to the action and choice of the people upon whom it is to operate, the determination of a question which may result in a want of uniformity in the operation of a law of a general nature."

49. The distinguishing feature of Vermont's local option law, according to the Vermont Supreme Court, was that it imposed a statewide penalty for retailing liquor while allowing towns to *opt out* of legal prohibition if a majority of their residents so desired. The Pennsylvania and Delaware laws, in contrast, effectively suspended those states' existing liquor laws pending the outcomes of county-level elections; the laws thus remained "a dead letter, until breathed into activity" by local electorates. *Bancroft v. Dumas*, 21 Vt. 456 at 464.

50. It is worth noting that Edward Corwin, in an important survey of antebellum constitutional thought, described *Rice v. Foster* and *Parker v. Commonwealth* as atypical decisions and the non-delegation principle as an "absurd doctrine." On the first point, it

seems odd to dismiss *Rice* and *Parker* as atypical decisions, given that five of the six state appellate courts that considered the non-delegation objection during the antebellum period deemed local option unconstitutional. On the second point, it may be true, as Corwin points out, that the non-delegation doctrine was rarely invoked before the mid-1840s. But it does not follow that the authors of the *Rice* and *Parker* opinions invented "a new dogma of constitutional law." In fact, the state judiciary's remarkably monolithic response to local option suggests that the policy violated a core principle of antebellum constitutional thought. That this principle was not clearly articulated in previous cases may well be explained by the fact that no legislature had previously attempted a reorganization of regulatory authority on the scale of the local option reform. See Edward S. Corwin, *Liberty Against Government: The Rise, Flowering and Decline of a Famous Judicial Concept* (Baton Rouge: Louisiana State University Press, 1948), 99–100.

51. 4 Del. 479 at 484.

52. The law provided an exception, however, for liquor used for medicinal and mechanical purposes, which could be obtained only through bonded agents. The texts of the various Maine Laws in effect as of 1856 are reprinted in Henry S. Clubb, *The Maine Liquor Law: Its Origin, History, and Results* (New York: Fowler and Wells, 1856).

53. The exemption for importers of foreign liquor was intended to avoid even the appearance of an interference with the federal commerce power. Although the Supreme Court, in the 1847 *License Cases* (46 U.S. 504), had ruled that local option laws were not inherently incompatible with the federal commerce power, several of the justices nonetheless raised questions about whether the states possessed the constitutional authority to interfere with the resale of foreign liquor imported under the federal tariff laws (which imposed duties on foreign liquor).

54. In the language of the Massachusetts prohibition law, "All intoxicating liquors kept for sale, and the implements and vessels actually used in selling and keeping the same . . . are hereby declared to be common nuisances, and are to be regarded and treated as such." Clubb, *The Maine Liquor Law,* 363–4.

55. Cooley, *Constitutional Limitations,* 583–4.

56. 33 Me. 558 (1852).

57. Ibid. at 560. Such provisions were relatively common in early American state constitutions. For an overview, see John C. P. Goldberg, "The Constitutional Status of Tort Law: Due Process and the Right to a Law for the Redress of Wrongs," *Yale Law Journal* 115 (2005): 559–64.

58. 33 Me. 558 at 561–2.

59. The Maine Supreme Court voided two more provisions of the law in the 1853 case of *State v. Gurney* (37 Me. 156) and the 1854 case of *Saco v. Wentworth* (37 Me. 165). The first provision required individuals found guilty of possessing illegal liquor to provide bonds and sureties before an appeal (in the form of a jury trial) would be permitted. The second provided that an individual's fine would double if he or she appealed from the judgment of a magistrate and was subsequently found guilty in a jury trial. As Judge Wells explained in *State v. Gurney,* the legislature had "no power to impair a right [the right to a jury trial] given by the constitution, [for] it belongs to the citizen

untrammeled and unfettered. If the legislature can impose penalties upon the exercise of the right, they may be so severe and heavy as practically to destroy it." 37 Me. 156 at 164.

60. More specifically, the New Hampshire court objected to the fact that the law: (1) conferred excessive authority on justices of the peace to order the destruction of property; (2) failed to guarantee a trial by jury for those accused of keeping illegal liquor; (3) interfered with the Contract Clause of the U.S. Constitution—as well as a similar state provision—by barring the enforcement of contracts or collection of debts involving liquor; (4) violated property rights guaranteed in the state constitution by barring suits against officials or other individuals who seized allegedly illegal stores of liquor; (5) failed to provide for the defendant's state constitutional right of appeal; (6) violated a state constitutional prohibition against the requirement of "excessive bail"; (7) failed to meet basic requirements of a "fair trial," including the opportunity to confront witnesses; and (8) violated the state constitutional right of citizens "to be secure against all unreasonable searches." For the full text of the New Hampshire Supreme Court's advisory opinion, see "The New Hampshire Liquor Law," *The Monthly Law Reporter* 5 (January 1853), 481. Also see "The Liquor Law in New Hampshire," *Western Law Journal* (April 1853), 336.

61. *Greene v. Briggs*, 10 F. Cas. 1135 (C.C.D.R.I. 1852). The litigation began when a New York man sued to recover liquor that had been seized by Rhode Island authorities. The federal court therefore took charge of the case under its diversity jurisdiction.

62. Ibid. at 1141–2.

63. Ibid. at 1140.

64. 1 Gray 1 (Mass., 1854).

65. 61 Mass. 53, 84–5 (1851). On the role of Shaw's *Alger* opinion in shaping the nineteenth-century conception of the police power, see Leonard W. Levy, *The Law of the Commonwealth and Chief Justice Shaw* (Cambridge, MA: Harvard University Press, 1957), 247–54; William J. Novak, *The People's Welfare: Law and Regulation in Nineteenth-Century America* (Chapel Hill: University of North Carolina Press, 1996),19–21, 144–5; Markus Dirk Dubber, *The Police Power: Patriarchy and the Foundations of American Government* (New York: Cambridge University Press, 2005), 104–14; Harry N. Scheiber, "Public Rights and the Rule of Law in American Legal History," *California Law Review* 72 (1984): 222–24.*

66. William Novak argues that because Shaw had upheld nearly "identical [nuisance abatement] processes" in earlier cases, his *Fisher v. McGirr* opinion must be seen as a singular departure from antebellum jurisprudential norms, which generally granted state and local officials wide leeway to maintain a "well-regulated society." *The People's Welfare*, 183.

67. Novak recognizes that the Maine Law differed from traditional forms of liquor regulation in that it "replaced local, discretionary liquor licensing with a formal, centralized, and uniform system of rules." However, he concludes his chapter on the antebellum prohibition movement by arguing that *Fisher* and other anti-Maine Law rulings launched a new constitutional epoch—one organized around the ideals of limited government and private rights. Certainly, Novak is correct that the Maine Law's

enforcement mechanisms differed from traditional forms of regulation. And yet it is difficult to see how the *judicial response* to the Maine Law can be described as a significant turning point in constitutional thought. Far from marking a new epoch in American constitutionalism, these decisions were broadly consistent with the local option and lottery grant decisions of the 1840s, in which antebellum judges had similarly refused to subordinate established constitutional limitations to a novel view of the public good. Novak, *The People's Welfare*, 180, 183, 184–8.

68. 1 Gray 1 at 47.

69. Ibid. at 27–9.

70. Ibid. at 33. It should be noted that some scholars have dismissed the early Maine Law decisions as mere procedural exercises with little bearing on the larger trajectory of constitutional development. Thus, Markus Dirk Dubber notes that Shaw's *Fisher* opinion focused on "secondary, procedural" matters while avoiding the critical constitutional question of "whether the state may interfere with the property rights of liquor owners through statutes that [prohibit] . . . the possession of liquor." But while Dubber is correct to a point—Shaw was indeed reluctant to specify the precise limits of the state's power to order the destruction of private property—it would be a mistake to conclude that Shaw dodged the most important constitutional questions raised by the Maine Law. On one critical point, at least, America's foremost theorist of the police power was clear: no threat to public morality, no matter how severe, could justify the state in effectively suspending the individual liberties embodied in the state's written constitution. 1 Gray 1 at 33. Markus Dirk Dubber, "Policing Possession: The War on Crime and the End of Criminal Law," *The Journal of Criminal Law and Criminology* 91 (2001): 944.

71. For additional state appellate decisions declaring the Maine Law unconstitutional in whole or in part, see *State v. Gurney* (37 Me. 156 [1853]); *Saco v. Wentworth* 37 Me. 165 [1853]); *State v. Snow* (3 R.I. 64 [1854]).

72. *Greene v. Briggs*, 10 F. Cas. 1135 at 1140.

73. Indeed, excerpts from the opinion, which appeared to many to offer an unequivocal endorsement of the temperance movement's aims, quickly became a staple of anti-liquor tracts. For typical examples, see Albert Barnes, *The Throne of Iniquity: Or Sustaining Evil by Law* (New York: National Temperance Society, 1852), 7–8; John Marsh, *The Triumphs of Temperance* (New York: John P. Prall, 1855), 10; Charles Jewett, "A Brief Plan of a Temperance Campaign" in *Speeches, Poems, and Miscellaneous Writings on Subjects Connected with Temperance and the Liquor Traffic* (Boston: John P. Jewett, 1849), 157–61.

74. Novak, for example, invokes the *License Cases* as further evidence that nineteenth-century judges regularly subordinated private rights to the wellbeing of the wider community. *The People's Welfare*, 176–7.

75. 25 U.S. 419 (1827).

76. 25 U.S. 419 at 449.

77. Harrison Gray Otis, "Memorial," in *Investigation into the Fifteen Gallon Law of Massachusetts* (Boston: J.H. Buckingham, 1839), 6.

78. 46 U.S. 504, 577.

79. On the larger significance of the *License Cases*, see, for example, David P. Currie, *The Constitution in the Supreme Court: The First Hundred Years, 1789–1888* (Chicago: University of Chicago Press, 1985), 225–6; Stuart Streichler, *Justice Curtis in the Civil War Era: At the Crossroads of American Constitutionalism* (Charlottesville: University of Virginia Press, 2005), 70–3; Felix Frankfurter, *The Commerce Clause under Marshall, Taney, and Waite* (Chapel Hill: University of North Carolina Press, 1937), 51–3.

80. Although all of the justices agreed that the license laws in question were not unconstitutional, they differed widely on the question of how to reconcile the states' licensing power with the federal commerce power. Taney and Catron, two of the Court's most ardent advocates of states' rights, took the position that the commerce power was a "concurrent power" and not the exclusive province of the federal government. On this view, the states were free to regulate commerce in any way they pleased, so long as their regulations conflicted with no specific acts of Congress. 46 U.S. 504 at 579, 607. Others, including McLean and Grier, apparently sought to deny that any valid regulation of health, safety, or morals—as determined by the legislature's intent—could ever be said to conflict with the federal commerce power. The two categories, in other words, were mutually exclusive, and within the category of "police" the states were sovereign. Ibid. at 592, 632.

81. Only Taney, who preferred to describe the liquor licensing power as an inherent attribute of state sovereignty, failed to cite the antiquity of the state license systems as evidence of their constitutionality. See 46 U.S. 504 at 583.

82. Ibid. at 627, 621.

83. Ibid. at 588–9.

84. Ibid. at 607.

85. Ibid. at 576–7, 590, 601, 619. The justices were Taney, McLean, Catron, and Woodbury. Woodbury seems to waver on this point, however. See 46 U.S. 504 at 620–1.

86. As Justice Woodbury pointed out, a person "could [still] import . . . for his own consumption and that of his family and plantations, and also . . . with [a] view of . . . storing them for a higher and more suitable market in another state or abroad." 46 U.S. 504 at 619–20. Also see McLean at 46 U.S. 591 ("It is said that the object of these laws is to prohibit the importation of foreign spirits. This is an interference which their language does not authorize. A license is only required to sell in less quantity than twenty-eight gallons. A greater quantity than this may be sold without restriction. But it is said, if the legislature may require a license for twenty-eight gallons, it may extend the limitation to three hundred gallons. In answer to this it is enough to say, that the legislature has not done what is supposed by the plaintiff's counsel it might do") and Daniels at 46 U.S. 617 ("The license laws . . . now under review impose no exaction on foreign commerce. They are laws simply determining the mode in which a particular commodity may be circulated within the respective jurisdictions of those states, vesting in their domestic tribunals a discretion in selecting the agents for such circulation, without discriminating between the sources whence commodities may have been derived. They do not restrict importation to any extent; they do not interfere with it either in appearance or reality; they do not prohibit sales either by wholesale or retail; they assert

only the power of regulating the latter, but this entirely within the sphere of their peculiar authority"),

87. Ibid. at 591.

88. Ibid. at 624. The similarity between Woodbury's *License Cases* opinion and the "*Cooley* Test" formulated by Justice Curtis in *Cooley v. Board of Wardens* is noted in Richard F. Hamm, *Shaping the Eighteenth Amendment: Temperance Reform, Legal Culture, and the Polity, 1880–1920* (Chapel Hill: University of North Carolina Press, 1995), 60.

89. 53 U.S. 299 (1851).

90. Clubb, *The Maine Liquor Law*, 299, 317, 320, 351, 377, 388, 407.

91. Ibid., 334, 358, 386.

92. *The Code of the State of Iowa* (Des Moines, IA: G.W. Edwards, 1873), 288.

93. Specifically, the Iowa Supreme Court held that the prohibition law did not exempt common carriers from civil suits aimed at recovering the value of liquor destroyed in transit. The upshot of the ruling was that liquor prohibition did not trump the existing common law rules governing common carriers; if carriers wanted to refuse shipments of liquor, the burden was on *the carrier* to demonstrate that the liquor was destined for illegal sale. *Bowen and King v. Hale*, 4 Iowa 430 (1857).

3. The Triumph of Evangelical Public Morality in the States

1. Redfield's 1854 opinion for the Vermont Supreme Court in *Thorpe v. Rutland and Burlington Railroad* is regarded as a classic of police powers jurisprudence, second only to Shaw's *Alger v. Commonwealth* opinion in its impact on doctrinal development. On the influence of Redfield's *Thorpe* opinion, see William J. Novak, *The People's Welfare: Law and Regulation in Nineteenth-Century America* (Chapel Hill: University of North Carolina Press, 1996), 109–10; Markus Dirk Dubber, *The Police Power: Patriarchy and the Foundations of American Government* (New York: Cambridge University Press, 2005), 85, 109, 115; Howard Schweber, *The Creation of American Common Law: Technology, Politics, and the Construction of Citizenship* (New York: Cambridge, 2004), 131–2.

2. *State v. Prescott*, 27 Vt. 194, 200, 201 (1855).

3. Ibid. at 197–8.

4. Ibid. at 201.

5. Novak, *The People's Welfare*, 179. Also see John J. Dinan, *Keeping the People's Liberties: Legislators, Citizens, and Judges as Guardians of Rights* (Lawrence: University Press of Kansas, 1998), 15–16; Michael Les Benedict, "Laissez-Faire and Liberty: A Re-Evaluation of the Meaning and Origins of Laissez-Faire Constitutionalism," *Law and History Review* 3 (1985): 327; Lawrence Friedman, *A History of American Law*, 2d Ed. (New York: Simon and Schuster, 2005), 269.

6. See, for example, Michael F. Holt, *The Rise and Fall of the American Whig Party: Jacksonian Politics and the Onset of the Civil War* (New York: Oxford University Press, 1999), 689–92; William E. Gienapp, *The Origins of the Republican Party, 1852–1856* (New York: Oxford University Press, 1987), 44–60; Ian R. Tyrrell, *Sobering Up: From*

Temperance to Prohibition in Antebellum America (Westport, CT: Greenwood Press, 1979), 260–4.

7. On the Republican party's enthusiastic support for the Maine Law in 1854 and 1855, see Gienapp, *The Origins of the Republican Party,* 47; Holt, *The Rise and Fall of the American Whig Party,* 863–4.

8. In New York, for example, the Whigs won the governorship in 1854, but only after acceding to the temperance forces' demand that the party nominate Myron Clark, a leader of the prohibition movement, for the job. See John A. Krout, "The Maine Law in New York Politics," *New York History* 17 (1936): 260–72; Gienapp, *The Origins of the Republican Party,* 153–60; Lex Renda, "Slavery, Liquor, and Politics: The Case of *Wynehamer v. The People,*" *Mid-America: An Historical Review* 80 (1998): 35–53.

9. Admittedly, the Republican party's unambiguous endorsement of the Maine Law was short lived. In the late 1850s, the party would begin to rethink the benefits of a close affiliation with the prohibition movement. See, for example, Eric Foner, *Free Soil, Free Labor, Free Men: The Ideology of the Republican Party before the Civil War* (New York: Oxford University Press, 1970), 241–2.

10. On the Vermont legislature of 1854–5, see Samuel B. Hand, *The Star that Set: The Vermont Republican Party, 1854–1974* (Lanham, MD: Lexington Books, 2003), 6–7; Holt, *Rise and Fall of the American Whig Party,* 871–2. On judicial selection in Vermont, see *The American Almanac and Repository for Useful Knowledge for the Year 1859* (Boston: Crosby, Nichols, 1859), 233.

11. Holt, *Rise and Fall of the American Whig Party,* 867–9; Cyrenus Cole, *A History of the People of Iowa* (Self-published, 1921), 309; Frederick H. Wines and John Koren, *The Liquor Problem in Its Legislative Aspects* (New York: Houghton, Mifflin, 1897), 97.

12. Only in Delaware did a state judiciary uphold the Maine Law in its entirety in the absence of a dominant Republican party presence. *State v. Allmond,* 7 Del. 612 (1858).

13. In 1855, for example, New York's Republicans nominated a leading temperance advocate, Bradford Wood, for a post on the state's highest court with the clear understanding that his first item of business, if elected, would be to confirm the constitutionality of the recently enacted prohibition law. Unfortunately for the state's prohibitionists, Wood was defeated by the Democratic nominee, Samuel L. Selden, who subsequently voted to declare the Maine Law unconstitutional. New York's Democrats, in turn, solicited and disseminated dozens of advisory opinions from leading jurists (many of the them closely affiliated with the Democratic party) who were willing to publicly express their doubts about the Maine Law's constitutionality. Gienapp, *Origins of the Republican Party,* 227–8. Several of the Democrats' advisory opinions are collected in Metropolitan Society for the Protection of Private and Constitutional Rights, *The Unconstitutionality of the Prohibitory Law Confirmed* (New York: McIntyre and Parsons, 1855).

14. *Wynehamer v. The People,* 13 N.Y. 378 (1856). For the New York justices' party affiliations, see Albert M. Rosenblatt, *The Judges of the New York Court of Appeals: A Biographical History* (New York: Fordham University Press, 2007); Renda, "Slavery, Liquor, and Politics," 44. The Democrats were joined in the *Wynehmer* majority by George F. Comstock, a judge elected to the Court of Appeals on the American party (or Know

Nothing) ticket. Renda speculates that Comstock may have sided with the Democrats in the hope that prolonging the prohibition debate would work to the Know Nothings' advantage.

15. *Wynehamer* has long been identified as an important precursor of the *Lochner*-era Supreme Court's substantive due process jurisprudence. See, for example, Edward S. Corwin, *Liberty against Government: The Rise, Flowering and Decline of a Famous Juridical Concept* (Baton Rouge: Louisiana State University Press, 1948),100–110.

16. See *Herman v. The State,* 8 Ind. 545 (1855); Charles E. Camp, "Temperance Movements and Legislation in Indiana," *Indiana Magazine of History* 16 (1920): 25–6; Emma Lou Thornbrough, *Indiana in the Civil War Era, 1850–1880* (Indianapolis: Indiana Historical Society, 1965), 68–9.

17. *Beebe v. The State,* 6 Ind. 501, 506 (1855). For additional background on Perkins, see John B. Knowland, *Sketches of Prominent Citizens of 1876* (Indianapolis, IN: Tilford and Carlon, 1877), 214–17; David J. Bodenhamer, Robert Graham Barrows, and David Gordon Vanderstel, *The Encyclopedia of Indianapolis* (Bloomington: Indiana University Press, 1994), 313.

18. Novak, *The People's Welfare,* 179; Dinan, *Keeping the People's Liberties,* 15–16; Benedict, "Laissez-Faire and Liberty," 327; Friedman, *A History of American Law,* 269.

19. As early as 1836, for example, Justin Edwards of the American Temperance Society had argued that liquor ought to be regarded as a public nuisance because its impact on the community was even more detrimental than that of traditional public nuisances like stagnant ponds, polluting factories, and stores of gunpowder: "A man has a stream of water upon his own land. He erects a dam which stagnates it, and occasions a pestilential atmosphere. This is a criminal offence, punishable by fine and imprisonment. Now, what is the principle of this case? . . . It is this: that what is, in itself, lawful, becomes a crime when its consequences are injurious to [the] community. Yet the injury in this case is infinitely less than that which is occasioned by selling intoxicating liquors." "License Laws, No. 12," *Christian Register and Observer* 15 (March 19, 1836), 48. For similar arguments, see Moses Stuart, "Professor Stuart on the Maine Liquor Law," *Christian Inquirer* 6 (Nov. 15, 1851), 1; Albert Barnes, *The Throne of Iniquity: Or, Sustaining Evil by Law* (New York: American Temperance Union, 1852).

20. That most antebellum Americans conceived of the power of nuisance abatement in relatively static terms is illustrated by the fact that the period's major legal commentators, in their discussions of public nuisance doctrine, often reproduced verbatim the list of "offences against the public police or oeconomy" found in William Blackstone's *Commentaries on the Laws of England.* See, for example, James Wilson, "Of Crimes, Affecting Several of the Natural Rights of Individuals," in *The Works of James Wilson,* ed. Robert Green McCloskey (Cambridge, MA: Harvard University Press, 1967), 2: 670–1; William Blackstone, *Commentaries on the Laws of England,* (Chicago: University Press of Chicago, 1769 [1979]), 4:163–75.

21. On the conviction among antebellum jurists that the police power was not plenary, but rather subject to common law and constitutional limitations, see, for example, Rodney L. Mott, *Due Process of Law: A Historical and Analytical Treatise of the Principles*

and Methods Followed by the Courts in the Application of the Concept of the "Law of the Land" (Indianapolis, IN: Bobbs-Merrill, 1926), 313–17; Edward S. Corwin, "The Basic Doctrine of American Constitutional Law," *Michigan Law Review* 12 (1914): 264–5.

22. *Alger v. Commonwealth*, 61 Mass. 53, 84–5 (1851). On the common law origins of Shaw's *Alger* opinion, see Harry N. Scheiber, "Public Rights and the Rule of Law in American Legal History," *California Law Review* 72 (1984): 222–4. As Shaw explained in *Alger*, the use of the police power to destroy obstacles to navigation was hardly innovative: "The law of England, as it had existed long anterior of our ancestors to America," recognized "the use of the sea-shores, for navigation and fishing, as *publici juris*, to be held and regulated for the common and general benefit; and this, although in many cases the right of soil was vested by private grant in an individual. . . . If . . . a wharf or other erection were such as to interfere essentially with the common right of navigation, it would be held by the common law to be a common nuisance, and could not be justified, even by the king's grant, unless sanctioned by an act of parliament. These rules and practices were familiar to the minds of our English ancestors at their emigration, and we may presume that the colonial government had them in view when, by a general act, it annexed the sea-shore to the upland, and made it the private property of the riparian proprietor." Also see Blackstone, *Commentaries*, 4: 167.

23. 27 Vt. 328 (1855). Redfield's dissent can be found in the companion case of *State v. Prescott*, 27 Vt. 194.

24. Significantly, Vermont's prohibition law contained all of the constitutionally problematic enforcement provisions discussed in the previous chapter: the law authorized the issuance of vaguely worded search warrants; gave magistrates the authority to order the summary destruction of liquor that appeared to be intended for sale as a beverage; placed the burden of proof squarely upon the property owner, requiring him or her to demonstrate that liquor was *not* intended for illegal resale; required the owners of forfeited liquor to post a hefty $200 bond before an appeal would be permitted; imposed relatively more severe penalties on individuals who lost their appeals; and barred the states' courts from hearing suits for the "recovery or possession of intoxicating liquor, or the value thereof." For the text of the Vermont statute, see Henry S. Clubb, *The Maine Liquor Law: Its Origin, History, and Results* (New York: Fowler and Wells, 1856), 404–7.

25. 27 Vt. 328 at 330–3.

26. Justice Curtis's 1852 *Greene v. Briggs* ruling, for example, is repeatedly cited in Lemuel Shaw's 1854 *Fisher v. McGirr* opinion. The New Hampshire Supreme Court's 1852 advisory opinion was also widely publicized. See, for example, "The New Hampshire Liquor Law," *The Monthly Law Reporter* 5 (January 1853): 481; "The Liquor Law in New Hampshire," *Western Law Journal* (April 1853): 336.

27. 27 Vt. 328 at 333, 343–4.

28. 27 Vt. 328 at 339.

29. Ibid. at 342. Emphasis added.

30. Ibid.

31. Ibid. at 337.

32. Ibid. at 346.

33. In 1853, the Rhode Island legislature reenacted a slightly modified prohibitory liquor law after its original Maine Law was ruled unconstitutional in the 1852 case of *Greene v. Briggs.* The 1853 law, while making it somewhat easier to appeal from the judgments of justices of the peace, left intact many of the original law's most controversial provisions, including the ban on suits against officeholders and others who seized privately held liquor. Following the state Supreme Court's 1854 *State v. Snow* ruling, the legislature again enacted a series of minor revisions. Significantly, this final revision left intact the law's core enforcement mechanism—the right of magistrates to order the summary destruction of liquor that they suspected was intended for resale. Nor did the final version modify the constitutionally problematic requirement that the owners of forfeited liquor post a hefty $100 bond before they would be permitted to appeal from the judgment of a magistrate (and receive a jury trial). For the text of the 1853 law, see Clubb, *The Maine Liquor Law,* 396–403. For the third revision, see *The Revised States of the State of Rhode Island and Providence Plantations* (Providence, RI: Sayles, Miller, and Simons, 1857), 194–202.

34. 5 R.I. 185 at 191. Emphasis added.

35. Ibid. at 192–3. Emphasis added.

36. 1856 Conn. Lexis 35 at 7–9. For the text of Connecticut's prohibitory liquor law, enacted in 1854, see *The General Statutes of the State of Connecticut* (New Haven, CT: John H. Benham, 1866), 692–705; and Clubb, *The Maine Liquor Law,* 299–311.

37. 1 Gray 1 at 27.

38. 25 Conn. 278 at 288–9. Emphasis added.

39. *Lincoln v. Smith,* 27 Vt. 328 at 345.

40. *State v. Brennan's Liquors,* 25 Conn. 278 at 288.

41. *Lincoln v. Smith,* 27 Vt. 328 at 345.

42. See John Samuell Ezell, *Fortune's Merry Wheel: The Lottery in America* (Cambridge, MA: Harvard University Press, 1960), 233–70; Charles W. McCurdy, "Justice Field and the Jurisprudence of Government-Business Relations: Some Parameters of Laissez-Faire Constitutionalism, 1863–1897," *The Journal of American History* 61 (1975): 970–1005.

43. *Moore v. The State,* 48 Miss. 147 (1873). The Reconstruction-era Mississippi Supreme Court was composed of three justices, with two justices necessary to form a quorum. The Court's third member seems not to have participated in *Moore v. The State.*

44. Ibid. at 160.

45. Ibid. at 161.

46. Ibid. at 162.

47. Ibid. at 174.

48. On the development of the idea of the "inalienable" police power, see Benjamin F. Wright, *The Contract Clause of the Constitution* (Cambridge, MA: Harvard University Press, 1938), 196–203. Wright concludes that the doctrine can be "vaguely" perceived in a handful of antebellum state decisions, but was not "clearly" recognized at the state level until after the Civil War. At the federal level, it was "not until 1878" that the Supreme Court handed "down a decision explicitly based upon the principle that there

are certain police or regulatory powers which the states may not contract away." Also see Stephen A. Siegel, "Understanding the Nineteenth Century Contract Clause: The Role of the Property-Privilege Distinction and 'Takings' Clause Jurisprudence," *Southern California Law Review* 60 (1986): 41–54.

49. 48 Miss. 147 at 162, 163, 168.

50. Ibid. at 172, 168.

51. Ibid. at 162.

52. The Court also bolstered its claim that the police power was inalienable with numerous citations to Theophilus Parsons's *The Law of Contracts.* Here, Parsons had suggested that a legislature could not, through the issuance of liquor licenses or lottery grants, alienate its ability to prohibit lotteries or liquor sales. Parsons provided little precedential support for this claim. Indeed, he relied heavily on the Supreme Court's 1850 ruling in *Phalen v. Virginia,* which had essentially dodged the question. As counsel for the lottery company in *Moore v. State* correctly noted, the cases cited by Parsons "in support of the doctrine stated in his text do not, in their facts, support the doctrine of the learned author." *The Law of Contracts,* 5th Ed. (Boston, 1866), 3: 567–8.

53. *Charles River Bridge v. Warren Bridge,* 36 U.S. 420 (1837).

54. 27 Vt. 140 at 156.

55. *Kellum v. The State,* 66 Ind. 588 (1879).

4. The Triumph of Evangelical Public Morality in the Supreme Court

1. On the WCTU's lobbying activities, see Ruth Bordin, *Frances Willard: A Biography* (Chapel Hill: University of North Carolina Press, 1986), 129–37; Gaines M. Foster, *Moral Reconstruction: Christian Lobbyists and the Federal Legislation of Morality, 1865–1920* (Chapel Hill: University of North Carolina Press, 2002), 84–90; Daniel Okrent, *Last Call: The Rise and Fall of Prohibition* (New York: Scribner, 2010), 16. Okrent notes that the WCTU was "undoubtedly . . . the nation's most effective political action group in the last decades of the nineteenth century."

2. On the WCTU's Department of Scientific Instruction, see Okrent, *Last Call,* 21–3.

3. On the Prohibition Party's influence in national politics, see Rebecca Edwards, *Angels in the Machinery: Gender in American Party Politics from the Civil War to the Progressive Era* (New York: Oxford, 1997), 41, 46–7, 81, 85; Foster, *Moral Reconstruction,* 31; Richard F. Hamm, *Shaping the Eighteenth Amendment: Temperance Reform, Legal Culture, and the Polity, 1880–1920* (Chapel Hill: University of North Carolina Press, 1995), 22–4. In the election of 1884, for example, the party consciously focused its electoral efforts in closely contested states such as New York, in the hope of forcing the Republican party to embrace the prohibitionist cause. That November, when Grover Cleveland became the first Democrat elected President in the post-Civil War era, many Republican leaders blamed the prohibitionists for their party's defeat. See Edwards, *Angels in the Machinery,* 41, 46–7.

4. On the political clout of the ASL, see K. Austin Kerr, *Organized for Prohibition: A New History of the Anti-Saloon League* (New Haven, CT: Yale University Press, 1985). The role of local Protestant congregations in funding and staffing the organization is also discussed in Ann-Marie Szymanski, *Pathways to Prohibition: Radicals, Moderates, and Social Movement Outcomes* (Durham, NC: Duke University Press, 2003), 63; and Okrent, *Last Call*, 36–7. Okrent notes that about 75 percent of the seats on the ASL's state boards were occupied by Baptist or Methodist clergymen. At its height, the organization dispatched speakers to as many as 30,000 congregations annually.

5. Peter H. Odegard, *Pressure Politics: The Story of the Anti-Saloon League* (New York: Columbia University Press, 1928).

6. An 1888 Prohibition party campaign tract explicitly cited the precedent of the 1850s realignment as reason to support the dry cause, confidently predicting that "1888 will be the [Prohibition party's] Fremont year and 1892 will be the Lincoln year." Quoted in Edwards, *Angels in the Machinery*, 43. Also see Edward J. Blum, *Reforging the White Republic: Race, Religion, and American Nationalism, 1865–1898* (Baton Rouge: Louisiana State University Press, 196–8.

7. By the 1890s, for example, virtually all of the Southern states had banned the lottery business, and by the early twentieth century most of the region was officially dry, thanks to a combination of statewide prohibition laws and successful local option votes. As Southern morals laws came more and more to mirror those of the Northern states, Southern lawmakers, too, had reason to worry about the corrupting effects of the interstate market in immoral commodities. In fact, for all their concern about local autonomy, Southerners soon discovered that they could not control their moral environments without federal assistance. For dates of prohibition enactment in the Southern states, see Michael Lewis, "Access to Saloons, Wet Voter Turnout, and State Prohibition Referenda, 1907–1919," *Social Science History* 3 (2008): 373–404. On the growth of Southern support for morals legislation, see Foster, *Moral Reconstruction*, 119–30. In addition, Edward J. Blum has argued that the cause of moral reform—and the efforts of the WCTU, in particular—played an important role in fostering sectional reconciliation after Reconstruction. See Blum, *Reforging the White Republic*, 174–98.

8. See, for example, Herbert Hovenkamp, "Law and Morals in Classical Legal Thought"; Lawrence Friedman, *A History of American Law*, 2d Ed. (New York: Simon and Schuster, 2005), 312; Michael Les Benedict, "Victorian Moralism and Civil Liberty in the Nineteenth-Century United States," in *The Constitution, Law, and American Life*, ed. Donald G. Nieman (Athens: University of Georgia Press, 1992).

9. For example, most states were by this time including reservation clauses in their corporate charters, which limited the effect of the Contract Clause by preserving the legislature's right to modify or revoke a charter under specified conditions. In addition, the Court had gradually narrowed the scope of the *Dartmouth College* holding, first by refusing to recognize the existence of implied exemptions in corporate charters, then by adopting a rule of construction to the effect that ambiguities in a charter should be resolved in favor of the state. For overviews of the Court's Contract Clause jurisprudence under Chief Justices Taney and Chase, see Stephen A. Siegel, "Understanding the

Nineteenth Century Contract Clause: The Role of the Property-Privilege Distinction and 'Takings' Clause Jurisprudence," *Southern California Law Review* 60 (1986–7): 35–54; James W. Ely, "The Protection of Contractual Rights: A Tale of Two Constitutional Provisions," *New York Journal of Law and Liberty* 1 (2005): 370–83; Stewart E. Sterk, "The Continuity of Legislatures: Of Contracts and the Contract Clause," *Columbia Law Review* 88 (1988): 647–700.

10. *Farrington v. Tennessee,* 95 U.S. 679, 682 (1877).

11. 94 U.S. 645 (1877).

12. Ibid. at 650.

13. 97 U.S. 25 (1878).

14. Ibid. at 33.

15. *Stone v. Mississippi,* 101 U.S. 814 (1879), 818, 821.

16. 101 U.S. 814 at 819.

17. See, for example, Ely, "The Protection of Contractual Rights," 396–9; Howard Gillman, *The Constitution Besieged: The Rise and Demise of Lochner Era Police Powers Jurisprudence* (Durham, NC: Duke University Press, 1993), 55–6; Herbert Hovenkamp, *Enterprise and American Law, 1836–1937* (Cambridge, MA: Harvard University Press, 1991), 27–34.

18. See, for example, Benjamin F. Wright, *The Contract Clause of the Constitution* (Cambridge, MA: Harvard University Press, 1938), 258; John E. Semonche, *Keeping the Faith: A Cultural History of the U.S. Supreme Court* (Lanham, MD: Rowman and Littlefield, 1998), 139; Melvin Urofsky and Paul Finkelman, *A March of Liberty: A Constitutional History of the United States,* 2d Ed. (New York: Oxford University Press, 2002), 503.

19. On the Louisiana Lottery Company's interstate operations, see John Samuell Ezell, *Fortune's Merry Wheel: The Lottery in America* (Cambridge, MA: Harvard University Press, 1960), 242–70.

20. On Congress's mostly futile attempts to prevent the lottery from using the mail during the 1870s, see Wayne W. Fuller, *Morality and the Mail in Nineteenth-Century America* (Urbana: University of Illinois Press, 2003), 192–206; Gaines M. Foster, *Moral Reconstruction: Christian Lobbyists and the Federal Legislation of Morality, 1865–1920* (Chapel Hill: University of North Carolina Press, 2002), 119–23.

21. "Arresting Lottery Men," *New York Times* (Nov. 12, 1879), 8.

22. "The Use of the Mails for Lottery Purposes," H. Exec. Doc. No. 22, 46th Cong., 2d sess. (Jan. 13, 1880).

23. For contemporary discussions of the failed attempt to repeal the Louisiana Lottery Company's charter, see: "Summary of Events," *The Friend* 52 (April 5, 1879): 272; "The Louisiana Lottery," *The Chicago Daily Tribune* (April 12, 1879), 5; "Home Secular Notes," *Christian Advocate* 54 (April 3, 1879): 220.

24. James C. Klotter, "Two Centuries of the Lottery in Kentucky," *The Register of the Kentucky Historical Society* 87 (1989): 416.

25. For corruption charges, see "The Louisiana Lottery," *Chicago Daily Tribune* (April 12, 1879), 5; Berthold C. Alwes, "The History of the Louisiana State Lottery Company," *The Louisiana Historical Quarterly* 27 (1944): 998.

26. *Louisiana State Lottery Company v. Fitzpatrick,* 15 F. Cas. 970, 980 (Cir. Ct., Louisiana 1879).

27. 101 U.S. 814 at 819.

28. Ibid. at 819.

29. Ibid. at 818.

30. Hovenkamp, *Enterprise and American Law,* 28.

31. See, for example, Thomas M. Cooley, *A Treatise on the Constitutional Limitations Which Rest upon the Legislative Power of the States of the American Union* (Boston: Little, Brown, and Co., 1868), 479. "No attribute of sovereignty is more pervading, and at no point does the power of the government affect more constantly and intimately all the relations of life than through this power. . . . The power to tax rests upon necessity, and is inherent in every sovereignty. The legislature of every free state will possess it under the general grant of legislative power, whether particularly specified in the constitution among the powers to be exercised by it or not. No constitutional government can exist without it . . ."

32. As the Court declared in one such case, handed down only two years after *Stone,* "where the [charter] language is clear, and the intention to grant the exemption apparent," tax exemptions remained beyond the power of the legislature to modify or repeal. *Asylum v. New Orleans,* 105 U.S. 362, 369 (1882). Also see *Wolff v. New Orleans,* 103 U.S. 358 (1881); *Louisiana v. Pilsbury,* 105 U.S. 278 (1882); *Ralls County v. U.S.,* 105 U.S. 733 (1882); *Louisiana v. Police Jury,* 111 U.S. 716; *Fisk v. Jefferson Police Jury,* 116 U.S. 131 (1885); *New Orleans v. Houston,* 119 U.S. 265 (1886); *Seibert v. U.S.,* 122 U.S. 284 (1887). And see the discussion in Wright, *The Contract Clause,* 94.

33. James P. Root, "Limitations on Legislative Contracts," *The American Law Register* 35 (1887): 67. Emphasis in the original. The logical connection between the two powers was repeatedly emphasized by Thomas Cooley, both in his judicial opinions and academic writings. See, for example, his opinion in *East Saginaw Manufacturing Co. v. City of East Saginaw,* 19 Mich. 259 (1869).

34. John William Burgess, *Political Science and Comparative Constitutional Law* (Boston: Ginn and Co., 1891), 239–40.

35. 111 U.S. 746 (1884).

36. 115 U.S. 650 (1885); 115 U.S. 674 (1885).

37. 115 U.S. 650 at 669.

38. 115 U.S. 650 at 672.

39. 115 U.S. 650 at 669. For subsequent applications of this doctrine see, for example, *Louisville Gas Co. v. Citizens' Gas Co.,* 115 U.S. 683 (1885); *St. Tammany Water Works Co. v. New Orleans Water Works Co.,* 120 U.S. 64 (1887); *City Railway Co. v. Citizen's Railroad Co.,* 166 U.S. 557 (1897); *Walla Walla v. Walla Walla Water Co.,* 172 U.S. 1 (1898). Also see the cases listed in Wright, *The Contract Clause,* 96.

40. 161 U.S. 646 (1896).

41. 161 U.S. 646 at 675.

42. Alfred Russell, "Status and Tendencies of the Dartmouth College Case," *The American Law Review* 30 (1896): 349.

43. 199 U.S. 473 (1905).

44. 199 U.S. 473 at 480. Emphasis added.

45. The view that *Dartmouth College* was wrongly decided—and that the Contract Clause was originally intended to apply only to private contracts and not to corporate charters—is clearly expressed in later editions of Cooley's *Constitutional Limitations.* See Cooley, *A Treatise on the Constitutional Limitations Which Rest upon the Legislative Power of the States of the American Union,* 3d Ed. (Boston: Little, Brown and Co., 1874), 279–80, note 2.

46. For a contemporary discussion of the incoherence of the turn-of-the century Court's Contract Clause jurisprudence, see, for example, Ernst Freund, *The Police Power: Public Policy and Constitutional Rights* (Chicago: Callaghan and Co., 1904), 360–9. As Stephen A. Siegel has pointed out, the 1890s witnessed an explosion of literature assessing "the present state of the *Dartmouth College*" principle. See "Understanding the Nineteenth Century Contract Clause: The Role of the Property-Privilege Distinction and 'Takings' Clause Jurisprudence," *Southern California Law Review* 60 (1986): 54, note 267.

47. For a contemporary discussion describing *Stone* as a critical turning point in the Court's rejection of the *Dartmouth College* doctrine, see Christopher G. Tiedeman, *The Unwritten Constitution of the United States: A Philosophical Inquiry into the Fundamentals of American Constitutional Law* (New York: G.P. Putnam's Sons, 1890), 60–66. Tiedeman concluded that the logic of *Stone* "could not be reconciled with the position of the Court in the Dartmouth College case." Rather, the Court had noticed "a change in public opinion" and had responded by bringing about "a consequent change in the constitutional rule."

48. See, for example, Gillman, *The Constitution Besieged*, Ch. 3.

49. Thus, Morton J. Horwitz argues that postwar judges used the common law category of public nuisance to mark the outer limit of Fourteenth Amendment economic liberties. Prohibition, on this view, was an easy case for the simple reason that the states had always enjoyed the power to abate unlicensed taverns as public nuisances. The Supreme Court's decision in *Mugler v. Kansas,* according to Horwitz, simply "illustrates how both state and federal courts had little conceptual difficulty in dealing with anti-liquor legislation. Since it was within the well-recognized category of protection of 'the public health, safety, and morals,' courts did not need to inquire further about the confiscatory consequences of such a statute." *The Transformation of American Law, 1870–1960: The Crisis of Legal Orthodoxy* (New York: Oxford University Press, 28–9.

50. See, for example, Gillman, *The Constitution Besieged,* 73.

51. As Owen Fiss explains, liquor prohibition "fell within the established boundaries of the police power because it did not prevent individuals from participating in a trade open to others." *Troubled Beginnings of the Modern State, 1888–1910* (New York: Macmillan, 1993), 263. Howard Gillman likewise argues that post-Civil War judges looked favorably on liquor bans because they viewed prohibition as a "class-neutral polic[y] that advanced a public purpose." *The Constitution Besieged,* 73.

52. 85 U.S. 129 (1874). The Court heard four cases involving state prohibition laws in the decade preceding the *Bartemeyer* decision, but none of these cases involved

Fourteenth Amendment challenges. The first three involved claims that state liquor regulations were in conflict with the federal excise on liquor, or vice versa. The last of the four raised a Commerce Clause challenge to a local license tax. *McGuire v. Massachusetts*, 70 U.S. 387 (1866); *License Tax Cases*, 72 U.S. 462 (1866); *Pervear v. Massachusetts*, 72 U.S. 475 (1866); *Downham v. Alexandria Council*, 77 U.S. 173 (1869).

53. 83 U.S. 36 (1873).

54. Field, J., dissenting. 83 U.S. 36 at 88.

55. 83 U.S. 36 at 49–50.

56. Ibid. at 61.

57. The origins of the *Bartemeyer* litigation are discussed in Charles Fairman, *Reconstruction and Reunion, 1864–1888* (New York: Macmillan, 1971), 1416–19.

58. 85 U.S. 129 at 134–5.

59. 85 U.S. 129 at 133. The right to sell liquor, according Miller, was "not one of the rights growing out of citizenship of the United States, and in this regard the case falls within the principles laid down in the *Slaughterhouse Cases*."

60. Field, J., dissenting. 83 U.S. 129 at 138. The key distinction between *Slaughterhouse* and *Bartemeyer*, according to both Bradley and Field, was that the Iowa law did not favor any single group or class of citizens over another; where the Louisiana legislature had attempted to "farm out the ordinary avocations of life," the Iowa legislature had instead barred *all* of the state's residents from pursuing an occupation it deemed injurious to public health and morals.

61. Fiss notes that where Field and Bradley had penned "passionate dissents in *Slaughterhouse*, . . . even they voted with the majority in *Bartemeyer*" on the grounds that the Iowa law was nondiscriminatory and targeted "the sale of articles deemed injurious to the safety of society." *Troubled Beginnings of the Modern State*, 263. Quoting Bradley, J., concurring. William M. Nelson likewise concludes that *Bartemeyer* relied "on the shared understanding that prohibition laws were not enacted so that the class of nondrinkers would improve their welfare at the expense of drinkers, but in order to enhance the well-being of all." *The Fourteenth Amendment: From Political Principle to Judicial Doctrine* (Cambridge, MA: Harvard University Press, 1988), 178. Also see Fairman, *Reconstruction and Reunion*, 1418–9. One of the few scholarly works to appreciate the difficulty of the constitutional questions confronting the Court in *Bartemeyer* is David P. Currie, *The Constitution in the Supreme Court: The First Hundred Years, 1789–1888* (Chicago: University of Chicago Press, 1985), 369–70.

62. 85 U.S. 129 at 133–4.

63. 83 U.S. 35 at 81.

64. Had the Iowa prohibition law not raised very different—and more troubling— due process questions than the Louisiana slaughterhouse law, Miller no doubt would simply have declared that the due process objection, like the privileges and immunities objection, was covered by the "principles laid down by this court in the *Slaughterhouse Cases*." Indeed, had Miller believed that valid police measures could not "deprive" citizens of liberty or property within the meaning of the Fourteenth Amendment, he no doubt would have used his *Bartemeyer* opinion to settle the question of prohibition's

constitutionality once for all instead of opening the door to future constitutional challenges. 85 U.S. 129 at 134, 133.

65. 80 U.S. 166 (1871).

66. Ibid. at 177–8. Emphasis in the original. On the *Pumpelly* decision's role in establishing a "dephysicalized" definition of property, see Horwitz, *The Transformation of American Law, 1870–1960*, 148.

67. Although *Pumpelly* had not involved a Fourteenth Amendment claim, Miller likely saw the Fifth Amendment term "taking" and the Fourteenth Amendment term "deprivation" as functional equivalents: if the destruction of use or value required compensation in one case, there was no logical reason why it should not be required in the other. The fact that postwar jurists often failed to distinguish between a Fifth Amendment "taking" and a Fourteenth Amendment "deprivation" of property is discussed in James W. Ely, Jr., *The Fuller Court: Justices, Rulings and Legacy* (Santa Barbara, CA: ABC-CLIO, 2003), 113.

68. 85 U.S 129 at 136.

69. 85 U.S. 129 and 137.

70. Hamm, *Shaping the Eighteenth Amendment*, 44–51.

71. Among the more influential "substantive" due process decisions of the 1880s were *In re Jacobs*, 98 N.Y. 98 (1885); *People v. Marx*, 99 N.Y. 377 (1885); *Millett v. People* 117 Ill. 294 (1886); *State v. Goodwill*, 33 W.Va. 179 (1889). For the argument that these decisions generally turned on the existence or absence of a valid public purpose, see Gillman, *The Constitution Besieged*, Ch. 2; Horwitz, *Transformation of American Law, 1870–1960*, 27–31; Eric R. Claeys, "Takings, Regulations, and Natural Property Rights," *Cornell Law Review* 88 (2002–3): 1549–1669.

72. On the origins of the "class" or "special" legislation doctrine, and its relation to the constitutional norm of due process, see Michael Les Benedict, "Laissez-Faire and Liberty: A Reevaluation of the Meaning and Origins of Laissez-Faire Constitutionalism," *Law and History Review* 3 (1985): 293–331.

73. *Railroad Commission Cases*, 116 U.S. 307, 331 (1886). Not until the 1890 decision of *Chicago, Milwaukee and St. Paul Railway v. Minnesota*, however, did the Court actually hold that the Constitution required judicial review of governmentally imposed railroad rates. 134 U.S. 418 (1890). On the evolution of constitutional doctrine in the area of railroad rate regulation, see Stephen A. Siegel, "Understanding the Lochner Era: Lessons from the Controversy over Railroad and Utility Rate Regulation," *Virginia Law Review* 70 (1984): 187–265.

74. *In re Jacobs*, 98 N.Y. 98 (1885). Significantly, the *Jacobs* Court pointedly refused to draw a bright line between the police and eminent domain powers. As Eric Claeys has written: "The court considered Jacob's arguments primarily under due process principles, but it also assumed that the due process clause followed takings principles." Claeys, "Takings, Regulations, and Natural Property Rights," 1580.

75. 98 N.Y. 98 at 105.

76. As the New York Court of Appeals explained in *In re Jacobs*, the "constitutional guarantee [of due process] would be of little worth, if the legislature could, without

compensation, destroy property or its value, deprive the owner of its use, deny him the right to live in his own house, or to work at any lawful trade therein." N.Y. 98 at 105. Also noteworthy in this regard is the general trend in the 1880s and 1890s towards recognizing that the amount of compensation owed in takings and due process cases should be calculated, not based on the value of the physical assets seized or regulated, but rather on the income that the property owner could expect to derive from those assets in the future. Perhaps the most important decision in this line was *Monongahela Navigation Company v. United States*, 148 U.S. 312 (1893). For a discussion of the general trend, see Horwitz, *Transformation of American Law, 1870–1960*, 148–51, 160–64.

77. Christopher G. Tiedeman, *Treatise on the Limitations of Police Power in the United States* (St. Louis, MO: F.H. Thomas Law Book Co., 1886), 307.

78. On the formation of national trade organizations in the brewing and distilling industries, and on their role in sponsoring constitutional challenges to the new wave of prohibition measures, see Hamm, *Shaping the Eighteenth Amendment*, 44–55.

79. *In re Zebold*, 23 F. 791, 795 (C.C.D. Kan. 1885). The law authorized county attorneys to order the summary abatement of illegal stores of liquor, as well as any other property that was suspected of being used in the manufacture or sale of liquor. A government that permitted the destruction of property in extrajudicial proceedings, the court declared, could only be described as "despotic."

80. *State v. Walruff*, 26 F. 178 (C.C.D. Kan. 1886).

81. Ibid. at 198–9. As Judge Brewer framed the issue: "I meet here the argument that, when private property is taken for public use, there is always a transfer of the use from one party to another; that here the use is not transferred, but only forbidden; and that this deprivation of the use is only one of the consequential injuries resulting from a change of policy on the part of the state from which no compensation or redress is allowed. . . . The argument is not sound. As a matter of fact, in condemnation cases, seldom is the particular use to which the property has been put transferred. Almost always that use is destroyed in order that another may be acquired. The farmer surrenders a part of his farm to the railroad company, not that the company may continue its use for farming purposes, but that the public may acquire the benefit in another direction. So, where land is flowed by a mill-dam. And thus it is generally. Here the use is taken away solely and directly for the benefit of the public. For no other reason, and upon no other ground, could it be disturbed. Of course, in this, as in other cases, some use remains to the owner; but here, as elsewhere, the use which is of special value is taken from him for the benefit of the public; and this is not a consequential, but a direct result."

82. Ibid. at 198–9.

83. Ibid. at 200.

84. On Brewer's personal religious convictions, see Linda Przybyszewski, "Judicial Conservatism and Protestant Faith: The Case of Justice David J. Brewer," *Journal of American History* 91 (2004): 471–96.

85. 26 F. 178 at 198–9.

86. Ibid. at 200.

87. 27 F. 883 (C.C.D. Iowa 1886).

88. 27 F. 883 at 886.

89. 28 F. 308 (C.D.C. Oregon 1886).

90. 28 F. 308 at 311–2. This is not to suggest that the lower federal courts adopted a monolithic approach in cases involving due process challenges to state prohibition laws. For a contradictory federal ruling, holding that a Georgia local option law did not amount to a "deprivation" of property within the meaning of the Fourteenth Amendment, see *Weil v. Calhoun*. That the author of the *Weil* opinion relied heavily on the Supreme Court's 1880 ruling in *Stone v. Mississippi*—a case that involved neither liquor nor the Fourteenth Amendment—to support this holding further illustrates the unsettled nature of federal doctrine. 25 F. 865, 872 (C.C.D. Georgia 1885).

91. On the origins of the *Mugler* case, and the brewing industry's role in the litigation, see Hamm, *Shaping the Eighteenth Amendment*, 49–55.

92. For an overview of the state judiciary's abandonment, in the postwar period, of the non-delegation principle, see Ellis Paxson Oberholtzer, *The Referendum in America* (New York: Scribner's Sons, 1912), 318–24. Ernest H. Cherrington reports that twenty-one states were under some form of local option during the late 1880s. *The Evolution of Prohibition in the United States of America* (Montclair, NJ: Patterson Smith, 1969), 184–236.

93. See Karen Orren, *Belated Feudalism: Labor, Law and Liberal Development in the United States* (New York: Cambridge University Press, 1991). Orren traces the roots of nineteenth-century labor law to feudal England and argues that judges reflexively insulated this culturally entrenched system of regulation from legislative interference.

94. 1887 U.S. LEXIS 2204.

95. 123 U.S. 623 at 669.

96. Ibid. at 661.

97. Ibid. at 662. Moreover, Field argued, it was unclear how the state's power to protect public health and morals could authorize the destruction of clearly innocent forms of property—including "bottles, glasses, and other utensils"—such as were subject to summary abatement under the terms of the Kansas law.

98. Ibid. at 678. Field also objected to the law on Commerce Clause grounds, arguing that a total ban on the sale of liquor, as applied to imported liquor, would amount to an unconstitutional interference with interstate commerce. The Court would be forced to confront this objection in *Bowman v. Chicago and Northwestern Railway*, discussed below. 125 U.S. 465 (1888).

99. This is not to suggest that opposition to *Mugler* was universal. But it is important to note that even the opinion's supporters recognized the decision as a departure from existing doctrine. Thus, a writer in the *American Law Register* expressed hope that *Mugler's* expansive conception of the police power would spell the end of "*laissez faire* democracy" in America; and yet the same writer acknowledged that *Mugler* and its progeny represented a "distinct advance . . . upon previous adjudications": "The difference between [*Munn v. Illinois*] and the liquor cases is, that in the former cases the right of State regulation of a public business was extended to *limiting* the prices to be charged in conducting it, while in the latter, the right of absolute *destruction* of the business and

of the value of the property invested in it was recognized. The latter cases were therefore a very material advance upon the former." A.H. Wintersteen, "The Sovereign State," *American Law Register* 37 (1889): 137.

100. Everett V. Abbot, "The Police Power and the Right to Compensation," *Harvard Law Review* 3 (1889): 205. Also see George Hoadly, "The Constitutional Guarantees of the Right of Property as Affected by Recent Decisions," *Journal of Social Science* 26 (1890): 53–5: "Those who are confident that it will be better and cheaper in the end to pay something . . . even for suppressing breweries and distillers . . . than to destroy them under the pretence of the exercise of an indefinite police power, or of an inherent right of government to control property devoted to a so-called public use, will find reason to consider whether . . . it ought not to be made more imperative upon courts to open their eyes to the violation of such rights, and to stretch forth their executive power to enforce them."

101. J.I. Clark Hare, *American Constitutional Law* (Boston: Little, Brown and Company, 1889) 2: 772, 776–7.

102. W. Frederic Foster, "The Doctrine of the United States Supreme Court of Property Affected By a Public Interest, and Its Tendencies," *Yale Law Journal* 5 (1895): 57.

103. Christopher G. Tiedeman, *A Treatise on the Law of Sales of Personal Property* (St. Louis, MO: F.H. Thomas, 1891), 513.

104. On the basic continuity of the nineteenth-century Court's approach to federalism questions, see Howard Gillman, "The Struggle over Marshall and the Politics of Constitutional History," *Politics Research Quarterly* 47 (1994): 877–86; "More on the Origins of the Fuller Court's Jurisprudence: Reexamining the Scope of Federal Power over Commerce and Manufacturing in Nineteenth-Century Constitutional Law," *Political Research Quarterly* 49 (1996): 415–37. For a dissenting view, arguing that the post-Civil War Court departed from the Marshall Court's understanding of the federal system, see Robert Lowry Clinton, "Judicial Review, Nationalism, and the Commerce Clause: Contrasting Antebellum and Postbellum Supreme Court Decision Making," *Political Research Quarterly* 47 (1994): 857–76.

105. The quotation is from the majority opinion in *Cook v. Pennsylvania* (97 U.S. 566, 574 [1878]). An alternative interpretation held that congressional silence with respect to a given subject should be interpreted as expressing Congress's desire that the subject remain unregulated.

106. 53 U.S. 299 (1851).

107. *Welton v. Missouri,* 91 U.S. 275 (1875); *Wabash, St. Louis and Pacific Railway Company v. Illinois,* 118 U.S. 557 (1886); *Pensacola Telegraph Company v. Western Union Telegraph Company,* 96 U.S. 1 (1877).

108. As one temperance activist complained in 1882, prohibition would never receive a "fair trial," so long as "the general government . . . by its power to regulate inter-state commerce" continued to guarantee "the importation of liquors into the state[s]." John B. Finch, "The Questions of the Jury Answered," in *The People Versus the Liquor Traffic: The Great Speeches of John B. Finch,* ed. Samuel D. Hastings (Chicago: International Order of Good Templars, 1882), 195.

109. As Barry Cushman has demonstrated, these two strands of late-nineteenth-century Commerce Clause doctrine were interconnected; the categories developed in the Court's "dormant" Commerce Clause decisions often provided the basis for the rulings with respect to the scope of Congress's "affirmative" commerce power. Prior to the *E.C. Knight* decision, for example, the distinction between "commerce" and "production" had received its fullest discussion in an 1888 dormant Commerce Clause decision involving Iowa's prohibition laws. *Kidd v. Pearson,* 128 U.S. 1 (1888). "Formalism and Realism in Commerce Clause Jurisprudence," *University of Chicago Law Review* 67 (2000): 1125–6.

110. 76 U.S. 41 (1870).

111. 100 U.S. 82 (1878).

112. 156 U.S. 1, 12–13 (1895). In a lone dissent, Justice John Marshall Harlan argued for a broader and less formalistic conception of the federal commerce power. Harlan reasoned that because the states, acting alone, were incapable of breaking up American Sugar, the practical effect of the majority's reading of the Commerce Clause would be to leave "the public . . . entirely at the mercy of combinations which arbitrarily control the prices" of "the necessaries of life." 156 U.S. 1 at 18–45.

113. This is not to suggest that these categories were purely "formalistic" in the sense of being developed in isolation from practical considerations. As Cushman has persuasively argued, the move on the part of the Court to clarify the boundary between the police and commerce powers was motivated by "frankly instrumental impulses": namely, "to secure a national market for the products of an increasingly vibrant and integrated economy, while at the same time preserving state and local prerogatives to regulate business in an era of comparative federal lassitude." "Formalism and Realism," 1126.

114. Ibid., 1126.

115. In *Wabash, St. Louis and Pacific Railway Co. v. Illinois* (1886), for example, the Court split 6–3 on the question of whether a state could prohibit railroads from setting high rates for "short-haul" trips where customers lacked a choice of competing rail lines. The case was a difficult one from the perspective of the Cooley Test, since the statute in question arguably affected rates on interstate, as well as intrastate, journeys. 118 U.S. 557.

116. In 1880, Illinois state contained thirty-six distilleries that produced a combined total of about $15 million worth of whiskey annually. *Report on the Manufactures of the United States* (Washington: Government Printing Office, 1883), 52. The Iowa law imposed criminal penalties on "any express company, railway company, or . . . person in the employ . . . of any common carrier" that transported liquor across the state line. Frederick Howard Wines and John Koren, *The Liquor Problem in Its Legislative Aspects* (New York: Houghton, Mifflin, 1887), 109; Dan Ebert Clark, "The History of Liquor Legislation in Iowa, 1878–1908," *Iowa Journal of History and Politics* 6 (1908): 503–608; Jerry Herrington, "Keokuk and the Prohibition Question, 1888–1889," *The Annals of Iowa* 46 (1983): 593–617; Hamm, *Shaping the Eighteenth Amendment,* 63–4.

117. *Hall v. Decuir,* 95 U.S. 485 (1878).

118. Most national leaders of the movement believed that a constitutional amendment would be necessary to authorize state importation bans. Thus, in 1882, J. Ellen Foster of the WCTU complained to a congressional committee that the states' lack

of constitutional authority to "control the importation and inter-state commerce" in liquor was "embarrassing very greatly the operation" of the prohibition laws that were still in effect. Quoted in "Temperance," *Friends' Review* 35 (1882): 461. Two years later, Senator Henry W. Blair of New Hampshire argued in the pages of the *North American Review* that the U.S. Constitution was "the great ally and protector of alcohol" and "the real stronghold" of the liquor traffic. Until the problem of imported liquor was addressed, Blair declared, state-level reformers would be doomed to repeat the fate of Sisyphus: "Why, then, is it that year after year the dreary work . . . goes on in every State; that the stone is rolled up the hill with infinite labor in the State only to be rolled down again by the force of national law at the top? Why is it that . . . wherever prohibition shall . . . succeed, national law is permitted to save the accursed traffic, and nullify laws enacted by the States for the preservation of the people?" "Alcohol in Politics," *The North American Review,* 138 (1884): 53–4.

119. 125 U.S. 465, 508 (1888).

120. 125 U.S. 465 at 508–9. Three justices, led by Harlan, dissented on the grounds that the Iowa law was necessary to achieve a valid "police" objective—i.e., the total prohibition of liquor sales. For Harlan and the dissenters, the deciding factor in the case was the Iowa legislature's *motive* in enacting the importation ban. Because the lawmakers' goal had been merely to protect the moral and physical health of the state's residents, the resulting law, Harlan insisted, should not be interpreted as interfering with Congress's power over commerce. To hold otherwise was to make the U.S. Constitution "operate as a license to persons doing business in one State to jeopard the health, morals and good order of another State, by flooding the latter with intoxicating liquors, against the express will of the people." 125 U.S. 465 at 509–24.

121. 135 U.S. 100 (1890). Relying heavily on John Marshall's *Brown v. Maryland* opinion, the Court reasoned that the right to import a traditionally legal commodity across state lines would be worthless if the importer was subsequently barred from re-selling the imported goods. Banning the right to *sell,* in other words, could destroy the interstate market in a commodity just as effectively as banning the right to import—and thus defeat the framers' goal of creating an unencumbered national market. 25 U.S. 419 (1827).

122. 135 U.S. 100 at 124. Iowa's prohibition regime also spawned a third noteworthy case, *Kidd v. Pearson,* in which the Court ruled that state bans on the *production* of liquor, unlike importation bans, did not conflict with the federal commerce power. Once liquor had been "lawfully called into existence," however, the regulatory authority of the state ended and that of the federal government began. In short, it would be "beyond the power of the State either to forbid or impede [the] exportation" of lawfully produced liquor. 128 U.S. 1, 18 (1888).

123. The quotation is from Frances Willard, leader of the WCTU. "Miss Willard Talks," *New York Times* (May 21, 1890), 1.

124. For contemporary accounts of conflicts between liquor retailers and local officials in the aftermath of the *Bowman* and *Leisy* rulings, see "Iowa Judges Differ," *New York Times* (June 18, 1890), 1; "Kansas Laws Defied," *New York Times* (July 4, 1890), 5;

"Effects of the Original Package Decision," *New York Times* (July 5, 1890), 4; "A Very Fruitful Field," *New York Times* (July 12, 1890), 2.

125. Joseph Shippen, "Original Packages and Prohibition," *The Chautauquan* (July 1890), 456.

126. In particular, party leaders believed that the efforts of overzealous temperance crusaders in Iowa and Ohio had produced Democratic victories in a pair of closely watched off-year gubernatorial elections in 1889. Richard Jensen, *The Winning of the Midwest: Social and Political Conflict, 1888–1896* (Chicago: University of Chicago Press, 1971), 102–21.

127. On the legislative history of the Wilson Act, see Hamm, *Shaping the Eighteenth Amendment,* 79–88. As Hamm points out, Republicans were more enthusiastic in their support of the measure than Democrats. And yet Democratic opposition was not particularly pronounced, perhaps because the measure augmented the police powers of the states (instead of imposing federal regulations), or perhaps because many Southern states were by this time under local option—meaning that Southern legislators, too, were increasingly concerned about the prospect of unregulated interstate shipments of liquor.

128. Wilson Act, Ch. 728, 26 Stat. 313 (1890).

129. In *Leisy,* Fuller had held that the Commerce Clause barred the state of Iowa from prohibiting the importation and sale of out-of-state of liquor that remained in its original package. Near the end of his opinion, however, Fuller suggested that Congress might "remove [this] restriction upon the state in dealing with imported articles of trade within its limits . . . if in its judgment the end to be secured justifies and requires such action." 135 U.S. 100, 123 (1890).

130. *In re Rahrer,* 140 U.S. 545 (1891).

131. 125 U.S. 465, 508 (1888).

132. 140 U.S. 545 at 561. The logical inconsistency of the *Rahrer* and *Leisy* opinions is discussed in Fiss, *Troubled Beginnings of the Modern State,* 275–8.

133. *In re Rahrer* seems to have been the first case involving an attempt by Congress to nullify the preemptive force of the Commerce Clause in the case of a particular state regulation of interstate commerce. The decision is regularly cited to support the claim that Congress possesses the constitutional authority to authorize state importation restrictions in such cases. See, for example, Joshua D. Sarnoff, "Cooperative Federalism, the Delegation of Federal Power, and the Constitution," *Arizona Law Review* 39 (1997): 241–44.

134. Robert Mather, "Constitutional Construction and the Commerce Clause," *The American Lawyer* (December 1897), 568. Significantly, even jurists who endorsed the constitutionality of the Wilson Act were forced to concede that the measure had all but obliterated the traditional distinction between regulations of "police" and "commerce." As a writer in the *American Law Review* explained, the underlying theory of the legislation seemed to be that "the line of reconciliation between the police power of the States and the commerce power of the Nation, is the cooperation of the State and National governments, for the most effective protection of the health, the morals and the safety of the people throughout the Union." Charles Carroll Bonney, "The Relation

of the Police Power of the State to the Commerce Power of the Nation," *American Law Review* 25 (1891): 168.

135. Ezell, *Fortune's Merry Wheel,* 248.

136. Fuller, *Morality and the Mail,* 192–206; Foster, *Moral Reconstruction,* 119–23.

137. *In re Rapier,* 143 U.S. 110, 135 (1894).

138. 96 U.S. 727, 735 (1878).

139. "The 'Central American Express,'" *New York Times* (Feb. 9, 1894), 4; "The Great Lottery Fraud," *New York Times* (Feb. 26, 1894), 4; "The New Anti-Lottery Campaign," *Outlook* (Feb. 10, 1894), 259.

140. "The Lottery and Florida Law," *New York Times* (Feb. 4, 1894), 4; "The Lottery Swindlers," *New York Times* (April 19, 1894), 4; "The Country to the Rescue of Florida!" *The Independent* (Feb. 8, 1894), 10.

141. Thomas M. Cooley, "Taxation of Lotteries," *Atlantic Monthly* 69 (April 1892): 523–34. Emphasis added.

142. Thomas M. Cooley, *The General Principles of Constitutional Law in the United States of America,* 2d Ed. (Boston: Little Brown, 1891), 151.

143. Indeed, in the period between 1890 and 1894 many of the nation's major periodicals—including the *North American Review,* the *Forum,* the *Atlantic Monthly,* the *Nation,* the *Independent,* and the *Outlook*—published multiple articles denouncing the Lottery's activities and advocating federal action. Following the expiration of the Lottery's Louisiana charter, for example, the *New York Times* published virtually day-by-day accounts of the company's efforts to secure a new foothold in Florida. At the same time, religious groups inundated Congress with petitions calling for new federal legislation; 157 petitions were sent to the first session of the Fifty-third Congress (1894–5) alone. See Ezell, *Fortune's Merry Wheel,* 264–5; Alwes, "History of the Louisiana State Lottery Company," 1083–5.

144. The text of the Animal Industry Act of 1884 is reprinted in *Reid v. Colorado* (187 U.S. 137 [1902]).

145. In the case of the Animal Industry Act, for example, Congress could plausibly claim that it was merely promoting an unencumbered national market in livestock by banning the introduction of a product that would, if left unregulated, destroy that market.

146. On the legislative history of the 1895 anti-lottery law, see Herbert F. Marguiles, "Pioneering the Federal Police Power: *Champion v. Ames* and the Anti-Lottery Act of 1895," *The Journal of Southern Legal History* 4 (1995–6): 50–4.

147. On the role of Southern religious leaders and politicians in promoting federal anti-lottery legislation, see Foster, *Moral Reconstruction,* 123–7. A leading figure in the push for federal anti-lottery legislation, for example, was the fiery New Orleans Presbyterian minister Benjamin Morgan Palmer—a man who was in other contexts a vigorous supporter of states' rights. Foster also notes that four Southern Democratic lawmakers—Edward W. Robertson of Louisiana, John H. Rogers of Arkansas, John J. Hemphill of South Carolina, and James H. Blount of Georgia—helped lead the push for federal postal regulations that denied lottery companies the use of the mails. Ibid., 19–20, 122–8.

148. *Champion v. Ames,* 188 U.S. 321 (1903), Argument of William D. Guthrie.

149. For the claim that the Court was evenly divided after the first two arguments, see Robert T. Swaine, *The Cravath Firm and Its Predecessors, 1819–1948* (New York, 1946), 1:743–4.

150. 188 U.S. 321 at 374.

151. 188 U.S. 321 at 364.

152. 188 U.S. 321 at 371.

153. 188 U.S. 321 at 372, 358.

154. 188 U.S. 321 at 357–8. Emphasis added.

155. See, for example, Alfred Russell, "Three Constitutional Questions Decided by the Federal Supreme Court During the Last Four Months," *The American Law Review* 37 (1903): 507: "[*Champion* holds that] the commercial power . . . is complete in itself, may be exercised to its utmost extent, and acknowledges no limitations other than are prescribed in the Constitution itself. Important consequences may flow from this decision. . . . Congress may [now] prohibit the transportation between states of goods manufactured in violation of antitrust laws"; "Trusts and the Lottery Decision," *The Independent* 55 (1903): 574: "Congress has power, under this decision, to prohibit transportation . . . and it may reasonably be inferred that the five justices of the majority would not attempt to restrain that power if it should be exercised to suppress evil practices injurious to the public welfare"; "Lottery Tickets and Interstate Commerce," *Yale Law Journal* 12 (1903): 453: "[I]t would seem that the effect of the decision will be far-reaching not alone in further defining the scope of interstate commerce, but in extending the police regulation of the central government at least to the extent of closer cooperation with the states." "The Lottery Case," *Columbia Law Review* 3 (1903): 411: "[T]he ground of the limitation [of the *Champion* decision] to lottery tickets . . . is not apparent. The powers of Congress must be totally independent of the policy of the states, and of any changes therein. Nor can the power to prohibit be limited to what is against public health and morals."

156. Edward B. Whitney, "The Latest Development of the Interstate Commerce Power," *Michigan Law Review* 1 (1903): 623.

157. William A. Sutherland, "Is Congress a Conservator of the Public Morals?" *The American Law Review* 38 (1904): 208: "[H]owever much we would welcome any legislation that would effectually wipe out the 'widespread pestilence of lotteries,' yet if the power to enact such legislation does not exist under the Commerce Clause . . . let us not attempt to stretch the Constitution to give that power to Congress. The Commerce Clause empowers Congress to regulate commerce, not the public morals. The very fact that nearly all . . . of the states have passed laws directed to the eradication of the lottery evil, and that such a result is universally desired, will prevent any popular outcry against this newly asserted power of the general government; the end will be deemed to justify the means. It must be remembered, however, that 'questions of power do not depend upon the degree to which it may be exercised.'" Also see "The Lottery Case," *Harvard Law Review* 7 (1903): 509: "[The *Champion* decision] marks the tendency towards an obliteration of state lines and a centralization of power in the federal government."

Barry Friedman and Genevieve Lakier have recently argued that *Champion*-era legal commentators who believed that the Court had endorsed a plenary congressional power to ban items from interstate commerce were guilty of misreading Harlan's opinion. In reality, they argue, Harlan did no more than endorse the use of the commerce power to enact "helper" laws—that is, laws that prohibit the interstate shipment of commodities that are universally banned at the state level. In the end, however, the question of Harlan's *intent* seems somewhat beside the point. The obvious effect of the opinion's sweeping language—the adjective "plenary" is used no less than five times to describe Congress's power over interstate commerce—was to shift the burden of proof from the advocates of a plenary commerce power to the advocates of an inviolable sphere of state sovereignty. "'To Regulate' Not 'To Prohibit': Limiting the Commerce Power," *The Supreme Court Review, 2012* (2012): 255–320.

158. Subjects successfully regulated under the newly expanded commerce power included prostitution and adultery (*Hoke v. United States*, 220 U.S. 45 [1913]; *Caminetti v. United States*, 242 U.S. 470 [1917]); impure food and drugs (*Hipolite Egg Co. v. United States*, 220 U.S. 45 [1911]); foreign "prize fight" films (*Weber v. Freed*, 239 U.S. 325 [1915]); and stolen automobiles (*Brooks v. United States*, 267 U.S. 432 [1925]).

159. On the origins of the "white slave" scare, see David J. Langum, *Crossing Over the Line: Legislating Morality and the Mann Act* (Chicago: University of Chicago Press, 1994).

160. *Hoke v. United States*, 220 U.S. 45 (1911); *Caminetti v. United States*, 242 U.S. 470 (1917). There were two dissenters in the latter ruling.

161. In 1898, the Court had given the Wilson Act an improbably narrow ruling, holding that it permitted states to ban only the *sale*—and not the importation—of out-of-state liquor. *Rhodes v. Iowa*, 170 U.S. 412 (1898).

162. The relevant passage, quoted in full, reads: "The fact that regulations of liquor have been upheld in numberless instances which would have been repugnant to the great guaranties of the Constitution but for the enlarged right possessed by government to regulate liquor has never, that we are aware of, been taken as affording the basis for the thought that government might exert an enlarged power as to subjects to which, under the constitutional guaranties, such enlarged power could not be applied. In other words, the exceptional nature of the subject here regulated is the basis upon which the exceptional power exerted must rest, and affords no ground for any fear that such power may be constitutionally extended to things which it may not, consistently with the guaranties of the Constitution, embrace." *Clark Distilling Co. v. Western Maryland Railway Co.*, 242 U.S. 311, 332 (1917). As Barry Cushman has observed, the Court never adequately explained how the *Clark Distilling* ruling could be reconciled with contemporaneous rulings, such as those dealing with admiralty jurisdiction, which denied Congress the power to delegate regulatory authority to the states. Indeed, in a case decided three years after *Clark Distilling*, the Court explicitly cited the framers' desire for uniform national regulations as a reason for voiding a federal law that authorized the states to establish their own rules to govern workmen's compensation in admiralty cases. *Knickerbocker Ice Co. v. Stewart*, 247 U.S. 251 at 281. Cushman, "Lochner, Liquor, and Longshoremen," 26–30.

163. *United States v. Hill*, 248 U.S. 420 (1919). The federal measure in question was known as the Reed "Bone Dry" Amendment. On its origins, see Hamm, *Shaping the Eighteenth Amendment*, 207–8.

164. 207 U.S. 463 (1908); 208 U.S. 161 (1908).

165. 247 U.S. 251 (1918).

166. Ibid. at 272. This is not to suggest that the *Hammer* majority created the distinction between harmful and harmless commodities out of thin air. For a carefully researched study of the doctrine's origins, see Logan E. Sawyer III, "Creating *Hammer v. Dagenhart*," *William & Mary Bill of Rights Journal* 21 (2012): 67–124.

167. Ibid. at 280–1.

5. Reexamining the Collapse of the Old Order

1. Thomas Reed Powell, "Some Aspects of Constitutionalism and Federalism," *North Carolina Law Review* 14 (1935): 16.

2. Classic studies include Morton G. White, *Social Thought in America: The Revolt Against Formalism* (New York: Viking Press, 1949); Morton Horwitz, *The Transformation of American Law, 1870–1960: The Crisis of Legal Orthodoxy* (New York: Oxford University Press, 1992); Edward A. Purcell, Jr., *The Crisis of Democratic Authority: Scientific Naturalism and the Problem of Value* (Lexington: The University Press of Kentucky, 1973), 74–94; Gary C. Jacobsohn, *Pragmatism, Statesmanship, and the Supreme Court* (Ithaca, NY: Cornell University Press, 1977).

3. On the coherence of *Lochner*-era constitutional thought see, for example, Howard Gillman, *The Constitution Besieged: The Rise and Demise of Lochner Era Police Powers Jurisprudence* (Durham, NC: Duke University Press, 1993); Barry Cushman, *Rethinking the New Deal Court: The Structure of a Constitutional Revolution* (New York: Oxford, 1998); Julie Novkov, *Constituting Workers, Protecting Women: Gender, Law, and Labor in the Progressive Era and New Deal Years* (Ann Arbor: University of Michigan Press, 2001). These more recent studies are indebted to an earlier generation of scholars who first challenged the progressive characterization of the *Lochner*-era Court. Important works in this first wave of *Lochner* revisionism include Charles W. McCurdy, "Justice Field and the Jurisprudence of Government-Business Relations: Some Parameters of Laissez-Faire Constitutionalism," *Journal of American History* 61 (1975): 970–1005; Alan Jones, "Thomas M. Cooley and Laissez-Faire Constitutionalism: A Reconsideration," *Journal of American History* 53 (1967): 751–71; Michael Les Benedict, "Laissez-Faire and Liberty: A Re-Evaluation of the Meaning and Origins of Laissez-Faire Constitutionalism," *Law and History Review* 3 (1985): 293–331.

4. Brian Z. Tamanaha, *Beyond the Formalist-Realist Divide: The Role of Politics in Judging* (Princeton, NJ: Princeton University Press, 2010), 27–44.

5. On the links between nineteenth-century evangelicalism and twentieth-century progressivism, see Eldon J. Eisenach, *The Lost Promise of Progressivism* (Lawrence: The University Press of Kansas, 1994); Robert M. Crunden, *Ministers of Reform: The Progressives' Achievement in American Civilization, 1889–1920* (New York: Basic Books, 1982).

From the 1890s through the 1910s, one can identify a number of prominent Americans who self-identified as both progressive and evangelical. Evangelicals affiliated with the Social Gospel movement, for example, believed that efforts to mitigate the social harms of industrial capitalism were inextricably linked to the campaign to reform public morals. The ties between evangelicalism and progressivism began to fray in the 1920s, however, as American Protestantism fractured into competing "liberal" and "fundamentalist" camps. Nonetheless, scholars including Eisenach and Crunden have shown that the vast majority of progressives—even those who spurned organized religion—were heavily influenced by the broader ideals of nineteenth-century evangelicalism. On the fracturing of American Protestantism in the early twentieth century, see George M. Marsden, *Fundamentalism and American Culture* (New York: Oxford University Press, 1982).

6. As early as 1913, Lippmann argued that the experiment with legal prohibition of alcohol was bound to end in failure: "To erect a ban doesn't stop the want. It merely prevents its satisfaction. And since this desire for stimulants . . . is older and far more deeply rooted in the nature of men than love of the Prohibition Party or reverence for the laws . . . people will continue to drink . . . in spite of the acts of a legislature." *A Preface to Politics* (New York: Mitchell Kennerley, 1913), 40.

7. *Missouri v. Holland,* 252 U.S. 416, 433–4 (1920).

8. As Morton Horwitz has written, it was Holmes, more than any other thinker, who "pushed American legal thought into the twentieth century" by demolishing the "late-nineteenth-century ideal of an internally self-consistent and autonomous system of legal ideals, free from the corrupting influence of politics." Horwitz, *The Transformation of American Law, 1870–1960,* 142. On Holmes's antipathy towards categorical modes of reasoning, see ibid., 109–44; White, *Social Thought in America,* 59–75; Thomas C. Grey, "Holmes and Legal Pragmatism," *Stanford Law Review* 41 (1988–9): 787–870.

9. G. Edward White, "The Integrity of Justice Holmes' Jurisprudence," *Hofstra Law Review* 10 (1982): 633–72, 649. As White notes, however, Holmes was not entirely consistent in observing his theoretical commitment to a deferential style of judging. See ibid., 652–3, 658–65.

10. 198 U.S. 45, 54 (1905).

11. 187 U.S. 606 (1903).

12. The outcome of the case was probably never in doubt, as the Court had previously upheld similar laws regulating the sale of stock on margin. See *Booth v. Illinois,* 184 U.S. 425 (1902).

13. 187 U.S. 606 at 608.

14. Ibid. at 609–10.

15. Ibid. at 609.

16. Ibid. at 609. Emphasis added.

17. 188 U.S. 321 (1903). Indeed, *Champion* and *Otis* were argued within a week of each other in mid-December 1902.

18. 198 U.S. 45 at 53, 54.

19. Ibid. at 55.

20. Ibid. at 53. Emphasis added.

21. On the progressives' embrace of Holmes's *Lochner* dissent, see G. Edward White, *Justice Oliver Wendell Holmes: Law and the Inner Self* (New York: Oxford University Press, 1993), 364–5.

22. 273 U.S. 418. See, for example, Cushman, *Rethinking the New Deal Court,* 80. Robert C. Post, "Defending the Lifeworld: Substantive Due Process in the Taft Court Era," *Boston University Law Review* 78 (1998): 1525. As Post has written, Holmes's *Tyson* dissent "essentially foreshadow[ed] the complete collapse of the doctrine as it would occur seven years later in *Nebbia v. New York.*"

23. The "business affected with a public interest" concept is first clearly articulated in *Munn v. Illinois,* 94 U.S. 113 (1877).

24. 273 U.S. 418 at 429.

25. 273 U.S. 418 at 439–40.

26. 273 U.S. 418 at 446. Emphasis added.

27. 273 U.S. 418 at 445–6.

28. Maurice Finkelstein, "From *Munn v. Illinois* to *Tyson v. Banton,*" *Columbia Law Review* 27 (1927): 783.

29. 247 U.S. 251 (1918).

30. *McCray v. United States,* 195 U.S. 27 (1904); *Weber v. Freed* (1911).

31. *Hoke v. United States,* 227 U.S. 308 (1914); *Caminetti v. United States,* 242 U.S. 470 (1917); *Clark Distilling Co. v. Western Maryland Railroad Co.,* 242 U.S. 311 (1917).

32. 247 U.S. 251 at 280–1.

33. Ibid. at 280–1. Emphasis added.

34. Ibid. at 281.

35. 253 U.S. 149 (1920).

36. 253 U.S. 149 at 165–6. The "special principles" remark was a reference to the majority opinion in *Clark Distilling v. Western Maryland Railroad Co.,* in which Justice White had remarked cryptically that the "exceptional nature" of the liquor problem might provide a justification for the delegation of congressional regulatory authority to the states. 242 U.S. 311, 332 (1917).

37. Mark De Wolfe Howe, ed., *Holmes-Laski Letters: The Correspondence of Mr. Justice Holmes and Harold J. Laski, 1916-1935* (Cambridge, MA: Harvard University Press, 1953), 1: 264; Robert M. Mennel and Christine L. Compston, eds., *Holmes and Frankfurter: Their Correspondence, 1912-1934* (Hanover, NH: University Press of New England, 1996), 90–1.

38. *Holmes-Laski Letters,* 1: 264.

39. John Dewey, "The Public and its Problems," in *John Dewey: The Later Works,* ed. Jo Ann Boydston (Carbondale: Southern Illinois University Press, 1981–), 2:318. Dewey was particularly struck by the fact that the South, the region most affiliated with the doctrine of states' rights, had enthusiastically supported national prohibition. The editors of the *New Republic* made a similar point, noting that many ardent supporters of property rights had adopted the principles of "the Bolsheviki" where liquor was concerned. "Prohibition as a Warning," *The New Republic* (Jan. 25, 1919), 359.

40. Some scholars date the critical jurisprudential shifts to the mid-1930s; others contend that the traditional order endured until 1937, or even into the early 1940s. For an account that puts critical turning point in the mid-1930s, see Cushman, *Rethinking the New Deal Court*. For accounts that view 1937 as the pivotal year, see William E. Leuchtenberg, *The Supreme Court Reborn: The Constitutional Revolution in the Age of Roosevelt* (New York: Oxford University Press, 1995); Bruce Ackerman, *We the People: Foundations* (Cambridge, MA: Belknap Press of Harvard University, 1991). For the view that "constitutional revolution" was completed only in the 1940s, see G. Edward White, *The Constitution and the New Deal* (Cambridge, MA: Harvard University Press, 2000). The question of causation is similarly rife with controversy. Although the old order's demise was long viewed as a response to "external" political factors—in particular Roosevelt's threat to "pack" the Court with pro-New Deal justices—much recent scholarship argues that the familiar "switch in time" narrative has little basis in fact. For the view that the revolution was primarily a response to external political pressure, see Leuchtenberg, *The Supreme Court Reborn*. For the view that the revolution is properly understood as the product of ideological and doctrinal developments internal to the legal community, see Cushman, *Rethinking the New Deal Court;* White, *The Constitution and the New Deal;* Horwitz, *The Transformation of American Law, 1870–1960.*

41. For Holmes's influence on the legal academy in the 1920s and 1930s, see, for example, Purcell, *Crisis of Democratic Theory,* 74–94.

42. The phrase "constitutional laxity" was coined by Edward Corwin in an article published in 1917. Corwin, "Social Insurance and Constitutional Limitations," *Yale Law Journal* 26 (1917): 431–443.

43. White, *The Constitution and the New Deal,* Ch. 7.

44. Howard Gillman, "The Collapse of Constitutional Originalism and the Rise of the Notion of the 'Living Constitution' in the Course of American State-Building," *Studies in American Political Development* 11 (1997): 197–215; Michael Kammen, *A Machine That Would Go of Itself* (New York: St. Martin's Press, 1994), 17–19.

45. On the emergence of the "living Constitution" concept in progressive political thought, see Gillman, "The Collapse of Constitutional Originalism"; White, *The Constitution and the New Deal,* Ch. 7; Morton J. Horwitz, "Foreword: The Constitution of Change: Legal Fundamentality Without Fundamentalism," *Harvard Law Review* 107 (1993): 33–76; Jonathan O'Neill, *Originalism in American Law and Politics: A Constitutional History* (Baltimore, MD: The Johns Hopkins University Press, 2005).

46. Roscoe Pound, "Liberty of Contract," *Yale Law Journal* 18 (1909): 467–8. Emphasis in the original.

47. Ibid., 468. The passage quotes from the New York Court of Appeals' decision in *Wynehamer v. The People* (striking down the state's Maine Law on due process grounds), as well as the U.S. Supreme Court's decision in *Mugler v. Kansas* (denying that prohibition violates economic liberties protected under the Fourteenth Amendment).

48. Ibid., 462.

49. Morris R. Cohen, "Legal Theories and Social Science," *International Journal of Ethics* 25 (1915): 470.

50. Ibid., 480–1.

51. Ibid. Emphasis added.

52. Brian Tamanaha has argued persuasively that Cohen and other academic critics of the early-twentieth-century judiciary drastically overstated the influence of this "mechanistic" conception of the judicial function. But while Tamanaha is convincing on this point, it is important to note that Cohen's critique actually centered on the claim that the Court was *selectively applying* what he termed the "phonograph theory" of the judicial function—that is, adjusting constitutional doctrine to accommodate social change in some areas while refusing to do so in others. Tamanaha, *Beyond the Formalist-Realist Divide*, 27–44.

53. Cohen, "Legal Theories and Social Science," 493. Cohen repeated the lottery example twenty years later at the height of the Court's confrontation with the New Deal. See Morris Cohen, "Constitutional and Natural Rights in 1789 and Since," *National Lawyers' Guild Quarterly* 1 (1938): 93. "In point of fact, no historian can deny . . . that in the making of our constitutional law there generally enters the personal opinion of the judge as to what is desirable or undesirable legislation. And this is inevitable, since the words of the Constitution cannot decide every issue. . . . To say, for instance, that the people of 1789 intended to give Congress power to prohibit lottery tickets but not to regulate insurance policies has no support in any words of the Constitution and runs counter to all that we know of the mores of the eighteenth century when lotteries were the foundation of charitable institutions and insurance underwriting was recognized as a form of gambling."

54. Corwin, "Social Insurance and Constitutional Limitations," 431–2.

55. Ibid., 434–5. Emphasis in the original.

56. Ibid., 434.

57. Ibid., 436.

58. Ray A. Brown, "Police Power—Legislation for Health and Personal Safety," *Harvard Law Review* 42 (1928–9): 897. Also see Brown, "Due Process of Law, Police Power, and the Supreme Court," *Harvard Law Review* 40 (1927): 943–68.

59. 261 U.S. 525 (1923).

60. Ibid., 880, 898.

61. Similar arguments can be found in the writings of Alpheus Mason and Albert Kales. Writing in 1934, Mason summarized the past four decades of constitutional development as follows: "In the 1890s it . . . came to pass that if property was threatened by labor activities, every resource of national executive and judicial power was available for its safeguard. . . . All this has attracted attention enough. Judicial review has been frequently criticized and attacked, but it still stands unimpaired. Apologists and eulogists have rallied to the Court's support urging that judicial review unlike British Parliamentarism furnishes protection for private rights against even legislative majorities. One may doubt this contention. . . . *Property rights in slaves and in liquor were annihilated without being paid for although Great Britain compensated for such losses. With us the erstwhile property owner enjoys only such consolation as he may gain from living in a community which thus rises to higher moral standards at his expense.*" A.T. Mason, "The Supreme Court of Yesterday and Today: A Government of Men and Not of Laws," *New Jersey State Bar*

Association Quarterly 25 (1934): 34–5. Kales, in turn, cited the abolition of liquor to make the point that the "inarticulate major premise" in the Court's police power rulings was that regulations deemed "consistent with the exigencies of the social order" would be sustained while those not so consistent would be invalidated. Thus, property in liquor—which the Court deemed inessential to the "social order"—could be abolished despite the fact that prohibition laws inflicted a "loss which would in general be regarded as confiscatory." Labor laws, in contrast, were subjected to a higher level of scrutiny, since society "rests upon success in commerce and industry." Albert Kales, "'Due Process,' the Inarticulate Major Premise, and the Adamson Act," *Yale Law Journal* 26 (1917): 519–49.

62. Morton Horwitz has documented the series of steps through which Hale and other academics associated with the Legal Realist movement steadily eroded the legitimacy of traditional due process concepts such as "confiscation" and "affected with a public interest." *The Transformation of American Law, 1870–1960*, 164–5, 195–8.

63. Quoted in ibid., 163.

64. Ibid., 196.

65. Robert Lee Hale, "Value and Vested Rights," *Columbia Law Review* 27 (1927): 524.

66. The economist John R. Commons, a scholar closely affiliated with the Realist movement, used the example of liquor prohibition to make essentially the same argument in his influential 1922 work, *Legal Foundations of Capitalism*. In particular, Commons criticized the emerging notion that judges deciding takings cases should calculate the market value of a business by taking into account its anticipated future earnings. This method of calculating value, Commons argued, was essentially circular, since a business's anticipated earnings depended on how the state would treat the business in the future. Market value, as the case of dry-county saloons and breweries clearly demonstrated, depended on a prior and evolving background of legal rules. John R. Commons, *Legal Foundations of Capitalism* (New York: McMillan Co., 1924), 190. Also see Horwitz, *The Transformation of American Law, 1870–1960*, 162–3.

67. Charles Warren, "What is Confiscation?" *The Atlantic Monthly* 140 (1927): 246, 248.

68. Ibid., 248.

69. Ibid., 249.

70. Collins Denny, Jr., "The Growth and Development of the Police Power of the State," *Michigan Law Review* 20 (1921–2): 173–214, 186, 188.

71. Malcolm P. Sharp, "Movement in Supreme Court Adjudication: A Study of Modified and Overruled Decisions," *Harvard Law Review* 46 (1933): 362, 374–5. Emphasis added. In the acknowledgements to the article, Sharp reports that his essay was begun "under a fellowship with Professor Felix Frankfurter"—a fact that may well account for the Realist overtones of the analysis.

72. A.H. Feller, "Moratory Legislation: A Comparative Study," *Harvard Law Review* 46 (1933): 1080.

73. Maurice H. Merrill, "Application of the Obligation of Contract to State Promises," *University of Pennsylvania Law Review* 80 (1931–2): 660–1.

74. Ibid., 664–5.

75. 290 U.S. 398 at 426. For an excellent overview of the origins of the *Blaisdell* litigation, see John A. Fliter and Derek S. Hoff, *Fighting Foreclosure: The* Blaisdell *Case, the Contract Clause, and the Great Depression* (Lawrence: University Press of Kansas, 2012).

76. Ibid. at 426–7.

77. Ibid. at 436. It is also worth noting that the state of Minnesota relied on *Mugler v. Kansas* to support the constitutionality of mortgage moratoria. Although *Mugler* was not, technically speaking, a Contract Clause case, the state's brief argued that Justice Harlan's opinion had established the state legislatures' power to determine when the "existence of [an] emergency" required the destruction or modification of settled property rights. Moreover, Harlan had made clear that this determination was not to be questioned by the courts, except where a particular police measure had "no real or substantial relation" to the emergency in question. Appellee's Brief, 40.

78. 290 U.S. 398 at 435.

79. Ibid. at 442–3. Emphasis in the original.

80. As G. Edward White has written, Hughes's *Blaisdell* opinion marked the first time that a majority of the Court had explicitly endorsed the "living Constitution" approach to constitutional interpretation. White notes that previous Court opinions had accepted that constitutional principles might, as a result of social change, be applied to circumstances not envisioned by the framers. *Blaisdell* broke new ground, however, by holding that altered social conditions might change the very meaning of the constitutional provision at issue. In the case of the Minnesota mortgage moratorium, Hughes's opinion held that the Contract Clause "meant something very different in the interdependent, depressed American economy of the 1930s from what it previously had meant." White, *The Constitution and the New Deal,* 211–15.

81. Hadley Arkes, for example, argues that Hughes "emptied [the clause] of its meaning in the course of interpreting" it. Richard Epstein echoes the charge: "The operative assumption [of Hughes's opinion] seems to be that questions of constitutional law are to be answered according to whether or not we like the Constitution as it was originally drafted. If we do not, we are then free to introduce into the document those provisions we think more congenial to our time. . . . By this standard a court can invest itself with the power of a standing constitutional convention." Hadley Arkes, *The Return of George Sutherland: Restoring a Jurisprudence of Natural Rights* (Princeton, NJ: Princeton University Press, 1994), 244; Richard A. Epstein, "Toward a Revitalization of the Contract Clause," *University of Chicago Law Review* 51 (1984): 735–6.

82. 290 U.S. 398 at 440.

83. As Gary Jacobsohn has observed, "Hughes did not cavalierly ignore the fact . . . that the founders had intended the [Contract Clause] to operate in times of emergency; rather, he redefined the nature of an emergency to make it conform to contemporary reality." *Pragmatism, Statesmanship, and the Supreme Court,* 189.

84. 290 U.S. 398 at 442.

85. Ibid.

86. Ibid. at 439.

87. For the argument that *Nebbia* marks the critical turning point in the Court's economic due process jurisprudence, see Cushman, *Rethinking the New Deal Court,* 79–92. For a dissenting view, arguing that *Nebbia* left much of the *Lochner*-era due process framework intact, see Gillman, *The Constitution Besieged,* 180–3.

88. Indeed, the briefs filed in *Nebbia* by the states of New York and Ohio—the latter participating as *amicus curiae*—both relied on Holmes to make the case that the Court should not substitute its own definition of a "public" economic concern for that of a state legislature. Ohio's brief quoted at length from the *Otis v. Parker* majority opinion, where Holmes had warned against the judicial tendency to read particular "ethical or economical opinions" into the Constitution. New York cited the same passage, as well as Holmes's famous assertion in *The Common Law* that "the felt necessities of the time" were ultimately more important than "syllogism" in "determining the rules by which men should be governed." Brief of John W. Bricker, Attorney General of Ohio, 16. Appellee's Brief, 26, 38.

89. 291 U.S. 502, 531 (1934).

90. Ibid. at 536.

91. Ibid. at 528.

92. Ibid. at 534.

93. Cushman, *Rethinking the New Deal Court,* 80.

94. 291 U.S. 502 at 537.

95. Thus, while Richard Epstein concedes that previous Court decisions had to some degree "confused" the boundary between public and private economic concerns, he nonetheless insists that the dichotomy reflected an empirically valid distinction between those businesses that tended towards natural monopolies and those that did not. Richard A. Epstein, *How Progressives Rewrote the Constitution* (Washington, DC: Cato Institute, 2006), 77–84; "In Defense of the 'Old' Public Health: The Legal Framework for the Regulation of Public Health," *Brooklyn Law Review* 69 (2004): 1436.

96. Thomas P. Hardman, "Public Utilities I: The Quest for a Concept," *West Virginia Law Quarterly* 37 (1931): 267–8; Finkelstein, "From *Munn v. Illiinois* to *Tyson v. Banton,*" 780, 783.

97. Hardman, "Public Utilities I: The Quest for a Concept," 262–3; Felix Frankfurter, "Mr. Justice Holmes: A Review of His Twenty-five Years on the Supreme Court," *Harvard Law Review* 41 (1927–8): 156; Thomas Reed Powell, "State Utilities and the Supreme Court, 1922–1930," *Michigan Law Review* 29 (1931): 830.

98. As a writer in the *Yale Law Journal* explained in 1930 (with a citation to Holmes's *Tyson* dissent), the "legal reasons" given by the Court for upholding or invalidating police regulations were "but henchmen who do valiant service for the overlords of public policy." The tortuous history of the "affected with a public interest" doctrine revealed that any attempt "to divide an order of interlocking industries, each of which produces for the market, into 'public' and 'private' businesses is a parlous adventure." Walton H. Hamilton, "Affectation with Public Interest," *Yale Law Journal* 39 (1929–30): 1103–4.

99. *Railroad Retirement Board v. Alton,* 295 U.S. 330 (1935); *Schechter Poultry Corp. v. U.S.,* 295 U.S. 495 (1935); *U.S. v. Butler,* 297 U.S. 1 (1936); *Carter v. Carter Coal Co.,* 298 U.S. 238 (1936).

100. 301 U.S. 1 (1937).

101. *U.S. v. Darby,* 12 U.S. 100, 124 (1941. Also see *Wickard v. Filburn,* 317 U.S. 111 (1942).

102. White, *The New Deal and the Constitution,* 225–33; Cushman, *Rethinking the New Deal Court,* 214–25.

103. *Wickard v. Filburn,* 317 U.S. 111 at 120.

104. Keith Whittingon, "The Death of the Legalized Constitution," in *Courts and the Culture Wars,* ed. Bradley C.S. Watson (Lanham, MD: Lexington Books, 2002), 35.

105. William Carey Jones, "The Child Labor Decision," *California Law Review* 6 (1918): 408, 410.

106. Thurlow M. Gordon, "The Child Labor Law Case," *Harvard Law Review* 32 (1918): 49, 54, 58.

107. Thomas Reed Powell, "The Child Labor Law, the Tenth Amendment, and the Commerce Clause," *Southern Law Quarterly* 3 (1918): 175–202. Also see Walter F. Dodd, "Extra-Constitutional Limitations on Legislative Power," *Yale Law Journal* 40 (1931): 1212. Dodd cited the Court's recent decisions on the question of whether "the power to regulate interstate commerce includes the power to prohibit" as evidence that the Commerce Clause "derives its real content" from the justices' idiosyncratic "considerations of wisdom and morality."

108. "States' Rights vs. The Nation," *New Republic* (June 15, 1918), 194–5.

109. O'Neill, *Originalism in American Law and Politics,* 33–4. For discussions of Corwin's impact on constitutional theory in the 1920s and 1930s, see Cornell W. Clayton, "Edward S. Corwin as Public Scholar," in *The Pioneers of Judicial Behavior,* ed. Nancy Maveety (Ann Arbor: University of Michigan Press, 2003), 289–315; Gary L. McDowell, "The Corrosive Constitutionalism of Edward S. Corwin," *Law and Social Inquiry* 14 (1989): 603–14; Richard Loss, "Introduction," in *Corwin on the Constitution,* ed. Loss (Ithaca, NY: Cornell University Press, 1981).

110. Edward S. Corwin, "Constitution v. Constitutional Theory," *American Political Science Review* 19 (1925): 295–6.

111. Corwin, "Constitution v. Constitutional Theory," 295–8; "Congress's Power to Prohibit Commerce: A Crucial Constitutional Issue," *Cornell Law Quarterly* 18 (1933): 485.

112. Edward S. Corwin, *The Commerce Power Versus States' Rights* (Princeton, NJ: Princeton University Press, 1936), 249, 267.

113. Ibid., 296.

114. Edward S. Corwin, *The Twilight of the Supreme Court: A History of Our Constitutional Theory* (New Haven, CT: Yale University Press, 1934), 180; Corwin, "Constitution v. Constitutional Theory," 299.

115. Corwin, *The Commerce Power Versus States' Rights,* 167, 248–9. For a contemporaneous critique of Corwin's "two horses" thesis, see Frank R. Strong, "Cooperative Federalism," *Iowa Law Review* 23 (1937): 459–518.

116. For the view that the Marshall Court's understanding of the federal system more closely resembled "dual federalism" than "cooperative federalism," see Howard

Gillman, "The Struggle over Marshall and the Politics of Constitutional History," *Politics Research Quarterly* 47 (1994): 877–86; Herbert A. Johnson, *The Chief Justiceship of John Marshall, 1801–1835* (Columbia: University of South Carolina Press, 1997), 73–4; Stephen M. Griffin, "Constitutional Theory Transformed," *Yale Law Journal* 108 (1999): 2115–2163.

117. *Champion v. Ames*, 188 U.S. 321, 358 (1903). Edward S. Corwin, "The Child Labor Decision," *The New Republic* (July 12, 1922), 177–9; Corwin, "Constitution v. Constitutional Theory," 296; Corwin, *Commerce Power v. States' Rights*, 104–7.

118. Thomas Reed Powell, "Comment on Mr. Corwin's Paper," *American Political Science Review* 19 (1925): 305.

119. Theodore W. Cousens, "The Use of the Federal Commerce Power to Regulate Matters within the States," *Virginia Law Review* (1934–5): 68, 75.

120. John Dickinson, "'The Defect of Power' in Constitutional Law," *Temple Law Quarterly* 9 (1934–5): 395, 397–8.

121. Morris R. Cohen, "What to Do with the Supreme Court," *The Nation* (July 10, 1935), 39–40. Law professor Douglas Maggs, writing in 1935, likewise described the upcoming "recovery legislation" cases as involving an essentially arbitrary choice between the *Hammer* majority's narrow definition of the commerce power and the more expansive definition of the *Champion* Court, which had been "neither overruled, nor . . . satisfactorily distinguished." Doctrine was now so "confused," in Maggs's view, that neither text nor precedent could determine whether the major New Deal measures were constitutional; the justices would simply have use their "sense of statesmanship" and "decide as they think best." Douglas B. Maggs, "The Constitution and the Recovery Legislation: The Roles of Document, Doctrine, and Judges," in *Legal Essays in Tribute to Orrin Kip McMurray*, ed. Max Radin and A.M. Kidd (Berkeley: University of California Press, 1935), 426, 403–4. For additional articles framing the New Deal constitutional debate as a clash between two irreconcilable lines of precedent, one originating in the morals cases and the other in *Hammer*, see D.O. McGovney, "Reorganization of the Supreme Court," *California Law Review* 25 (1937): 402–3: "The [*Hammer*] majority . . . was forced to very narrow and technical distinctions to justify this decision in view of decisions in other cases [upholding federal laws prohibiting] the shipment in interstate commerce of lottery tickets, prostitutes, stolen automobiles—although lotteries, prostitutes, and stealing, within the States, are exclusively within State control. . . . In decisions on New Deal legislation the Court has continued to give the power of Congress over commerce [this] narrow and power-denying interpretation." "Recent Decisions," *N.Y.U. Law Review* 13 (1935–6): 288: "In declaring the Child Labor Act unconstitutional, the court held that Congress had no authority to exclude from interstate commerce goods which effect no evil in their sale in the state of destination. . . . But such commodities as liquor, lottery tickets, and stolen automobiles, all of which Congress has excluded without successful attack, are not evils *per se*, but become evils by some combination of facts within the borders of the states. In denying Congress the right to prevent the use of interstate commerce to promote the evil of unfair competition within the states the judiciary has taken upon itself to judge between evils." "Editorial Notes,"

Brooklyn Law Review 5 (1935–6): 463–4: "[In *Champion*] the principle was established that Congress could safeguard commerce from the pollution of immoral matter. . . . The broader basis of the decision was the Court's reluctance to interfere when Congress saw fit to adapt its commerce power for moral welfare purposes. . . . [But in *Hammer*] prior decisions were distinguished upon the ground that the statutes previously considered had been designed to prevent moral evils in the state of destination. . . . [I]t is difficult to understand why Congress can manipulate its commerce power for the prevention of evils in the state of destination, and cannot do the same as regards the state of origin. . . . The Court [has] consciously walked into a no-government land or a twilight zone where neither state nor federal government [can] act because each would usurp the powers of the other." Howard E. Wahrenbrock, "Federal Anti-Trust Law and the National Industrial Recovery Act," *Michigan Law Review* 31 (1933): 1052–3: "Prior to the Child Labor case little question would have been raised that Congress could control interstate commerce for welfare ends. The cases upholding federal statutes [dealing with liquor, lotteries, prostitution, and pure food and drugs] seemed to leave little room to question such power."

122. See, for example, William MacDonald's *New York Times* review of Corwin's *Twilight of the Supreme Court.* "The Supreme Court and the New Deal," *New York Times* (Dec. 23, 1934), BR7.

123. Walton H. Hamilton and Carlton C. Rodee, "Police Power," in *Encyclopedia of the Social Sciences,* vol. 12, ed. Edwin R.A. Seligman (New York: Macmillan, 1934), 190–92.

124. Charles A. Beard and William Beard, *The American Leviathan: The Republic in the Machine Age* (New York: Macmillan, 1931), 602–14.

125. "Ex Parte Snatch," *Time* (March 15, 1937), 36–7. The essay was a condensed version of a law review article by Professor Thomas A. Cowan, "Ex Parte Snatch," *Illinois Law Review* 31 (1937): 737.

126. The Federal Kidnapping Law (or Lindbergh Law), which used the commerce power to impose federal criminal penalties for kidnapping in instances where the kidnappers crossed state lines, was upheld in *Gooch v. United States,* 297 U.S. 124 (1936).

127. "Ex Parte Snatch," 37.

128. James William Moore and Shirley Adelson, "The Supreme Court: 1938 Term," *Virginia Law Review* 26 (1939): 15.

129. Peter H. Irons, *The New Deal Lawyers* (Princeton, NJ: Princeton University Press, 1982), 250.

130. Respondent's Brief (Brief for Government Officers), 129. Emphasis in the original.

131. Ibid., 136–7. Emphasis added.

132. Ibid., 136–7, 128.

133. 298 U.S. 238 at 308–9. In dissent, Justice Cardozo, joined by Brandeis and Stone, endorsed the government's contention that the subjects regulated in the Guffey Act bore an "inescapable . . . relation" to interstate commerce. To bar the federal government from regulating prices and working conditions in the coal industry would be

to create a "vacuum" of power, thus leaving "many a public evil incidental to interstate transactions . . . without a remedy." Ibid. at 329, 326.

134. 299 U.S. 334 (1937).

135. Amicus Brief of United States, 38–9.

136. Citing *Champion* and *Hoke*, the brief concluded that "it was because of the evil character of the traffic regulated and not because of any inherent evil in the objects" themselves that the Court had upheld the use of the commerce power to reach subjects such as lotteries, prostitution, and auto theft. Ibid., 31.

137. 247 U.S. 251 at 271.

138. This point is discussed at length Edward H. Levi, *An Introduction to Legal Reasoning* (Chicago: University of Chicago Press, 1948), 67–8.

139. Hughes's opinion emphasized the fact that the Ashurst-Sumners Act had "substantially the same provisions as the Webb-Kenyon Act," and that "[t]he course of congressional legislation with respect to convict-made goods has followed closely the precedents as to intoxicating liquors." 299 U.S. 344 at 350–1.

140. Ibid. at 347–8.

141. Ibid. at 351.

142. Ibid. at 352.

143. Ibid. at 349. "Horse Collars," *Time* (Jan. 11, 1937), 16. *Kentucky Whip* was widely noticed by contemporary observers, with many hailing the ruling as a transformative decision. Also see "Editorial," *The New Republic* (Jan. 13, 1937), 312; Franklin Waltman, "Politics and People: Wide Effect on Proposed Legislation Expected After Supreme Court Bans Prison Goods," *Washington Post* (Jan. 5, 1937), 2; "Editorial," *Nation* (Jan. 9, 1937), 30. More recently, William Ross has argued that the Court's decision to uphold the Ashurst-Sumners Act played an important role in killing Roosevelt's Court-packing plan (which, by an accident of timing, was announced at around the same time *Kentucky Whip* was handed down). Ross notes, for example, that Senator Henry Ashurst was both chair of the Senate Judiciary Committee—the Committee to which the Court-packing bill was referred—and a sponsor of the convict labor bill. Ashurst's lukewarm support of the Court-packing bill has long been cited as a reason for the plan's failure, and Ross observes that Ashurst soured on the Court-packing plan at about the same time that the Court upheld his signature bill. William G. Ross, "When Did the 'Switch in Time' Actually Occur? Re-Discovering the Supreme Court's 'Forgotten' Decisions of 1936–7," *Arizona State Law Journal* 37 (2005): 1185–6.

144. 301 U.S. 1 (1937). Another pivotal 1937 decision which clearly built on the logic of the Court's earlier morals rulings was *Steward Machine Co. v. Davis*, which upheld the unemployment compensation provisions of the 1935 Social Security Act against a Tenth Amendment challenge. Like Justice Harlan, whose *Champion* opinion had declared that the states' inability to address a great national "evil" might provide sufficient constitutional grounds for federal regulation, Justice Cardozo emphasized that the states had attempted to address the problem of unemployment compensation, but had ultimately been unable to do so, "whether through timidity or for other motives [such as the fear that businesses would migrate to neighboring states]." In such a case, Cardozo reasoned,

nothing in the Constitution prevented "the states and the nation [from] joining in a cooperative endeavor to avert a common evil." 301 U.S. 548, 588–9 (1937).

145. Ibid. at 37–8. The "close and substantial relation" test, as Richard Friedman has observed, was first formulated by Hughes himself in the 1914 *Shreveport Rate Cases.* Writing for the majority, Hughes had held that the commerce power could reach "intrastate" activities—such as rates on intrastate rail journeys—when such activities could not easily be disentangled from interstate commercial activity. Until the *Jones and Laughlin* decision, however, it was generally assumed that activities relating to "production" or "manufacturing" were, by definition, not "closely" or "substantially" related to interstate commerce. 234 U.S. 342 (1914). Richard D. Friedman, "Switching Time and Other Thought Experiments: The Hughes Court and Constitutional Transformation," *University of Pennsylvania Law Review* 142 (1994): 1964.

146. As Hughes's majority opinion explained, for the Court to "shut [its] eyes" to the potentially "catastrophic" effects of labor unrest in the nation's largest steel-producing firms would be to decide the case "in an intellectual vacuum." 301 U.S. 1 at 41.

147. Although, to be sure, the Court's decision to uphold the application of the Wagner Act to a tiny clothing manufacturer in the jointly decided *Labor Board v. Friedman-Harry Marks Clothing Co.* raised serious doubts about the viability of the distinction between direct and indirect effects. 301 U.S. 58 (1937).

148. 307 U.S. 38 (1939).

149. 297 U.S. 1 (1936).

150. Indeed, many sections of the *Carter Coal* brief were reproduced verbatim, including the discussion of the federal lottery act of 1895. Brief for the United States, 82–3.

151. Ibid., 39–40.

152. Ibid., 88–9. Emphasis added.

153. The administration lawyers clearly believed they had discovered a winning argument; they repeated the point almost verbatim in another section of the brief, noting that the prevention of "unreasonably low prices . . . and disorderly marketing in commerce" was "much more closely related to the underlying objectives of the Commerce Clause than the protection of the public against immorality, crime, and disease." Ibid., 40.

154. Ibid., 39.

155. Ibid., 112–18.

156. 307 U.S. 38 at 48.

157. Ibid. at 54.

158. Ibid. at 56. In an article that appeared too recently to be fully addressed in the present study, Barry Cushman has argued that the pre-1937 Court relied on concepts derived from due process analysis to define the scope of the prohibitory commerce power. In particular, Cushman maintains that the Court adopted a broader view of the prohibitory commerce power when the law in question targeted an inherently dangerous or noxious item, such as liquor, that did not trigger a compensation requirement when seized or destroyed by state or local officials. Although Cushman is persuasive on this point, it must be pointed out that the due process distinction between noxious and

innocent property remained highly controversial in the decades after its original formulation in *Mugler v. Kansas*. To the extent that the Court's Commerce Clause jurisprudence came increasingly to rely on this distinction, then, it seems likely that the effect was not to reinforce the underpinnings of the dual federalism framework, but rather to accelerate their erosion. Barry Cushman, "Carolene Products and Constitutional Structure," *The Supreme Court Review*, 2012 (2012): 321–377, 342–4.

159. Instead, he merely quoted a twenty-year-old bit of dictum, from *Wilson v. New* (1917), in which the Court had suggested that the federal government's power to prohibit the interstate traffic in liquor and lottery tickets did not imply a similar power over "flour, dry goods . . . pig iron, steel rails, or most of the vast body of commodities." This, in turn, was followed by a quotation from *Hammer* in which the majority had warned against using the commerce power to invade the purely "local" sphere of production. Ibid. at 55.

160. 312 U.S. 100 (1941).

161. Appellee's Brief, 31, 35–6.

162. Brief for United States, 64.

163. Ibid., 62.

164. Ibid., 62.

165. 312 U.S. 100 at 115.

166. Ibid. at 115–6.

167. Ibid. at 116–7.

168. Ibid. at 124.

169. Ibid. at 116.

170. The Court's decision the following year in *Wickard v. Filburn* made clear that the commerce power could reach even wholly intrastate, non-commercial activity—such as an individual farmer's decision about how much wheat to produce for his own private consumption—provided the activity in question, when viewed in the aggregate, could be said to exert a "substantial effect" on interstate commerce. 317 U.S. 111, 129 (1942).

171. Edward S. Corwin, "The Passing of Dual Federalism," *Virginia Law Review* 36 (1950): 22, 17.

172. In Epstein's words, "What failed in *Darby* was not the language of the Constitution, but the willingness of the Justices to accept the theory of limited government on which it was based." Epstein, "Proper Scope of the Commerce Power," 1449.

173. 312 U.S. at 116.

174. Gillman, "Disaster Relief, 'Do Anything' Spending Powers, and the New Deal," *Law and History Review* 23 (2005): 443–50, 450. On the role of the emergency powers and "stream of commerce" precedents, see Richard D. Friedman, "The Sometimes-Bumpy Stream of Commerce Clause Doctrine," *Arkansas Law Review* 55 (2003); 981–1001; Michele Landis Dauber, *The Sympathetic State: Disaster Relief and the Origins of the American Welfare State* (Chicago: University of Chicago Press, 2013); Griffin, "Constitutional Theory Transformed," 2131. Griffin goes so far as to suggest that decisions upholding emergency economic measures during World War I were "the only

precedent[s] the New Dealers could find to justify" their expansive conception of federal regulatory authority.

175. As Fuller put the point, "Our form of government may remain notwithstanding legislation or decision, but, as long ago observed, it is with governments, as with religions: the form may survive the substance of the faith." 188 U.S. 321, 372, 375 (1903).

Conclusion

1. Oliver Wendell Holmes, Jr., Digital Suite of the Harvard Law School Library (http://library.law.harvard.edu/suites/owh).

2. See, for example, Richard A. Epstein, *How Progressives Rewrote the Constitution* (Washington, DC: Cato Institute, 2006); Randy E. Barnett, *Restoring the Lost Constitution: The Presumption of Liberty* (Princeton, NJ: Princeton University Press, 2004); Hadley Arkes, *The Return of George Sutherland: Restoring a Jurisprudence of Natural Rights* (Princeton, NJ: Princeton University Press, 1994); Gary L. McDowell, *The Language of Law and the Foundations of American Constitutionalism* (New York: Cambridge University Press, 2010); Patrick M. Garry, *An Entrenched Legacy: How the New Deal Constitutional Revolution Continues to Shape the Role of the Supreme Court* (University Park: Pennsylvania State University Press, 2008); Bradley C.S. Watson, *Living Constitution, Dying Faith* (Wilmington, DE: ISI Press, 2009).

3. Barry Friedman, *The Will of the People: How Public Opinion Has Influenced the Supreme Court and Shaped the Meaning of the Constitution* (New York: Farrar, Straus, and Giroux, 2009), 382–3. Also see Stephen M. Griffin, "Constitutional Theory Transformed," *Yale Law Journal* 108 (1999): 2130–31.

4. Bruce Ackerman, *We the People: Foundations* (Cambridge, MA: Belknap Press, 1991); *We the People: Transformations* (Cambridge: MA, Belknap Press, 1998). Admittedly, the "rights revolution" of the 1960s and 1970s has scrambled the terms of the debate somewhat, to the extent that modern-day liberals are more likely than their New Deal-era predecessors to envision a strong role for the judiciary in the constitutional system. And yet even the postwar expansion of civil rights and liberties is regularly characterized as a natural outgrowth of the New Deal revolution. Once the Court had banished the nineteenth-century shibboleths of economic rights and dual federalism, the argument goes, the way was open for a reconstituted judiciary to impose the substantive values of postwar liberalism on the American polity. As Ken Kersch has written, the collapse in the New Deal period of "traditional . . . constitutional principles" created an intellectual vacuum which was quickly filled by the rise of "modern constitutional theory." Where nineteenth-century constitutional theory was firmly anchored in "the nation's founding texts . . . and writings about those texts," modern constitutional theory consists of "a succession of ingeniously serviceable legitimating rhetorics for whatever progressive-spirited reform imperative is imagined to be of moment." *Constructing Civil Liberties: Discontinuities in the Development of American Constitutional Law* (New York: Cambridge University Press, 2004) 339.

5. Morton G. White, *Social Thought in America: The Revolt against Formalism* (New York: Viking Press, 1949). Although scholars have quibbled with various aspects of White's account, his basic framework continues to shape scholarly thinking about the origins of the living Constitution. For broadly similar treatments of the subject, see Edward A. Purcell, Jr., *The Crisis of Democratic Authority: Scientific Naturalism and the Problem of Value* (Lexington: The University Press of Kentucky, 1973), 74–94; Morton Horwitz, *The Transformation of American Law, 1870–1960: The Crisis of Legal Orthodoxy* (New York: Oxford University Press, 1992); Gary C. Jacobsohn, *Pragmatism, Statesmanship, and the Supreme Court* (Ithaca, NY: Cornell University Press, 1977); Louis Menand, *The Metaphysical Club* (New York: Farrar, Straus, and Giroux, 2001).

6. McDowell, *Language of Law*, 9–11.

7. Ibid., 10; Arkes, *Return of George Sutherland*, 244.

8. Epstein, *How Progressives Rewrote the Constitution*, 136–7.

9. For a nuanced examination of the relationship between constitutional theory and state-building in the early twentieth century, see Kersch, *Constructing Civil Liberties*.

10. In the words of the antebellum Massachusetts Temperance Society, the American constitutions, properly interpreted, recognized "no immoral rights." Massachusetts Temperance Society, *Twenty-Sixth Annual Report* (Boston: Cassady and March, 1838), 71.

11. For the claim that the period of the founding was an age of "darkness and ignorance," see Justin Edwards, "Fifth Annual Report of the American Temperance Society," in *Permanent Temperance Documents of the American Temperance Society* (Boston: Seth Bliss, 1835), 212.

12. Epstein, *How Progressives Rewrote the Constitution*; Arkes, *The Return of George Sutherland*; Michael S. Greve, *Real Federalism: Why It Matters, How It Could Happen* (Washington, DC: AEI Press, 1999); *The Upside-Down Constitution* (Cambridge, MA: Harvard University Press, 2012); David E. Bernstein, *Rehabilitating Lochner: Defending Individual Rights against Progressive Reform* (Chicago: University of Chicago Press, 2011).

13. McDowell, *The Language of Law*; Watson, *Living Constitution, Dying Faith*.

14. Barnett, *Restoring the Lost Constitution*; Arkes, *The Return of George Sutherland*.

15. Thomas G. West, "Progressivism and the Transformation of American Government," in John A. Marini and Ken Masugi, eds., *The Progressive Revolution in Politics and Political Science: Transforming the American Regime* (Lanham, MD: Rowman and Littlefield, 2005), 13–34.

16. Robert H. Bork, "Courts and the Culture Wars," in *Courts and the Culture Wars*, ed. Bradley C.S. Watson (Lanham, MD: Lexington Books, 2002), 3–14; Christopher Wolfe, "The Supreme Court and Changing Social Mores," in *Ourselves and Our Posterity: Essays in Constitutional Originalism*, ed. Bradley C.S. Watson (Lanham, MD: Lexington Books, 2009), 153–74.

17. For an important exception to this trend, arguing that the New Deal revolution can be justified on broadly originalist grounds, see Jack Balkin, *Living Originalism* (Cambridge, MA: Belknap Press of Harvard University Press, 2011).

18. Ackerman, *We the People: Transformations*, 306–16.

19. On the "constitutional moment" concept, see Ackerman, *We the People: Foundations.*

20. Robert Post and Reva Siegel, in their recent work on "democratic constitutionalism," have advanced a theory of legitimate constitutional change that shifts the focus from sudden "moments" of constitutional transformation to the much lengthier periods of public mobilization that inevitably precede such "moments." See, in particular, "Roe Rage: Democratic Constitutionalism and Backlash," *Harvard Civil Rights-Civil Liberties Law Review* 42 (2007): 380.

Acknowledgments

It is a pleasure to acknowledge the teachers, colleagues, friends, and family members who have contributed in ways large and small to the completion of this book. I am particularly indebted to Gary Armstrong, Alan Holiman, and Rein Staal, who encouraged me to ask big questions about the relationships between politics, ethics, and religion. Karen Orren introduced me to the field of American political development and encouraged me to pursue research at the intersection of religion and constitutional law. Whether in the role of advisor, mentor, or friend, Karen has always given generously of her time, providing exactly the right combination of criticism and encouragement. I continue to draw inspiration, not only from the high quality of her scholarship, but from her dedication to asking the most basic and important questions about the nature of the American political regime. Andy Sabl, Scott James, and Clyde Spillenger provided many valuable suggestions for improving an earlier version of the manuscript. Their respective expertise in the fields of political theory, political development, and legal history saved me from countless errors. I am also grateful to Evan Gerstmann and John Parrish, who listened to an early synopsis of my historical argument and convinced me that I had something to say about constitutional theory in the present.

More recently, Mark Graber, as well as the anonymous outside readers selected by Harvard University Press, provided detailed and helpful comments on the entire manuscript. Others who read and commented on parts of the manuscript, usually in the form of conference papers, include Grier Stephenson, Chris Shortell, Tom Burke, Ann-Marie Szymanski, Curt Nichols, Matthew Brogdon, and Jeffrey Polet. Several colleagues in the Chapman University political science department—including Lori Cox Han, Angeliki Kanavou, Don Will, Gordon Babst, Nubar Hovsepian, Art Blaser, David Shafie, and Richard Ruppel—provided invaluable advice and encouragement during the time when I was struggling to complete the manuscript while simultaneously adjusting to life as an assistant professor. Two outstanding Chapman political science majors, Beau Bryant and Bobby Konoske, helped with tracking down legal citations and compiling the index. I am grateful as well to Michael Aronson of Harvard University Press for his unwavering support for this project.

Finally, I owe a special thanks to my family: to my parents and parents-in-law for their steadfast love and support; to my brother, Paul, for his valiant—if ultimately unsuccessful—attempts to fix my golf swing (and for reading parts of the manuscript); to Neal Turnage for his encouragement and friendship over the years; to Bill Turnage, who read an earlier version of the manuscript and shared some helpful firsthand insights on the nature of judging; and most of all to my wife, Heidi Hyun, whose kindness, optimism, and generosity of spirit know no bounds. This book is for her.

Index